Emily Cruwys Sharland, Nicholas Ferrar

The Story Books of Little Gidding

Being the religious Dialogues recited in the great Room, 1631-2

Emily Cruwys Sharland, Nicholas Ferrar

The Story Books of Little Gidding
Being the religious Dialogues recited in the great Room, 1631-2

ISBN/EAN: 9783337130602

Printed in Europe, USA, Canada, Australia, Japan

Cover: Foto ©ninafisch / pixelio.de

More available books at **www.hansebooks.com**

THE STORY BOOKS OF LITTLE GIDDING

BEING
THE RELIGIOUS DIALOGUES RECITED IN THE GREAT ROOM,
1631–2

From the Original Manuscript of
NICHOLAS FERRAR

With an Introduction by
E. CRUWYS SHARLAND

NEW YORK
E. P. DUTTON AND CO.
31 WEST TWENTY-THIRD STREET
1899

To
The Glory Of God
AND TO THE MEMORY OF

ROSETTA LOUISA STIRLING,

GRAND-DAUGHTER OF ROSETTA FERRAR,

AND A LINEAL DESCENDANT

OF THE FERRARS OF

LITTLE GIDDING

PREFACE

THE Story Books of Little Gidding consist of five manuscript folio volumes, mostly in Nicholas Ferrar's own handwriting, and were all bound by Mary Collet in black morocco with gilt edges. The penmanship, which is exquisite, possesses a few noticeable peculiarities, such as the accent over the article "a"—(á)—and the brace which connects "ct" and "st"—("affection," "stand," &c. A distinctive feature, also, of these and all other writings done at Little Gidding, is the heading of every page with the sacred monogram, I H S.

The history of the Story Books, so far as it is known, is as follows. In the year 1631 (1632) the first volume was completed and presented, first to old Mrs. Ferrar, afterwards, by her wish, to Mr. and Mrs. Collet's eldest daughter, Mrs. Joshua Mapletoft, of Margetting, Essex. In the course of the next few years three other volumes were compiled at Little Gidding, copies of which were most probably transcribed and forwarded to this much-loved absent member of the family; for her uncle Nicholas had assured her (p. liv.) "that of every good thing that God shall impart to us, you shall ever have as liberal and free a communication as wee can possibly make you." The fifth volume is a duplicate of the first part of Vol. II., made for some other absentee. These five books were carefully preserved for two hundred years by generations of Mapletofts, together with "The Great Concordance" (as it was called in Miss Mapletoft's will), or Harmony of the Four Gospels, made and bound by Mary Collet; a cabinet presented to the family by King Charles I., a silk purse also given by the King, and a few books and relics of less importance and later dates.

At the death of Miss Anne Mapletoft of Canterbury, at an advanced age, in 1856, these heirlooms passed into the hands of another descendant of the Ferrars and Mapletofts, Mrs. Henry Solly Hodges, of Tiverton, Devon, by whom they were reverently cherished for over thirty years. But when Mrs. Hodges died, in the year 1888, leaving all her Little Gidding treasures to a cousin who was living in New South Wales, they were sent to that distant land with much regret, for it was feared that in after years they would be lost sight of, and their association with Little Gidding completely destroyed. This view of the matter having been set before Mr. H. Mapletoft Davis, he decided, after much consideration, to send the Ferrar relics back to England, stipulating that they should be disposed of either to a descendant of the family or to the trustees of some public institution.[1] In accordance with these terms, the treasures were distributed in the following manner :—

Charles I.'s cabinet was purchased by the Queen, and is now at Windsor Castle.

The trustees of the British Museum bought the "Great Concordance," three of the Story Books, an abridged MS. Life of N. Ferrar, in paper cover, copied from other sources, and a Cambridge Commonplace Book of later date.

The other two Story Books, viz., Vol. III., and the duplicate of Vol. II., pt. 1, had been bespoken by the Governors of Clare College, Cambridge (Nicholas Ferrar's own College), but they courteously resigned their claim in favour of Lady Lyell, a lineal descendant of the Ferrar family,

---

[1] A copy of the first edition of Dr. Peckard's "Life of Nicholas Ferrar" was placed with the Story Books, &c., by Mr. Richard Mapletoft in 1791. In the beginning of the book he desired that this copy might be always kept with the other volumes, and it was sent back to England with them in 1893, but was unaccountably lost shortly afterwards.

who is now the possessor of these two volumes, and of the purse given by King Charles I.

The present volume is a copy of Vol. I. and the first part of Vol. II., from the original books in the Manuscript department of the British Museum.

Should these Stories meet with acceptance, the series will be completed by the publication of a second volume, containing Vol. IV., on Temperance (Brit. Mus.) ; Vol. III., Charles the Fifth's Relinquishment of this World (by the kind permission of Lady Lyell) ; and the latest records of the Little Academy, compiled after the death of its venerable Founder, and copied into the second part of Vol. II. (Brit. Mus.) To these will be added (by the kind permission of the Archbishop of Canterbury) a copy of an original Manuscript by John Ferrar,[1] now in Lambeth Palace Library.

[1] There is no doubt that Ferrar is the correct spelling of the name. Mr. Michael Ferrar, one of the present representatives of the family, says that Gwalkeline de Ferrariis was Master of the Horse to William the Conqueror. His surname, as was usual in those days (and later), was taken from his estate known as *Ferraria*, the plural of the Latin *Ferrarium*, iron-mine or iron district, at or about Ferrières, a town near Liège. The members of the family were all *de Ferrariis*—that is, "of the Iron lands" or "Iron mines." Gwalkeline's son Henricus was made Earl de Ferrars, (shortened from Ferrariis), and got grants of land in very many— fifteen or twenty—of the counties of England. His descendants branched out into numerous families, and some of them spelt their names properly, Ferrars and Ferrar : others, according to custom, were careless and spelt it Ferrers, Farrar, Farrer, &c. Nicholas, the elder and younger, used Farrar, and sometimes Farrer : but the correct form, Ferrar, appears to have been used in the latter's lifetime, or soon after his death (in 1637), and continued so to be used by the Huntingdon family till they disappeared from the county some one hundred and fifty years ago. Nicholas Ferrar's father got a special grant of arms and crest on 29th December, 1588, from Queen Elizabeth, still used by the family. And the motto is the same as that of the ancient Ferrars :—

"Ferré va Ferme"—"Go firmly shod."

INTRODUCTORY SKETCH

THE following short history has been entirely derived from two biographies, edited by the Rev. J. E. B. Mayor, at Cambridge, in 1855, entitled "Nicholas Ferrar, Two Lives; by his Brother John and by Dr. Jebb" (a friend and contemporary).

Nicholas Ferrar, the saintly and gifted compiler of these religious exercises, was born on the 22nd day of February, A.D. 1593. From his elder brother, John, his faithful and loving biographer, we learn that he was "a lovely child, fair and of bright hair like his mother. The Bible was the book in the world, to him dear and precious. The next book, the Book of Martyrs, he took great delight in, and the story of Bishop Ferrar he had perfect, as for his name's sake."

He was confirmed at the early age of five, on which occasion he managed to slip unnoticed from his place a second time, and thus secured a double portion of the bishop's blessing for himself. "I did it," he said, " because it is a good thing to have the bishop's prayers and blessing twice, and I have got it."

Even when he was but six years of age little Nicholas "fancied being a clergyman." Once when Mrs. Ferrar and her maids were making little bands for the children, trimmed with lace, "he came very soberly to his mother, and earnestly prayed her that his bands might have no lace upon them, but be made little plain bands. 'Why, child,' saith she, 'will you not have your bands made like the rest of your brothers?' 'No, I pray you, dear mother,' said he, 'let mine be such little plain bands as Mr. Antony Wotton wears; for I will be a preacher as he is.' Mr. Wotton was then newly come into the parlour to visit Mr. Ferrar and his wife (as he once a week, if not oftener, used to do), and he and Mrs. Ferrar heartily laughed at the child's earnestness in that particular, for he would have no nay."

Although noted for bodily activity and grace, and also possessed of a vigorous temper of mind, he never enjoyed good health, being subject from infancy to aguish attacks.

When he was about to be sent to school (being then only in his eighth year) "it pleased God to permit a sore and grievous temptation to befall Nicholas Ferrar, that wonderfully perplexed his body and mind, 'Whether there was a God, and how to be served.' One night, which was cold and frosty, he riseth out of his bed, for sleep he could not, and goes down to a green grass-plat in the garden, and throws himself upon his face on the ground, and with extreme perplexity of grief, sobs, sighs, and abundance of tears, earnestly with all his strength, humbly begged of God that 'He would put into his heart the true fear and care of His Divine Majesty, and that this fear and love of God might never depart out of his mind, and that he might know how he must serve Him.' After much bitter weeping he felt his heart much eased, and comforts began to come to it, and to have an assurance of God, and the doubt began to pass away, and his heart was much cheered. He then rose up, and went up to his chamber to bed again, but could not sleep but little; yet found he daily more and more confirmation in his soul, and so had all his lifetime after a more than ordinary fear of God in him, and His presence, which continued in him to his dying day." Another biographer (John Worthington) writes: "Two things especially, in that night's holy exercise were so imprinted in the heart and mind of the child that they came fresh into his memory every day of his life. (This he told me more than once, two or three years before his death.) The one was the joy and sweetness which he did in that watching night conceive and feel in his heart. The other was the gracious promise which God made to him, to bless and keep him all his whole life, so that he would constantly fear God and keep His commandments."

The next event of importance was the entrance of Nicholas

Ferrar at a school, "where one Mr. Brooks, an excellent man for discipline, had introduced so extraordinary a way of teaching and living, that I am apt to believe" (says Dr. Jebb) "the thoughtful, pious child did there receive the first impressions and dispositions to that regular and religious course of life he so many years after heightened and formed in his own family into a greater and nobler figure of the good old Christian discipline."

"This Mr. Brooks had lived and preached with much esteem in London, but following the example of Jo. Gerson, the famous chancellor of Paris, he forsook the noise of a great city to preside over children in a country retirement, believing his charitable pains abundantly rewarded by the prayers of such happy innocents. He procured able masters in their several kinds: a master of music, a writing master, and a choice one for grammar learning, reserving to himself a governing inspection over the scholars and over the tutors themselves. Above all, they had their times for conning and repeating the Church catechism, the psalter, the epistles and gospels, for which this youth's vast memory served him to good purpose and to his great consolation, when many years after he travelled and fell desperately sick among those who take it for a mark of heresy in a traveller to carry about him an English Bible. None of the scholars performed their tasks of this kind (neither indeed of any kind) so constantly, carefully, and easily as he. Sometimes at those repetitions he would deliver observations of his own that could not have been expected from his years (which yet, that it may not seem incredible, was no more than St. Augustine's Adeodatus would often do, whose prodigious wit, the father himself protests, amazed him to think of it). He did so naturally comprehend and retain everything, that while he conquered the greatest difficulties, he neglected not the least parts of useful education. Shorthand he learnt exactly, and his masters were even proud of him, and gave him this commendation, that he could do what he pleased. Yet he had so little vanity and took so little pleasure in hearing himself commended, that he would often weep and forsake his meals when they would applaud him, and so unawares expose himself to the envy of his schoolfellows; so that if his other virtues were gained by exercise, it looked as if his modesty and humility were born and bred with him."

When Nicholas Ferrar was in his thirteenth year, Mr. Brooks thought him more than ripe for the University, and placed him at Clare Hall, Cambridge. It was by no means unusual at that time for boys of his age to be promoted from school to University.

Nicholas Ferrar was at first entered as a pensioner at Clare Hall, in order "that he might be more strictly obliged to study and exercise. But soon after, the fellows would needs have him fellow-commoner, *that he might be their companion*, as they expressed themselves. His tutor (Dr. Lindsell, afterwards Bishop of Peterborough, and at last of Hereford) would invite his learned friends to be present at hard trials of his memory, and other his extraordinary faculties. And though a friendly foe (as one calls a great expectation) was raised upon him, yet he often performed things greater than were expected, either in declaiming (which he was chosen to execute on the Coronation Day, St. James' Day, July 25, 1610, in the College Hall), or in disputing, or which way ever they turned him, for he was all obedience. He was no sooner Bachelor of Arts but the Master of Clare Hall and the other electors were pleased to invite this young fellow-commoner into a fellowship, and chose him by unanimous consent at their next election. Whilst he lived at the college, his life was the example not only of his equals but of his superiors. It must be no little indisposition that kept him at home when he heard the five o'clock bell ring to chapel. His chamber might be known by the last candle put out, and by the first lighted in the morning. As his parts were excellent, so his industry was admirable, but his piety at his years was incomparable; and what made this still more illustrious was that his fervours of devotion were so tempered and well governed by a rare judgment and discretion, when he was not above twenty years old, that he seemed to possess this in a more eminent height than any one of his other virtues. So good a conduct in his affairs, with such undoubted integrity, gained him universal esteem, with a powerful influence upon all his particular friends; and this good-natured youth would be overjoyed to use that interest as a reconciler, if any difference happened among them, or to divert them from any ill-chosen resolution. His good old tutor would often change his mind upon his advice, and then would tell others of the society pleasantly, that *if his pupil took them to task, he would alter them too."* It was during his residence at Clare Hall that he used to visit frequently his eldest sister, Susanna Collet, who, with her husband and family, was living at Bourne, about ten miles from Cambridge. "This sister he loved entirely, she being a lover of learning—often resorted to her house, and his tutors and fellows—had divers young nieces, bred up with their mother, trained up in daily reading chapters in the Bible and David's psalms, whom he instructed in all good things, with exhortations in writing and letters." This he ever continued to do until the day of his death.

In the autumn of 1612, when Nicholas Ferrar had been about three years a graduate, his aguish attacks obtained such hold upon him that his physician ordered him to "change the air of England and go beyond sea for the recovery of his health, and a necessary diversion from his incessant studies," expressing the opinion that "nothing but travel could preserve his life, and that scarce would prolong it beyond his thirty-fifth or thirty-sixth year"; but, by the blessing of Providence, his very temperate manner of life caused him to be spared to rule his household at Little Gidding until he had overpassed the age of forty-four.

His parents were very unwilling to part with him, and so were many of his fellow-students, who "loved him as a brother." But his tutor persisted in taking a hopeful view of his case, bidding them all "hope comfortably to see him again, not only improved in health and learning, but grown in grace, a stock few of our young travellers increase abroad."

In the following April, through the introduction of Dr. Scott, then Master of Clare Hall, and sub-almoner to the King, Nicholas was appointed one of the gentlemen to attend the Princess Elizabeth, who was newly married to the Elector Palatine, and was about to be conducted to the Palatinate. Before leaving Cambridge, however, he was created Master of Arts, the University conferring his degree upon him before Midsummer, by extraordinary favour. Three days after his departure, a remarkable paper was found in his study, of which his brother John transcribed a copy in his diary. It was this: "Since there is nothing more certain than death, nor more uncertain than the time when; I thought it the first and chief wisdom for a man to prepare himself for that which must one day come, and always to be ready for that which may every hour happen; especially considering how dangerous an error is here, which cannot be amended; neither is any man anything the nearer death for it. It is, then, a thing of exceeding madness and folly to be negligent in so weighty a matter, in respect whereof other things are trifles. I here confess my own wretchedness and folly in this, that through the common hope of youth have set death far from me; and persuading myself that I had a long way to run, have more carelessly walked than I should. The Good Lord be merciful unto me.

"Indeed, I have a long way to run, if death stood still at the end of three score years; but God knows if he be not coming against me, if he be not ready to grasp me, especially considering the many dangers wherein I am now to hazard myself, in every one of which death dwells, and if God keep me not, I know in some of them he will entrap me.

"If the good Lord be merciful unto me, and bring me safe home again, I will all the days of my life serve Him in His holy Name and exhorting others; yea, in His tabernacle, and in His holy sanctuary will I serve Him, and shall account the lowest place in His house better and more honourable than the greatest crown in the world.

"But I know my sins have deserved all His plagues and

punishments, that any soul may suffer, but I most humbly beseech God to pardon them for Jesus Christ's sake, and by His only merits and precious death I know my sins are forgiven me ; yea, it may be God will take me away in the beginning of my day, it may be in this my journey. I hope He that hath begun this mind in me will continue it in me, and make me to walk so as I may always be ready for Him, when He shall come, either in the public judgment of all the world, or in private judgment to me by death. This is my purpose, and this shall be my labour. I thank Thee, O blessed Lord God, for of Thee cometh this mind ; it is not of myself, but from the inspiration of Thy blessed Spirit.

"And you, my most dear parents, if God shall take me from you now, I beseech you be of good comfort, and be not grieved at my death, which I undoubtedly hope shall be to me the beginning of eternal happiness, and to you no loss, for you shall with inestimable joy receive me in the kingdom of heaven, to reign there with you and my dearest brother, Erasmus, and your other children that are departed in the Lord. If I go before, you must come shortly after : think it is but a little forbearance of me. It was God that gave me to you, and if He take me from you, be you not only content, but most joyful, that I am delivered from this vale of misery and wretchedness. I know that through the infinite mercy of my gracious God it shall be my happiness, for I shall then, I know, enjoy perpetual quietness and peace, and be delivered from those continual combats and temptations which afflict my poor soul. O Lord, Thou knowest I may truly say, *that from youth up Thy terrors have I suffered with a troubled mind.* My soul hath been almost rent through violent temptations that have assaulted it ; for to Thy glory, O Lord, will I confess my own weakness and the great danger Thou hast delivered me from. *It was Thou, Lord, that hast kept me, else had they devoured my soul and made it desolate.* And this God who thus hath kept me ever since I was born, ever since I came out of your womb, my most dear mother, will preserve me to the end, I know, and give me grace that I shall live in His faith, and die in His fear, and rest in His peace, and rise in His power, and reign in His glory.

"I know, my most dear parents, your tender affection to your children, and therefore I fear your grief if God take me away, and therefore write and leave this, that you might know your son's estate, and assure yourselves (for on the truth of God's infinite mercy am I confident in the hope of my salvation) that though he be dead to you, yet he is alive to God.

"I most humbly beseech you to pardon me in whatsoever I have at any time displeased you, and forgive me. I most humbly beseech God to bless and keep you, and give you a happy life here and everlasting life in the world to come.

"Your most humble and obedient son,
"N. Farrar.

"Postscript.—My dearest brothers and dearest sisters, if I live you shall find me a faithful, loving brother unto you all; if I die, I beseech you by the fear of God, by the duty to our parents, by the bond of nature, by the love you bear me, that you all agree in perfect love and amity, and account every one the other's burthen to be his. So may plenty and prosperity dwell among you. So prays your faithful, loving brother,
"N. F.

"If I die, I desire that the value of £5 of my books may be given to the college. The rest I leave to my father's and mother's disposing; yet I desire that in them my worthy tutor Lindsell and cousin Theophilus may be remembered; and if any of my sisters' sons prove a scholar, the rest may be given to him."

"This tenth day of April, 1613, being Sunday."

Contrary to his foreboding and in answer to the earnest prayers of his parents and friends, Nicholas Ferrar lost his disposition to ague after the sea voyage. From the time that he landed at

Flushing with the suite of the Princess, he was a man of note and observation; for whilst his biographer (Dr. Jebb) tells us that the Princess's tour was "a triumph," and that "she was all along royally feasted"; he also adds that "he (Nicholas) as an ornament of her train, was much caressed." But Nicholas had his own purpose of life always set steadfastly in his heart; and although he was earnestly implored to go to Heidelberg, where the Count Palatine kept his court, with the assurance that he "stood fair" for the Princess's secretary; yet he made answer "that he aimed at lower things, and was not qualified for such an employment." Whereupon he bade farewell to the Princess, and pursued his travels by another route.

Even whilst in attendance on the Princess in Holland, Nicholas found time to study the manners and industries of the people, their forms of worship (which were very numerous), and particularly all remarkable instances of God's providence—"the miracles of His mercy and justice in rewards and punishments which are illustriously visible in the histories of every country, though many such rich observations are buried in oblivion among us for want of reading them." As soon as he left the court at Amsterdam he proceeded to Hamburg, where he was so hospitably entertained by the English merchants that he made it a rule never to taste wine or strong liquor, for fear he should be called upon to exceed his rule of temperance. "At first they tempted him, but he knew how to defend himself, and when they discovered his temperance in eating and drinking they left off importuning him; acknowledging that 'he was in the right way, though they could not hit it.'" At Leipzic he studied for a time at the University, and during his stay there he "made inquiries for the ablest masters in every art, whom he would gain entirely, if gold and good words could gain them, to teach him their mystery. Among other curious arts which he learnt abroad he was taught the skill of artificial memory." His fame from town to town seemed to precede him, so that he was obliged to retire into some small neighbouring village, to avoid having too many visitors.

At this time many German towns were full of the plague. It fell out, therefore, that at one part of his journey Nicholas was detained in quarantine for forty days, and these days, by God's appointment doubtless, were our forty fast days in Lent. "Here he had leisure enough to recollect his thoughts, to revise his (shorthand) notes, and to reduce his observations into method. He spent this time of fasting very agreeably. In the morning he went up into a neighbouring mountain, where abundance of wild thyme and rosemary grew; there with a book or two and with his God, whom he met in the closest walks of his mind, having spent the day in reading, meditation, and prayer, he came down in the evening to an early supper (his only set meal) of oil and fish. He omitted not his offices and exercises of devotion morning and evening and at midnight in his travels, for to serve and please his Maker was the travail of his soul. He needed not many books, who was his own concordance, and had the New Testament in a manner without book. And if the time and place would not serve him to kneel, yet then and there he made the lowest prostrations of soul and spirit."

Whilst in Italy his life was on more than one occasion, both in sickness and accident, most miraculously preserved. He was a man of mark wherever he went. At Padua, whilst studying physic intensely, he became so well known that he was overburdened by visits, especially by those of his own countrymen; for (as his biographer quaintly puts it) "it is the Englishman's fault when he is abroad to lose his time in quest of his mother tongue." Nicholas, therefore, removed into some quiet country place, changing his residence frequently, and then returning to Padua or Venice for a few weeks at a time. He was exceedingly anxious to visit Rome, but was told by some who came from the English College there that "the Jesuits had him in the wind," and had been supplied with a careful description of his person and manners, as they believed him to have come abroad with some great design. Rome was not in those days a safe place for Protestants, but Nicholas Ferrar contrived to travel there very privately on foot, reaching the great city upon Monday in Holy Week. "When there, he changed his lodgings every night, and stayed but ten days, which he managed as advantageously as possible to take a view of everything very remarkable."

Leaving Rome he went to Marseilles, and after having been detained there by a very serious illness, he set sail for Spain in a small English vessel. Whilst on board he was the means of delivering them, by his courage and maritime knowledge, from becoming overpowered by a Turkish privateer, for he persuaded them all to fight, and "was as active as any tarpaulin of them all."

Soon after he reached Madrid, Nicholas heard by some means that his family were involved in serious difficulties, from which he alone could extricate them. Accepting the situation as one which demanded immediate action, he sold some jewels (for he was out of funds and waiting for a remittance from his father) and started off on foot to walk to St. Sebastians, whence he could take ship for England. The journey was wearisome, and beset by many dangers, and when at length he reached the coast the winds were contrary for some days longer. The English factors were very kind to him, for though they knew him not, "they discerned him to be a gentleman of very great worth and experience." Every day they pressed him to command their purses, and at last he was glad to accept a loan of £10. Many of his new friends accompanied him aboard when a fair wind allowed him to set sail; so having bidden them kindly farewell, a few days brought him safely to Dover. As soon as he had leaped ashore, Nicholas threw himself flat upon his face and rendered most humble thanks to God for so many preservations abroad during the five years in which he had been absent from his native country. "So posting from Dover to London, and finding his father's door open, he entered the house in his Spanish habit.

His father, seeing one in that garb kneeling and begging his blessing, demanded *Who he was;* for he did not know him. He named himself, at which the good old man, who did not dream of his coming, felt all the transports of an affectionate father. Thus after about five years' absence in travel he returned home with a far better constitution than he carried abroad, and was received by all his friends with all the satisfaction imaginable."

A short time after his return, Nicholas Ferrar had some thought of going back to Cambridge; but his parents were now growing old, and besought him not to live from them. His brother John was deputy of the Virginia Company, of which Sir Edwin Sandys was Governor; and soon Nicholas was hard at work in the interests of this new-found world. Within two months of his return from abroad he and Sir Edwin Sandys had "contracted so near a friendship that they were seldom asunder." That this friendship was of life-long endurance there is proof in the fact that before Sir Edwin died he charged his lady to take Nicholas Ferrar's counsel in all her affairs. At Little Gidding Church there is still to be seen a silver flagon, on which is inscribed, " What Sir Edwin Sandys bequeathed To the remembrance of freindship, His freinde hath consecrated To The Honour of God's Service, 1629." And on the handle, " For the Church of Little Gidding in Huntingdonshyer."

Old Mr. Ferrar was himself "a lover of plantations," having been intimate with Sir Walter Raleigh, Sir John Hawkins, Sir Francis Drake, and other noble adventurers who could tell him of foreign heathendom. He and his two sons, John and Nicholas, were shareholders in the Somer Islands. We are told that he "lent his great parlour and hall for the governors of the Virginia Company to meet in weekly, and was much joyed to see his son (Nicholas) as heartily affording his assistance to Sir Edwin as he entreated it in this hard work. Nay, his care and charity could not confine itself to Virginia, for he and his ingenious brother, Mr. John Ferrar, frankly bestowed two shares of land they had in Bermuda for the maintenance of a free school there, whither they also sent a great number of bibles and psalmbooks for the children." As long as the Virginia Company existed, John and Nicholas Ferrar worked continuously and faithfully in its behalf, and it was no small grief to them when the Company was disbanded. John Ferrar writes of it in the following terms: "The Virginia business was close followed and put on Sir Edwin Sandys and Nicholas Ferrar by that Parliament; and the Parliament, so sensible of the great benefit and happiness that might in short time happen to England in many respects, and what an affrightment the Spaniard took at the then reputation of the action, that the House resolved to take all into their consideration, and the Lords joined in the business, and they would have confirmed the company and plantation by Act of Parliament. But King James then sent them a message, *that he had and would take it into his serious consideration and care, and by the next Parliament they should all see it, he would make it one of his masterpieces, as he said it well deserved to be.* And thus the matter then stood; but God knows these were but fair words, as the event showed, for all was let loose and to go to six and seven, as the proverb is, which requires a long story, not here to be inserted."

Whilst all this public business was being transacted, good old Mr. Ferrar had died, in 1620, leaving his son Nicholas sole executor, a duty which he carried out with all care, love, and fidelity, " being a continual stay and comfort to his dear mother."

" In 1624 he was chosen a Parliament man (member for Lymington), so great was his reputation and worth"; and during the year that followed he was actively engaged in the affairs of the Virginia Company. "The Parliament sat, and Nicholas Ferrar being in many things made of the committee, often was chosen by the committee to make report of such things to the House. All of which he performed so well and so pleasingly that there was great notice taken of him." Notwithstanding all these righteous efforts, "the colony languished, and the most flourishing plantation in the world was almost blasted under new lords and new laws."

"If at this time his hands were full of the public business, they were overloaden with the private affairs of his own family, which, according to the advertisement given him abroad, he found at his coming home involved in such difficulties as nothing but the infinite mercies of God and the wisdom of this great man, which was designed to be God's instrument in it, could have wrought their deliverance." His brother John's estate had become deeply involved through the desertion of his friends and partners; but Nicholas undertook the satisfaction of his creditors, and never rested until he had freed him of all his liabilities. It is believed that he spent £3,000 of his own estate before this could be effected; and, instead of bemoaning his own loss of money, he composed a beautiful prayer of thanksgiving for the occasion, which was offered up solemnly and constantly by the family on the last day of every month. About this time two offers of advancement were made to Nicholas Ferrar, both of which he refused. A certain Mr. Briggs, mathematical lecturer in Gresham College, having been appointed Savilian Professor at Oxford, strongly recommended Mr. Ferrar to the Company of Mercers as his successor. "But he humbly refused the offer, alleging that *he had other intentions and aims, if it pleased God to ripen them to a happy issue.*"

The other offer which he declined at this time was that made to him by a rich merchant, one of the Virginia Company, who begged him to accept for his wife his only child and heiress, and £10,000 with her. At first Nicholas told the father that "he was not worthy to enter into the honourable state with so much wealth"; but the disappointed man pressed his proposal upon him, declaring himself to be in love with him. Whereupon Nicholas assured him that "*he was resolved not to marry at all* (though he knew the world and the Church too well to speak or think dishonourably of that estate in his clergy friends). So resolute he was to deny himself in anything that might in the least obstruct his great design of retiring and sharing his estate, so as to enjoy it only in common with his many relations."

In 1625 the great plague broke out in London, and a death having occurred next door, Nicholas conveyed his aged mother to her daughter's house at Bourne, in Cambridgeshire. He would not quit the town himself, even when there died 4,000 a week, until he had paid all debts and cleared the estate of all engagements.

His mother had bought a lordship the year before—Little Gidding, in Huntingdonshire—to which he dismissed his brother John, to make ready a place of quarantine for himself, as he feared the infection for his mother, and entreated her to remain a month longer at Bourne. However, she so greatly longed to see him after all the risks he had encountered for the sake of herself and the rest of her family, that she rode to Gidding, fifteen miles from Bourne, within three days of his arrival there. Their meeting is graphically described: "Their greeting was like that of old Jacob and his son Joseph, after his father had given him over for lost, while he was providing for the support of the family. Such an interview must needs be passionately kind and zealously devout, both of them blessing God, and she again and again blessing her son."

Mrs. Ferrar's first care was to go into the church and there return humble thanks to Almighty God for His mercies before entering the house. But Nicholas prevented her, saying that the church had been profanely used as a barn and hog-stye, and needed cleansing. Upon this his mother was the more urgent, and having made an entrance, she knelt, weeping and praying, for a quarter of an hour, after which she entreated her son to have the church cleansed without delay; upon which business the workmen entered on the following day. "A month being overpast, and no danger appearing of infection by her son's coming out of the fatal city, she sent for her children and grandchildren and other her dear relations from Bourne, that they all might live and serve God together at this their new purchase. Seating themselves there, it required much cost and time to repair the old crazy house, and to make it a convenient habitation for a religious and numerous family (consisting of above forty persons), of whom above half were so descended from the old gentlewoman that they kneeled to her morning and evening for her blessing. Then Mr. Nicholas Ferrar, who was as it were the soul that inspired the whole family with piety, began to bring all their affairs, both spiritual and temporal, into as good order as could be expected and as the sadness of the times did either permit or exact of them; the church being now made fit for use, and in those additions of structure or ornament which were made to the church there were none of the family that had not a hand, and they that through absence could not do it themselves had a stone laid by some other hands."

The vicar of Steeple Gidding, their next parish, proved so friendly that he and they were a blessing to each other. The prayers of the Church were divided into services for three times a day, Nicholas Ferrar having obtained special leave from Bishop Williams (the bishop of the diocese, and an old acquaintance) to have the litany used daily, "it being the time of the plague, and the deplorable city now the common object of the kingdom's prayers." The vicar of Steeple Gidding, "like a true spiritual guide, walked with his own flock after him to officiate at that church. Thus they began already to taste the delicious fruits of peace and quietness, and they found by this little experience how much the pleasant solitariness of the place (for their family was in a manner all the parish) contributed to the serenity of their thoughts and the piety of their devotions. At this rate they spun out that part of the unhealthy summer and all the long winter at Gidding."

In the following year, at Easter, Mrs. Ferrar went to London, to bid farewell to all her friends there, " expecting to see them no more till the great Easter morning at the resurrection"; for she had resolved to remain at Little Gidding, by God's grace, for the remainder of her life, and there to be buried. The great house in London was let, and all things in order for her return to Gidding a fortnight after Whitsuntide. As Whitsunday drew near, Nicholas Ferrar came "to a full determination of entering into that religious life which he had so long and so ardently thirsted after." For a week beforehand he fasted much and slept little; and spent Whitsun-eve in his room in prayer. All this attracted not the notice of his friends, because he had often done so before. He acquainted no one with his intention except his old tutor, Dr. Lindsell, "who was ravished with joy"; but early on Trinity Sunday morning he went to King Henry the Seventh's Chapel at Westminster Abbey with Dr. Lindsell, and was there ordained deacon by Bishop Laud, who received him with great joy, believing that he was about to lay his hands on a very extraordinary person. The same evening Nicholas Ferrar went to his mother and asked leave to read to her a paper written on vellum and signed by himself; "it was the solemn vow he had made to Almighty God, that *since He had afforded so many gracious deliverances from so many perilous attempts of the devil and man upon his soul and body, and since now his family was rescued from a ruin so deplorable and unavoidable, if God had not been infinitely good to them; he would now separate himself to serve God in this holy calling, to be the Levite himself in his own house, and to make his own relations, which were many, his cure of souls.*" His mother, and those of his relations who were present, were amazed and delighted. His good old mother wept, beseeching Almighty God "*to fill him every day more and more with His Holy Spirit, and to grant him a long life, as an unspeakable blessing to her and her whole family.* They all answered him, that *they also by God's assistance would set themselves with greater care and diligence than ever to attend the one thing necessary.*"

The news of this step soon reached the city and Court, and Nicholas was offered preferment in the Church, which it was supposed he would not refuse, although he had declined advancement in the State. But he had not undertaken that which he would lightly lay aside. "He returned his most humble acknowledgments to those honourable peers, promising to pray for their prosperity, *but as he had already parted with all propriety in his temporal estate by sharing it equally with his kindred for their common good, so he would employ his talent or half-talent (for he alone had a mean opinion of his own abilities) to make them partakers of the true spiritual treasures.*"

So, having bidden farewell to the world in that great city of London, they returned to Gidding, where Mrs. Ferrar set about beautifying their little church. The floor was boarded and the walls wainscotted. On Sundays and Saints' Days the cedar wood communion table was adorned with "carpets of blue silk embroidered with gold." The pulpit and reading-desk—of the same height—were hung with fine blue cloth, "richly laced and fringed with vallans about each of them." The floor upon which the altar stood was raised, and covered with "sky-coloured silk," and the benches round the chancel with "blue taffety." On week days the carpets were of tapestry and green cloth. "There was a brass font set up, and a large eagle of the same to hold a fair Bible. She thought the house of God the only place on which such costly furniture was not ill bestowed; and in this her son not only approved but animated her devotion."

As soon as the church was in order, a school was provided, for which purpose an ancient dove-house was dispigeoned; for, having no harvest of their own, they did not think it fair to "harbour so many little thieves to devour their neighbours' corn." To this schoolhouse the children from other parishes had liberty to come and be trained with their own children; "where they might learn virtue as well as grammar, music, and arithmetic, together with fair writing." For all his nieces and female relations Nicholas Ferrar provided rooms and out-of-door pleasure grounds to suit all ages and conditions; for the three schoolmasters and the boys "convenient lodgings" were fitted up, his own room being placed in the midst of the house, so that "he could hear and see good order observed." One room was kept as an infirmary, "that if any of all his young company should fall sick they might be removed thither out of harm's way." Ample provision was made for recreation, for running, vaulting, and shooting at butts with bows and arrows.

The young women, of whom there were nine or ten, always wore black stuff, "all of one grave fashion, always the same, with comely veils on their heads. They were curious at their needles, and they made their scissors to serve the altar or the poor. They were fine surgeons, and they kept by them all manner of salves, oils, and balsams: a room they had on purpose to lock up these and cordial waters of their own distilling. All which, being as freely given by them to the country folks as themselves freely received all from God and their kind uncle, they were sure not to want customers; which every year cost them a good round sum. None of them were nice of dressing with their own hands poor people's wounds, were they never so offensive; but as for prescribing physic, their uncle understood it well himself, yet he never practised it, and he forbid them to tamper or meddle with it. And together with helps for the body the virgins were expert and ready to administer good counsels, prayers, and comforts to their patients for their souls' health.[1] To take off the

---

[1] In 1642, when the King visited Little Gidding for the second time, he was seated in the great Parlour, examining the Great Book that was being made for the Prince, with the latter (Prince Charles, of Wales) on one side of him and the Palsgrave on the other; the Palsgrave "went to one of the Gentlewomen, and taking her by the Hand, said Lady, you shall do me the favour to go and shew me the Fine Almes-house that your grandmother erected for 4 poor widows as I have been told: so she led him through the room into it: and the other courtiers followed to see it." ... "Then said the Palsgrave (to the King) Sir, there is one thing more worth your seeing: what's that said the King? The curious lodgings in the Alms-house provided for 4 poor widows, by the Old Gentlewoman Mother of the Family: what said the King, have you been there already before me: I meant to see them before I went: Sr., I will lead you the way, said the Palsgrave: so the King followed: then coming into the room, I will believe

burthen of household affairs from his aged mother's shoulders, her son ordered his four nieces to be the managers; yet so as it might prove a burthen to none of them, but rather a recreation to them all, he contrived that every sister should be sole governess but one month in four, and then Mary's better part was not to be taken away from her who acted the part of their Martha. Nor was she often called away, being not to apply her hands to anything servile, but only to carry in her head, to give the servants directions and cause herself to be obeyed by them, to book every farthing of their weekly expenses, allowing every small matter its column in their account-book; so they could cast an eye on what they gained or spent in every little necessary at the end of the month or year. This made his nieces, several of whom resolved to marry, not only perfect accountants but good housewives too. The land was all let out in parcels to their tenants, who by agreement were to serve the house with some provisions at constant rates. Their diet was neat and frugal, yet with variety enough accommodated to every one's health and constitution."

Weekly Routine at Little Gidding.

Sunday.

4 A.M. in summer.⎫ They all rose, and having quietly
5 A.M. in winter. ⎭ dressed, the daughters and younger children resorted to the great room,[1] and there repeated to

your Judgmt. another time said the King: Its passing neat and well kept, and of good Example; Sr., said one, it resembles much the Chapel, each being all wainscotted and pillared and arched: Sr., said the Palsgrave to the King, Oh how often should I have been glad to have had such a Lodging: I believe you, replied the King, so going out at the back-door into the garden." (From an old contemporary MS. in the possession of Sir Richard Tangye.)

[1] The "great room" was handsomely furnished with hangings; at its upper end was "a great large compass window" looking out

Nicholas Ferrar (who was always ready for them) "such chapters and psalms as each were to give an account of without book." They then retired "and made their selves all more comely in their best attires."

9 A.M. The bell rang to church. All the family assembled in the great room and sang a hymn to the organs; "which ended, each person said some sentence of scripture, such as they thought good, and so all went down to church in decent order, two and two together, the three masters in gowns leading the way, the young youths in black gowns following them. Nicholas Ferrar led his mother, his two brothers, John Ferrar and Mr. Collet, going before her (after the children), and then followed their sister Collet and her daughters, and so all the servants, two by two: each as they came into the church making low obeisance,[1] taking their places, the masters in the chancel, and the boys kneeling upon the upper step, which ascended up into the chancel from the church; the reading-place and pulpit standing, each opposite to the other, by two pillars, at the ascent into the chancel, the one on the right hand, the other on the left, close to each side of the wall: old Mrs. Ferrar and all her daughters going into an isle of the church, that joined on the north side, close at the back of the reading-place, where all the women sat always. Nicholas Ferrar being in his surplice and hood (for so in it he always went to church) stepped up into the reading-place, and there

upon the church, which stood at the end of the garden, and in this window stood each little company whose turn it was to recite the hour's service. In the midst of the room stood a little table, "at which stood a great chair (upon which table lay the Holy Bible and a Common Prayer-Book). There each standing at the back of the chair, said some one sentence of Scripture," &c. In this room, also, the family always assembled before going to Church.

[1] "At the entering thereof (that is, of the church) he (N. F.) made a low obeisance; a few paces farther, a lower; coming to the half-pace (which was at the east end, where the table stood) he bowed to the ground, if not prostrated himself."

they said divine service, and responses were made by all present, and the reading psalms were done so.

This performed, being returned home, those that had the office (which were the elder nieces and some others of the family) in summer time went and sat in a gallery, in winter in a room where a good fire was. Then they called the psalm-children to them, to hear them repeat their psalms. A penny was given to every child for each psalm well repeated.

10.30 A.M. The minister of Steeple Gidding, having repeated divine service in his own church first, came to Little Gidding with his parishioners. The bell then rang, and the family with the psalm-children met him. Nicholas Ferrar read the second service "at the communion-table with an audible voice," a psalm was sung, and the Vicar preached.

12 NOON. The psalm-children dined, standing on each side of long tressel tables. Mrs. Ferrar and her daughters and others were present until grace had been said, and the servants had "brought in the baked pudding and other meat, the old gentlewoman setting the first dish upon the table." After grace, some of the family remained until the children had finished, when they were dismissed to go to their homes and attend afternoon service with their parents in their own parish churches.

Meanwhile, dinner was being served in the great dining-room,[1] a hymn having been first sung, accompanied by the organs.

After dinner, every one did as they pleased.

2 P.M. The bell rang, all the family assembled and went to Steeple Gidding Church, a distance of a quarter of a mile, to hear a sermon. On their return they went up into the great

---

[1] "In the great dining-room, which was also the receptacle for strangers, there were divers tablets, fairly written in great letters, hung round the room; which were of the same use with the travellers' table-books, to receive any sentence their friends and visitants had a mind to insert or by way of good counsel bestow upon them."

room, and all the psalms which on week-days were said at set hours were repeated at one time. This done, every one did as they pleased.

5 P.M. in summer. ⎫ Supper-time. The bell rang, the family
6 P.M. in winter. ⎭ assembled in the great parlour, and sang while the meal was being set on the table.

At supper one of them read aloud a chapter, "and then another that had supped went to the desk and read a story out of the Book of Martyrs."

"Supper done, grace said, in summer all again went out where they pleased; in winter they warmed themselves if they pleased, a great fire being made in the room to heat it all over; those that would, had candles and went away, and Nicholas Ferrar, his mother, and the elder people found some good discourse or other to pass the time with."

8 P.M. Prayers in the great room. Then the children asked the old gentlewoman's blessing, and went to bed. Every one bid each other good-night, and the elder ones went to their chambers or closets—"for it was an order that none must after prayers go up and down, but keep their chambers."

Sunday's work was so arranged that no servant was kept from church, and as much freedom as possible was given from bodily employments. For dinner, ovens were heated, and the food set in them before church-time. After evening service, "the spits were laid down for meat to be roasted at the fire" for supper.

On the first Sunday in the month, as well as on all the great festivals, the Holy Communion was celebrated in Little Gidding Church; and on that day the servants (having communicated) stood at the lower end of the table, and dined with the family.

Week Days.

4 A.M. in summer. ⎫ They rose, and as soon as dressed
5 A.M. in winter. ⎭ went to the great room to recite their psalms and chapters to Nicholas Ferrar.

6 A.M. At this hour the short services, recited throughout the day at almost every hour, began. There were certain psalms for each hour of the day, and also one of the heads of the concordance [1] of the four evangelists to be recited; after which the following hymn was sung to the organ :—

> Thus angels sang, and so do we,
> To God on high all glory be :
> Let Him on earth His peace bestow,
> And unto men His favour show.

Each of these hourly services occupied but a quarter of an hour; the elder nieces and others of the family were divided in companies, to recite the services by turns.

All the family went to the church, which was only about 40 paces from the house, three times a day, viz., for matins, at about 6.30 a.m.; for the litany only, at 10 a.m., and for evensong at 4 p.m.

After matins all the family seem to have attended the 7 o'clock hourly service in the great room, and then the children's breakfast took place. As soon as it was over, the young

---

[1] THE CONCORDANCE OF MR. FERRAR'S MAKING.

"The book was divided into 140 heads. He every day spent one hour in contriving it, and directed his nieces that attended him in what manner they should cut the pieces out of the Evangelist, and so and so to lay them together as to make and perfect such a head or chapter. When they had first cut out those pieces with their knives or scissors, then they did neatly and exactly fit each verse that was so cut out to be pasted down on sheets of paper; and so artificially they performed it, that it looked like a new kind of printing to all who saw the books when they were finished; so finely were all the pieces joined together, and with great presses for that purpose pressed down upon the white sheets of paper. . . . But the work grew daily into greater perfection by the care and judgment of Mr. Ferrar; nay, the old gentlewoman herself became a handicraft-woman to help it forward."

The heads of the Concordance were so arranged, that the whole of it was recited once a month.

children, and the youths with their masters went off to the schoolhouse, "which was near adjoining to the house."

"The old gentlewoman set herself down in a chair, and this was her constant place for most part of the time any were there, and some or other of her daughters: her grandchildren were always there. Others, as young or old and such as were too young to go to school yet, sat there, and in great silence, either at their book or otherwise; and the others, some to their needleworks, others to learn what they were to say the next day. And each hour had commonly some employment or other for them; the making the concordance[1] (*i.e.*, a Harmony of the Gospels), their singing, their playing on their instruments, their writing, ciphering; and so never idle. And for the variety of employments, Nicholas Ferrar entertained a bookbinder's daughter, of Cambridge, to learn of her the skill and art of bookbinding and gilding, and grew very expert at it, as the king, having received books of her binding, said, *he never saw the like workmanship.*"

11.15 A.M. Dinner was served at this hour as soon as the 11 o'clock service had been recited. The order of dinner and supper was always the same: a hymn sung with organs playing to it while the meat was being set on the table. Grace said, all standing; after some time they all sat down, and one whose turn it was read at dinner and supper-time some part of history, such as was appointed; either some chronicles of nations, journeys by land, sea voyages, and the

---

[1] The "Concordance Chamber" was a "long, fair, spacious room, wherein were large tables round the sides of the walls, placed for their better conveniency and contrivement of their works." In it, also, were "two very large and great presses, which were turned with iron bars, for the effecting of their designs." The walls were "all coloured over with green pleasant colour varnished, for the more pleasure to their eyes, and a chimney in it for warmth, as occasion served." Each member of the family and "some other good friends of their kindred, gave each their sentence which should be written round the upper part of the walls of the room."

EIKON BASILIKE.

Bound at Little Gidding by Mary Collet.

like. The reasons and the method of them I shall, for the better satisfaction of the historian, set down.

"*Finding silence at meals-time unpleasant, and common discourse for the most part unprofitable, it is agreed that there shall be always something read during meal-times. And because the mind, then being in most men altogether intent upon the refreshment of their bodies, doth not willingly admit any serious speculation, it is thought fit that the reading shall be always of some easy and delightful matter, such as are history and relations of particular actions and persons, such as may not only furnish the mind with variety of knowledge in all kinds, but also stir up the affections to the embracements of virtue. The performance of this shall be by the two young daughters and four boys, every one in their course, whereby a particular benefit it is hoped will arise to the whole, and they shall by these means be brought to read any book well and gracefully. They that are to read shall immediately upon the coming into the dining-room have a mess of broth sent them, which when they have eaten, they shall begin their reading, standing at the north end of the table, and continue so reading until the rest of the children have supped; when another, after they have repeated their gospels, shall take the book, and the first go to their meal and, in regard of their forbearance, shall always have the advantage of some more than their fellows had. For the better retaining in memory of that which shall be read, it is agreed that a summary collection shall be kept in writing of those things which are judged worthy of observation out of that book. The drawing of this abstract shall be the work of one of the parents or masters, but the transcribing it fair may be by any of the children; and every noon, presently after collation, shall be made a repetition of that which was formerly read. The manner of this repetition, whether it shall be by examination of the younger, or by the elders relating it and application of things, is left to the judgment of the directors of those exercises to proceed according as the nature of the subject, time, persons and other occasions shall require. The ordinary and constant charge of this matter is committed to John and Mary Ferrar*

***

and for assistance and supply when they cannot, to Susanna Collet; the mother and the eldest daughters are desired always, as occasion serves, to give their help."

"When dinner and supper were ended the reader ceased; and then, grace said, one boy, whose turn it was that meal, repeated a story without book, such as Nicholas Ferrar had compiled for them, and fitting their capacities. These were short, pleasant, and profitable; good language and no less good matter, teaching them something of worth, exciting to virtue and the hatred of vice: and by this the young ones learned to speak gracefully and courageously."

After dinner and these performances every one did as they pleased.

1 P.M. The bell tolled for the boys to go to school. Mrs. Ferrar sat till 4 o'clock in the great chamber, superintending, as before, the employments of the hours.

4 P.M. Evensong at the church.

5 P.M. Supper in the great parlour, after which they were all at liberty to do as they would.

8 P.M. The bell rang to prayers in the great chamber. Then the children went to bed, and the elders to their own rooms, as on Sunday.

The Night Vigils.

Nicholas Ferrar always considered that he and his family had received extraordinary favours and blessings of God, for which they were bound to render Him thanks beyond that which was the usual practice or custom amongst men. In this he was approved and confirmed by the opinion of grave and learned divines whom he consulted, and he was also acting "upon the invitation of that worthy servant of Christ, Mr. George Herbert,[1] his most entire friend and brother (for

---

[1] Nicholas Ferrar and George Herbert held great intercourse by letter and "loved each other entirely," but John Ferrar mentions their "having but once had personal conference with each other."

so they styled each other)." He therefore established a regular course of nightly vigils in his house, in which he was gladly joined by many members of his household. All were free to please themselves in this matter, and none were thought less well of for not taking a part. Every night two watchers at least took their turns; they began at nine at night and continued their prayers until one in the morning. The watchers kept in their several apartments or oratories, the men's rooms being far removed from the women's. Sometimes the watch was kept by one of the daughters, with a sister or else one of the maidservants who desired to watch. At other times one of the men would keep the vigil, assisted by one at least of the boys, for they were always eager to be allowed to watch with their elders, although their uncle did not permit them to do so more than once a week, nor were the young women allowed to watch oftener. At one o'clock they knocked at Nicholas Ferrar's door (if it was not his vigil), bidding him good morrow and placing a lighted candle outside, for it was his custom to rise at that hour, go to his study, and continue in prayer and meditation until six o'clock. Twice in the week he took the vigil, and in later years three times. In the summer time he and the boys kept their watch in the church; at one o'clock the latter laid themselves down upon a bench to sleep, whilst their uncle continued his prayers and meditations; they did not leave the church until five o'clock. "Now the matter was this they chiefly insisted on in their watch, and was the length of it: that they two that watched should carefully and distinctly say all David's psalms over in those four hours' time, from

Both John and Nicholas Ferrar assisted Mr. Herbert considerably in carrying out the work of restoration at Leighton Church, in which they were also subsequently helped by their cousin, Mr. Woodnoth. When Mr. Herbert died (in 1633) he bequeathed to "his dear brother Ferrar" the manuscript of his poem "The Temple," of which Nicholas brought out two editions in the course of a year.

nine to one o'clock, they having both a glass and the clocks to let them know how the night passed away. One of the watchers said one verse of the psalm and the other the other verse interchangeably by way of responsal. They performed it on their knees all the time, except at some spaces of time and intermission which they used, when they in winter went to the fire to warm themselves, when extreme weather was. For in their rooms near them they had fires all night, and were otherwise provided that they took no cold to endanger their health, of which Nicholas Ferrar in all things was most careful. These watchers went not to their naked beds at all, but lay down upon them till six o'clock and then rose. This was to inure them, upon any occasion that might happen, that they could do well without going into a bed."

They kept up a fair amount of visiting with their neighbours, though it soon became understood that they did not wish to go abroad often to see them; but whenever any of them were pleased to afford their company at Little Gidding Hall, they were civilly and pleasantly treated. A glass of wine or tankard of ale was always offered to all comers of any note; many came for the novelty of the thing, many more because they knew the merit of Nicholas Ferrar, and esteemed it an honour to become acquainted with him. Hardly a day passed in which some considerable person did not come to visit him, so that he had hundreds and thousands of visitors at several times. "Several persons of honour and many great scholars of other persuasions (Romish priests and the like) addressed themselves to discourse with him and discover his opinions, in which he had no reserves as one exactly well set in his principles for the most Apostolic Church of England."

On one occasion the family were to have been honoured by a visit from the Queen, but the roads were impassable when the visit was planned. Her Majesty, having heard from the

King that there was "a Protestant family that outdid the severest monastics abroad," despatched a gentleman to Little Gidding to observe all that he could of their manner of living, and " to bring her a clear account of their manner of life; which he did so much to the admiration of the Queen, that she very much regretted the disappointment of her own journey."

When the King's standard was set up at Nottingham, however, being told on his journey that he was not far from Little Gidding, his Majesty rode thither with the Prince of Wales, Prince Rupert, the Duke of Richmond, and many other valiant and noble men. The King spent his time in reading their harmonies of the gospel, whilst the rest of the party visited various rooms and partook of refreshments. The family presented the King with some devout books which they had bound, concerning which he was pleased to say "*he never saw such workmanship.*" "At parting, he prayed *the blessing of God might be upon them*, and he desired their hearty prayers; wherein they never failed him at the public offices in their little chapel, till by the fury of the oppressor they were driven away."

In 1634 old Mrs. Ferrar died, after a peaceful and good old age enjoyed at Little Gidding, where she had been the loved ruler and example of her children and grandchildren. The household changed from time to time, as its younger members grew up and went out into the busy world. But the religious, happy life continued, and reflected its holy influence on all around it. Of the poor we learn that "the adjoining ministers, when they came to Gidding, protested that *a mighty change was wrought not only on the children, but on the men and women who sat hearing their children reading and repeating at home. And whereas heretofore their tongues were exercised in singing either naughty or lewd or else vain ballads that much estranged their young minds from the ways of virtue, now they heard the streets and doors resounding with the sacred poetry of David's harp which drove away the evil spirit from Saul.*"

Of the many visitors to Nicholas Ferrar, we are told that

"seldom any parted from him but with satisfaction, and it can hardly be imagined what lasting fervours of devotion many carried away with them that spent but a few hours in that happy society. For it was one establishment in this family, which had set itself thus heartily for heaven, whatever strangers were in the house (though some perhaps of a different communion), yet that they would keep their set times of going to prayers in the church. And if such as came to see their devotions were pleased to join with them, they were a great deal the more welcome on that account."

Some men of birth and fortune actually feigned having lost their way in the dark and strayed to the house to beg for a night's shelter, whilst they had really sent their servants on to a neighbouring village to wait them there next morning. Their stratagem succeeded, and they were quickly set down to a good supper.

Every day Mr. Ferrar would himself interview those poor people who came to the house for relief; he would inquire who were sick in any of the neighbouring villages, and send them comforts. "He made the point of applying the best remedies to wounded consciences one great and main end of his studies, and with his most affectionate pains would assist others in these distresses, till he had, as it were, begotten them anew to God. He understood it the better as having undergone himself, in his own tender age, many and grievous temptations."

It was in the year 1637 that Nicholas Ferrar was taken from his earthly home to a better and a heavenly one. His illness was but of a month's duration: on Friday, November the 3rd, he began to suffer from fainting fits, and at once made provision for the continuation of the daily services at Little Gidding Church, feeling assured that he should not any more be able to perform his part there. Some three days before his death, lying in his bed about 8 o'clock in the morning, he called his brother, John Ferrar, his sister Collet and all his nieces to him, saying, *Brother, I would have you*

INTRODUCTORY SKETCH   xxxix

go to the church, and at the west end of the door, where we go into the church, I would have you measure from the half pace, where we go into the church, of stone you tread upon seven foot to the westward, and at the end of that seven foot there let my grave be made. His brother, looking very sadly upon him, with his eyes full of tears (and so all the standers-by did), he went on, saying, *Brother, that first place of the length of seven foot I leave for your own burying-place, you are my elder ; God, I hope, will let you there take up your resting-place, till we all rise again with joy. When you have measured out the place for my grave, then go and take out of my study those three great hampers full of books that have stood there locked up these many years. Carry,* said he, *those hampers to the place of my grave, and upon it see you burn them all;* and this he spake with some vehemency and passion of indignation. *Go, let it be done, let it be done, and then come again all of you to me.* So it was performed, and a great smoke, bonfire, and flame they made ; and it being upon a hill, the towns round about and men in the fields came running up to the house, supposing some great fire had happened at Little Gidding. When they saw what was doing, that it was an infinite sort of books burning, and that Mr. Nicholas Ferrar was like to die, as they heard, they went their ways home, and within a few days it was by rumour spread abroad at market-towns all the country over that *Mr. Nicholas Ferrar lay a-dying, but could not die till he had burned all his conjuring-books, and had made a great fire of them upon the grave he would be buried in.*" (See " Story Books," vol. i. p. 119 *et seq.*) On Sunday, the 3rd of December (Advent Sunday), he received his last Communion, after making " a full and lively confession of his faith and state of soul." Throughout the day " he applied himself again to the work in which he resolved to live and die, and that was confirming his family in the ways of piety, more particularly directing this last sermon of his to his most beloved nieces, his two virgin disciples, that *they should be steadfast and commit themselves to the guidance of their Lord God and Jesus Christ their Master.*" At one o'clock on Monday morning, December the 4th, whilst the prayer was being used by those who knelt round his bed, "that God would be pleased to send His holy angels to carry his soul to heaven," he was taken from them, at the very hour at which he constantly rose to praise God and to pray to Him.

"As one of the company said, *He ended the Christian Sabbath upon earth to begin the everlasting one in heaven.*"

"His body is buried in peace, but his name liveth for evermore."

LITTLE GIDDING CHURCH.

Showing the graves of John and Nicholas Ferrar.

INTRODUCTION TO THE STORY BOOKS.

THE origin of the Religious Exercises contained in these Story Books has been well described by Dr. Jebb, who prefaces his account of them with a paragraph on the versatility of Nicholas Ferrar's mind. "Though he was far from one of the volatile or *bird-witted* (as one ingeniously calls that sort of men that are ever hopping from bough to bough, and can never fix upon anything), yet he would never be long in any of his studies or in any employment, but keep (as exactly as his many accidental occasions would give him leave) such and such hours for such and such affairs; and out of doubt this was best for his body and mind. 'Tis certain he found a real advantage in shifting the scenes, besides a new pleasure and refreshment at every turn, though, if occasion were, he could set himself day and night to any task and never give over till he could say '*'Tis perfect.*'"

One of these diversions was the compilation of divine interludes, dialogues, and discourses in the Platonic way, planned by him for the purpose of warning his family from the "Christmas games and wilder sports, which could hardly subsist without riot and extravagant license. On All Saints' Day they began, and at Christmas, on every holiday, they proceeded in gracefully repeating and acting their Christian histories, taken both out of ancient and modern historians," and framed (we are told) in opposition to the legends of Rome.

INTRODUCTION TO THE STORY BOOKS

These stories were carefully copied out by each actor from Nicholas Ferrar's transcription of them, and generally committed to memory. But now and then, through want of time, or inability to learn the task, the story was read aloud (see Story Books, p. 82). At the end of each recital there was a free discussion of the lessons to be learnt from the day's storying, except on rare occasions when the stories occupied so much time in the telling that the usual debate had to be abandoned (see p. 138).

The younger members of the Little Academy were treated with leniency; their stories were often very short, and sometimes they had already been related by one of their elders (see pp. 36, 37, 57).

At another time the singing of a hymn would be accepted as a sufficient contribution towards the day's entertainment (see p. 88).

As to the manner in which the story books were compiled, it is quite evident that Nicholas Ferrar, the VISITOUR, and master of the ceremonies, took careful notes of each day's proceedings, or deputed some one else to do so; after which he formed them into "colloquies, with forcible applications of all to their own circumstances; and for that very reason (because they are so adapted to the private constitution of this family) the books themselves (which are two or three large folios) are not fit to be published, though they are well and properly worded."

This is the account given of them by Dr. Jebb, who also writes in an early part of the same memoir, concerning Mrs. Collet's daughters, "If ever women merited the title of *the devout sex*, these gentlewomen won it by their carriage, and deserved to wear it; though to come to many particulars would so oppress the modesty of some yet alive, that such instances of their devotion are not yet to be made public."

After the lapse of 260 years all details which would once have been accounted too personal for publication have now become historical; and it is with the cordial consent of the present representatives of the family that these records of the conversations and aims of the Little Gidding Academy are for the first time published in their entirety.

The importance which was attached to the continuance of these religious exercises by those who in the first instance promoted them, is worthy of attention. Just before the death of old Mrs. Ferrar, in 1634, when these meetings had, from one impediment and another, been discontinued for more than two years, "finding that the intimation of her desires by word of mouth did not prevail for the renewing and prosecution of this intermitted work, she proceeded to the expressing of them by writing, with such lowliness of intreaty where she had the right of command, as the particular declaration thereof (so writes Nicholas Ferrar after his mother's death), oppressing the modestie of the surviving, must be buried in her grave." In this paper she enjoined all her family to bring about, as much as lay in their power, "a full accomplishment of all those holy desires which she made overture of; amongst which this of storying being found upon record, signed with her own hand, to be one of the principal that she intended, it was concluded that it must necessarily be proceeded in" (see Story Books, vol. ii. part 2, Brit. Mus.).

Nicholas Ferrar, also, when he lay a-dying, counselled the younger members of his family to "remember all that he taught them in their books called the children's morning and night precepts, and their story books, and to keep in heart diligently their psalms and concordances" (see John Ferrar's Life of his Brother).

THE LITTLE ACADEMY

DRAMATIS PERSONAE

FIRST VOLUME

The Founder, Grandmother, or *Mother* . . . Mrs. FERRAR.
The Guardian . . . . . . JOHN FERRAR.
The Visitour . . . . . NICHOLAS FERRAR.
The Good Wife . . . SUSANNA MAPLETOFT (*née* COLLET)
(though not mentioned in these volumes).

FIRST COMBINATION.

The Foure Mayden Sisters.

The Cheife . . . . . MARY COLLET.
The Patient . . . . . ANNA COLLET.
The Cheerefull ⎫ . . MARGARET and ELIZABETH COLLET
The Affectionate ⎬ (which was the former and which
⎭ the latter does not transpire).

SECOND COMBINATION.

The Moderatour . . . Mrs. COLLET (*née* SUSANNA FERRAR).
The Obedient ⎫ . . Two of the three Younger Sisters,
The Submiss ⎭ HESTER, JOYCE, and JUDITH.

SECOND VOLUME

The Cheife becomes *The Mother* in the place of her Grandmother, who resigns.
The Humble . ANN MAPLETOFT, seventh child of Mrs. JOSHUA MAPLETOFT (*née* SUSANNA COLLET).

& was y:e same Day, wherein y:e Church celebrates y:t great festivall of y:e Purification of y:e Mayden Sisters Longing to be Imitators of those glorious Saints, by whose Names they were (called) for All those Saints Names, &c. she, y:t was elected Abb:ss that of y:e Blessed Virgin Mary) Saving entred into a Joynt Covenant betweene themselves, & some others of Neerest Blood (as according to those severall Relations they stiled Foundee, Guardian & Visito:rs) for y:e performance of divers Religious Exercizes: Least as sweet Liquo:rs are oftentimes Corrupted by

CONTENTS

FIRST VOLUME OF THE MANUSCRIPT

I
	PAGE
THE FEAST OF THE PURIFICATION, 1630 (1631)	1

II
ASH WEDNESDAY, 1630 (1631)	3

III
EASTER, 1631	11

IV
CHRISTMASTIDE, 1631—ST. STEPHEN'S DAY	19

V
CHRISTMASTIDE, 1631—ST. JOHN THE EVANGELIST'S DAY	39

VI
CHRISTMASTIDE, 1631—HOLY INNOCENTS' DAY	59

VII
CHRISTMASTIDE, 1631, DECEMBER 29TH	72

CONTENTS

VIII
CHRISTMASTIDE, 1631 91

IX
CHRISTMASTIDE, 1631 103

SECOND VOLUME OF THE MANUSCRIPT

X
ST. LUKE'S DAY, 1632 154

XI
ALL SAINTS' DAY, 1632 173

XII
ST. ANDREW'S DAY, 1632 208

XIII
CHRISTMASTIDE, 1632 246

XIV
CHRISTMASTIDE, 1632—ST. JOHN THE EVANGELIST'S DAY 267

XV
CHRISTMASTIDE, 1632—HOLY INNOCENTS' DAY . 279

LIST OF ILLUSTRATIONS

NICHOLAS FERRAR. *Engraved by C. J. Tomkins, after the picture by Janssen at Magdalene College, Cambridge* . . . . *Frontispiece*

    PAGE

EIKON BASILIKE. *Bound at Little Gidding, by Mary Collet* xxxii

LITTLE GIDDING CHURCH. *Showing the graves of John and Nicholas Ferrar* . . . xl

FACSIMILE OF PART OF A PAGE OF THE FIRST VOLUME OF THE STORIES IN NICHOLAS FERRAR'S HANDWRITING xlv

MRS. FERRAR. *From the picture by Janssen in the possession of Lady Lyell, painted in her sixty-second year* 1

MRS. COLLET AND CHILD. *From the picture in the possession of Lady Lyell* 154

INSCRIPTION AND LETTERS IN FIRST VOLUME.

JOHANNES COLLET,
FILIUS
THOMŒ COLLET,
PATER
THOMŒ, GULIELMI, & JOHANNIS,
OMNIUM SUPERSTES
NATUS
QUARTO JUNIJ, 1633,
DENASCITURUS
QUANDO DEO VISUM FUERIT,
INTERIM HUJUS PROPRIETARIUS,
JOHN COLLET.

Elizabeth Kestian given me by my dear cosen John Collet. I desier it to be given to my dear cosen Dr. John Mapletoft.

MOST DEARE AND HONOURED GRANDMOTHER,
The finishing of this Book in the return of the self-same Festival in which it began, having, amongst many other Considerations, brought to remembrance the Love you that Day shewed in bestowing the best of your Roomes and Furniture upon us for the Performance of this and other good Exercizes, have made us judge that the first fruits of our Labours in every kind are due to you, by whose Bounty wee have received the Opportunitie of beginning and con-

tinuing in them. Wee most humbly beseech you, therefore, favourably to accept now in writing that which you were so favourably pleased to approve in the rehearsing, and together with it our faithfull acknowledgement that wee doe owe to you as the great instrument of GODS Mercy, not onely the Convenience and Opportunitie, but even the very Abilities themselves that are in us towards the performance of this or any other good thing; considering that the vacancie of time, the meanes of Instruction, and all other necessarie concurrent helps, have had their prime and cheif rise from and by meanes of your Love, and on your Love and Life doe even at this present mainly depend. Besides, for that whereunto this particular exercise is chiefly intended: the Discoverie of those false Opinions wherewith the world misleads all Mankind, especially our weaker sex,—wee have received both by your precepts and example, if not the greatest and weightiest, yet surely the most proper and effectual Arguments and Motives that could have beene brought. You have forsaken all those Affections, Imploiments, and Delights, wherein the world perswades the cheif content of womens minds should ly, and you have censured them as vanities at the best, as sins and great ones, as they are commonly pursued. You have taught us often that which wee hope shall ever remaine as firme written in our minds as in this Book, That there is nothing but the Practizes of Vertue and Religion that can in the end yeeld comfort: all other things will turn to Bitternes at the last. Wee know your experience hath beene more large and full then most others in these matters, and therefore cannot but beleive your judgement to bee right; and upon this ground have beene the rather encouraged to the contempt of that which is indeed contemptible, and to the endeavouring after those things which are alone worthy Love and Honour. Wee are bold, deare Grandmother, to refresh these things upon this occasion, the rather as it were by the recording thereof to oblidge our selves to the following both of your Example and Advise, the Benefits whereof in the Continuance of the Life wee most humbly beseech GOD of his infinite Mercie long to continue to us and your whole Familie.

Your most Bounden Daughters,
The Sisters,
MARY AND ANNA COLLET.

2 Februarie,
1631.

MY DEARE CHILDREN,

What I have taught is true. Use carefully therefore now and ever the time and Opportunities that GOD offers you for the attainement of wisedome and encrease of Vertue. As for matters of Huswifery, when GOD puts them upon you it would bee sin either to refuse them or to perform them negligently, and therefore the ignorance of them is a great shame and Danger for women that intend Marriage. But to seek these kinds of Businesses for pleasure, and to make them your delights, and to pride yourselves for your care and curiositie in them, is a great vanitie and Folly at the best, and to neglect better things and more necessarie by pretence of being imployed in these things is surely, though a common Practize, yet a peice of sinfull Hypocrisie. Doe them therefore, when GOD puts them upon you, and doe them carefully and well, and GOD shall reward you, however the things themselves bee but meane, accepting them at your hands as if they were greater matters, when they are done and undergone out of Obedience to his Command. But let your Delight bee onely in the better part. As for your Book, I kindly accept it; and although I have heard you very jealously deny the communicating it with any, yet because I suppose you esteeme your Sister Mapletoft all one with yourselves, I would have you send her this Book, which I doubt not will bee both of Profit and comfort to her.

GOD continue and encrease you in every good way and thing, till you come to Perfection in Christ Jesus.

Your Mother,
MARY FARRAR.

INSCRIPTION AND LETTERS

To our Dearest Sister,

With the same Love that is given by our most honoured Grandmother, doe wee make the Conveyance of this Book unto you, our dearest Sister, professing faithfully that wee esteeme our Paines as well imployed in thus parting with it to you as wee should have done in keeping it for ourselves, so much doe wee love and prize the Grace of God that is in you, and the gracious Benediction of God which wee have received by your meanes, a most worthy and faithfull Brother; to whose good judgement wee doe freely submitt this little work, beseeching him to give us Notice of what hee there shall find amisse.

And so beseeching God to perfect his goodnes in you by the full Restitution both of inward and bodily Health, wee rest,

    Your faithfull
     Sisters,

2 Februarie, 1631.   Mary and Anna Collet.

Who both dyed Virgins, resolving so to live when they were young, by the Grace of God. My much honoured Aunt Mary, who took care of me and my Brother Peter and Sister Mary after the death of our reverend and pious Father, Mr. Joshua Mapletoft, dyed in the 80th year of her age.

        John Mapletoft.

Jan. 22, 1715.

My Deare and Worthy Neice,

The equall joy and Benefitt which I have in and by you make mee as gladly give you my part as your Sisters have done theirs of this Book, and to add my further promise, which their joynt consent doth ratifie, that of every good thing that God shall impart to us, you shall ever have as liberal and free a communication as wee can possibly make you; which not onely our Love but your own desert binds us to, whilest you continue what you are by the performance of your Duty, the great Comfort and Ornament to our Familie.

God make you to encrease in all his graces and Blessings. Amen.

Your Unkle,
Nicholas Farrar.

This Book was presented by my great Grandmother, my honoured Mothers two Sisters (the daughters of John and Susanna Collet), and their Unkle Nicholas Farrar, who was my God father, to my ever honoured Mother, Susanna Mapletoft, the same year in which I was born. And I desire my Son, to whom I do give it, with the great Concordance and other story Books, that they may be preserved in the Family as long as may be.

John Mapletoft.

Jan. 23, 1715.

MRS. FERRAR. *After Janssen.*
From the picture in the possession of Lady Lyell.

BOOK I

I

THE FEAST OF THE PURIFICATION, 1630 (1631)

Formation and design of the Little Academy.

IT was the same Day wherein the Church celebrates that great Festivall of the Purification, that the Mayden Sisters, longing to bee Imitatours of those glorious Saints by whose Names they were called (for all bare Saints Names, and shee that was elected CHEIFE, that of the Blessed Virgin Mary) having entered into a joynt Covenant betweene themselves and some others of neerest Blood (which according to their severall relations they stiled FOUNDER, GUARDIAN, and VISITOUR) for the performance of divers religious exercizes, least, as sweet Liquours are oftentimes corrupted by the sowrenesse of the Vessells wherein they are infused, there should arise in their hearts a Distast or Abuse of those excellent things which they purposed; they therefore resolved, together with the Practize of Devotion, to intermingle the study of wisedome, searching and enquiring diligently into the knowledge of those things which appertaine to their Condition and Sex.

Finding in themselves, and observing in others that doe sincerely pursue vertue, that the greatest barre of Perfection was Ignorance of the truth, whereby through misapprehension many prejudiciall things were embraced, and many most behovefull to their ends and most delightfull in performance were not onely neglected but abhorred: which, having by many particulars experimented in themselves, doubting that they were alike abused in most of those things which wee have received by Tradition from our Fathers, they determined with firme promises each to other to make a particular survey of those opinions and practizes which the world recommends or disallows, weighing them not in the scales of common Judgement, but of true and right Reason, according to the weights and by the standard of the Scripture; wherein being excellently versed, so as they were able to repeat by heart both the Booke of Psalms and most part of the New Testament, they found that there was neither Action nor Opinion that could bee propounded but might receive a clear solution and direction from that Booke.

Wherefore, not upon presumption of their own Abilities, but on Confidence of GODS gracious assistance to their humble and diligent Indeavours, they agreed every day at a sett houre to conferre together of some such subject as should tend either to the information of the understanding or to the exciting of the Affections, to the more ready and fervent prosecution of vertues and better performance of all such duties as in their present or other Course of Life hereafter should be required of them.

The first proceedings, as it alwaies happens in great Attempts that have no presidents to direct, were both in forme and substance farre short of that whereunto they were in the end reduced.

Wherefore, as Artists upon the full accomplishment of their workes cast aside the first draughts, so silencing what was lesse exactly done, I shall goe on with the recording of things from that time which themselves accompt the beginning, being about the end of May. Onely, by way of introduction, as Porches were anciently sett in the Fronts of greater Buildings, I will sett downe the passages of two or three severall daies, which may well serve for a preface to the Reader for this following booke, as in truth they were maine arguments to the Confirmation of their minds who were the Actours of this and other noble undertakings.

II

ASH WEDNESDAY, 1630 (1631)

*Pirrhus—Trajan—The Lady of the Lights—The Courtiers'
Penny Tax.*

ON Ashwednesday, therefore, although for the better suiting of their bodies to their Hearts and their Hearts to the Meditations of the Day they forbore the refreshment of corporall Food, yet so much the more desirous to feast their minds in the Fast of their Bodies, meeting at their appointed time and place, together with that other Company which were alwaies Auditours, and sometimes at least one of them partener Actours, in these Exercizes,

The CHEIFE began thus :—

My dearest Sisters and sweet Companions, the Solemnity of this day inviting us to sober thoughts, I shall desire our stories may be such as both befitt the season and tend to a serious Confirmation of our well chosen resolutions. And that so much the rather, because if you shall agree thereunto wee will make this Day the beginning of our exercize, accounting this weeke already past but as the tuning of Instruments before the Musick, harsh Jarring to sweet Harmony. The whole company seeming by cheerefull gesture to approve the matter, the GUARDIAN in all their behalfes made answere :—Faire CHEIFE, the motion is, like yourselfe, most acceptable, and worthy to be so. Wherefore, in GODS Name doe you make enterance, and wee all will, to the best of our Abilities, second you, both in Cloth and Colour, as the Proverbe is. Whereupon she thus proceeded.

That brave King and Captaine Pirrhus, whom Haniball judged the worthiest Chieftaine next Alexander that ever the world had, boyling with ambitious desires of enlarging his Dominions and encreasing his Honnours, brought one day into Consultation amongst his Captaines and other Freinds, the resolutions of warring upon some of his Neighbours, against whom hee had rather made then found a just Quarrell. The whole Counsaile gave their votes according to the Kings mind, onely one excepted, named Cineas, a man of long robes, who, excusing his Ignorance in martiall matters, besought his Majesty that, waving all arguments touching that subject, hee might freely demand some few questions of him. To which the King graciously condescending, Cineas sayd, Sir, when you have overcome these against whom you are now bent, what will your grace further doe? Marry, quoth the King, if wee heerein prove successefull, the whole state of Greece must submitt to our Empire. Bee it so, sayth Cineas; will you rest there? Nay, verily, quoth Pirrhus; but then immediately will wee goe against the Romanes, and if wee overthrow them, then Italy shall be the fruit of our Labours and hazard. A noble and happy Conquest, says Cineas; but when this shall be effected, what shall wee then doe? Why then, quoth the King, wee shall not doubt to sett on the Carthaginians. And suppose you have overcome them, what then? Why then, quoth hee, all Africa shall be ours. In a blessed houre, replied Cineas; and what shall wee then doe? Pirrhus, now growne a wearie, halfe in anger, half in mirth, Oh Cineas, sayth hee, then will wee give our selves to rest and quiet, to Banquets and Games, and enjoy all the happines which wee shall have purchased. If that, sayd hee, dread Soveraigne, bee the upshott of your intents and aimes, who forbid you now to accomplish the same with saving of all that Labour and hazard which wee shall undergoe, and perhaps bee overwhelmed with? How can it bee conformable to your excellent wisedome to fetch a large and wearisome Course about for the attainement of those pleasures into the fruition whereof you may immediately enter, if you please? If a happy and delightfull life bee that you aime at in the end, why doe wee not without delay take our part thereof?

This sayd Cineas. And though Pirrhus could not gainesay, yet could hee not follow the prudent advise of this wise Counsellour but, led on stifly by his confused and blind desires, after some yeares spent in extremities toyle and anguish of mind and body, was miserably slaine by a piece of Timber cast downe from the top of a house by a womans hand. But his tragicall end is not that which I have recounted this story for, but the proposall of Cineas his argument to convince the madnes of us Christians that, professing the service of GOD out of a pure heart and good Conscience to bee the maine and upshott of all our desires and aimes, doe notwithstanding all by a joynt Conspiracy, as it were, in folly sett that part to be performed in the Catastrophe of our Life, giving our youth and present times to the pursuit of vanities, spending the strength and vigour, both of mind and body, in a violent race cleane contrary to that path at the head whereof the prize is sett, which wee pretend to seek. But let us no more, my dearest Sisters, bee as Children tossed to and fro with every windy and frothy argument of the Lovers of this world, but come to a cleare and stable resolution touching the leading of our lifes henceforth. If the service of the world and the Flesh bee good and beneficiall, and worthy our soules, that fetch their Originall from heaven, why, then, lett us sett seriously thereabout, loosing no time, gett what wee may of the pleasures and profitts they afford and perhaps offer a liberall tast unto us, and herein let us sett up our rest. If we say Nay, but though for a while wee shall be glad to bee partakers of this worlds delights, yet on no hand will wee take them for our Portion, but purpose in the end bidding adue to them all as, with greatest Honour to her and joy to our selves, wee see our dearest Grandmother to have done; why, then, what silly fondness will it bee not to beginne even from this very instant to follow that Course which in the end wee resolve to take, and to endeavour the attainement of those things which wee know onely to bee worthy keeping: Wisedome, Temperance, Patience, Meekenes, Humility, and the rest of those heavenly ornaments. As for the vaine Fancies in apparrell, the licorish appetites in Diet, foolish imployments of our minds and times in gauds and trifles, peevish venting of humours, and all the like infirmities which vex our weake sex, why should wee not from this very houre bid an utter defiance unto them, since at the last wee meane with shame to casheere them as our reproach and danger? If it will be honourable and good in our gray haires, how much more now in youth, to bee wise and vertuous?

Here the CHEIFE stayd, and having for a good space sett her eies on the ground, at last with a cheerefull eie viewing the Company round about—Your thoughtfull Countenances (sayd shee) give Testimony that I have sayd too much, and perhaps in other manner then I ought, and therefore I will no further increase your wearinesse or my owne fault.

Not so (replied the GUARDIAN) most worthy CHEIFE, but rather the excelleney of the matter and your answerable handling of it hath bred this solemne alteration on our parts; so as though wee could gladly heare your discourse till the starres should appear, yet that wee may not at present overcharge yours nor our owne memories, desirous to beare away that which you have already sayd, wee are content to yeeld to your desires.

Whereupon the CHEIFE arose and took the PATIENT by the hand, and sett her downe in the Chaire, saying, To you belongs, deare Sister, by some better recounted story to make satisfaction for that which I have been wanting in.

To whom the PATIENT replied: Whatsoever shall this day, worthy CHEIFE, bee sayd on this subject must be but descant on the song which you have now sett. And in proof thereof

I shall tell you an example tending to that purpose,—That every man in his place should bee carefull to perswade his owne office without delay.

Trajan, that incomparable Emperour, being on a day in speedy March against some Barbarians that had broken into the Romane Pale, a poore Widdow pressing through the middest of his guard, casting her selfe on her knees, tooke hold of his stirrop, and with a showre of teares besought him to doe her justice of one that had cruelly murdered her onely son. The Emperour bad her rise, saying that at his returne hee would doe her justice to the full. But now, Mother, sayd hee, my hast is too great. Whereupon the old Woman replied, Suppose you come not back againe, who then shall doe mee right? That shall my successour, sayd Trajan. Alas, Sir, sayd shee, if he should faile mee too, shall not you then remaine indebted to Justice and to mee? But in case that thy successour doe mee right, shall his Justice free thee? Nay, shall it not rather augment thy fault? Happy will it be for him if all that hee can doe suffice to discharge himselfe, which is more, as thou perceiveth, then thou now canst doe. The Emperour hearing this dismounted presently, and sent for the Accused, did the widdow Justice according to her desire and his owne duty, and afterwards discomfited his enemies and returned with great honour. This was one of those noble Acts which made this Emperour so famous and beloved, as after ages, out of Compassion that such incomparable vertues should be damned, feined Trajans soule to bee returned out of hell by St. Gregory the great his Prayers. But surely, wherever his soule bee, the wisedome and worth of his actions ought to be imitated by us, never putting of the doing of right and Justice which wee are bound to performe.

The PATIENTS story was of all much commended, and the CHEIFE, taking the CHEEREFULL by the hand, Although (sayd shee) the mends of my defects bee already made by this renowned Story, yet that it may bee with greater advantage, I shall desire you, sweet Sister, to fitt us with some of those excellent ones which you are Mistresse of. Whereupon the CHEEREFULL made answere: I am at the most but a steward that keepe others wealth, but because I know with their good liking I may make use of that which is in my store, I shall tell you an example to perswade us not to deferre the bestowing of our Almes and the exercize of our Charity (as the manner of too many is) to the period of our lives; but whilest opportunity serveth to bee ready to distribute and willing to communicate, according to the Apostles Counsell and encouragement, laying up in store a good Foundation against the time to come. To this purpose shall my story bee, whereof, however the Fact may bee doubtfull, the morall, I am sure, is most profitable.

A great Lady, high both in Bloud and Riches, but much more high and happy in the Vertues of her Sonne, by Dignity a Bishop, and in holy Conversation a Saint, being oftentimes pressed by him to the exercize of Charity in an overflowing measure, still putt him off with the large bequest that shee intended in her will to good uses, which shee conceived would bee as acceptable to GOD and profitable to her selfe as any present distribution. Her good son, perceiving that by solid arguments he was not able to perswade her, bethought himselfe by a more plain and materiall kind of proofe to convince her. One night, therefore, having invited her to supper at his pallace, which hee studiously protracted, at her getting into the Coach to returne home, it being very late and darke shee called for torches to attend and guide the way. The Bishop, who had purposely commanded there should bee none ready, desired her to lett the Coachman drive on easily. To which when shee made answere that all the way being bad needed light, but especially the passage of the bridge, which was very perilous, the Bishop counselled her to proceede, saying that he would send the lights after, which should overtake her by that time shee came to the Bridge. Whereunto with much passion she replied. That will I not hazard, sayd she, by any meanes; for suppose wee should bee on it before wee are aware? There would then perhaps need more then lights to helpe us out againe, and to remedy the hurt that might befall us. I will not therefore stirre, sayd shee, till I have the Torches before mee. The Bishop, seeing that it wrought as hee wished, with great humility besought her to consider whether it were not fitt to observe the same Course in that which was of farre more importance, sending her good works and Almedeeds before her by the performance of them in her Life time, rather then to leave them till the last houres, which might happily, as it did many others, by sudden approach prevent her expectation. Which if it should, Madam (sayd hee) I cannot say how certainely you might promise yourselfe to accomplish what you intend. Many more and greater hazards of disappointment must needs bee undergone then that which you now feare from me. But, howsoever, this I am certaine, that at best the lights can but follow, which will bee nothing like, either for Comfort or safety in so dreadfull a passage, as to have it nightly shining before you. The good Lady, beeing a woman of deepe understanding, after shee had well pondered the matter, told her Son that the Causes were indeed so like that shee ment to hold the same Course in both, and therefore, sayd shee, let mee now have the torches alongst with mee to prevent bodily danger, and come you tomorrow, and take order for the providing of as much Light as may bee for the conducting of my soule in that darke and fearefull passage of death.

You have, deare CHEEREFULL (sayd the GUARDIAN), passed our expectations in this story. Let us heare (sayd the CHEIFE) what the AFFECTIONATE intends, and I doubt not, honoured GUARDIAN, but you shall have further matter of Commendation. My Story (sayd the AFFECTIONATE) being short and to perswade the sparing of faults, I should make a double one to trouble you with a preface.—A certaine Courtier having obtained of the Prince towards the repaire of his decaied Fortunes a charter to exact a penny for every defect in Man or Beast that passed the gates of the Citty, his Officers seeing one come limping by, called to him for their due. Hee, pretending that it was but a casuall stirring, refused to pay, whereupon, drawing nearer to him, the Officers perceived a blemish in his eies, and so required twopence. He offered the first penny; for the last hee began stoutly to maintaine that, seeing his sight was perfect, the blemish was not in Compasse of their Charter. They as resolutely claiming as hee denying, by misfortune his hatt fell off, and some soreness appearing on his head, they then told him they would have threepence. Which in the end the poore man was forced to doe, that might at first have gone cleare for a penny. How often hath it happened so with mee in the foolish defence of errors, multiplying the guilt and putting upon my selfe the necessity of discompting by fourefold sorrow and shame that which at first a light acknowledgement would have redeemed. Its best therefore at the first to make the amends of that which is done amisse. So I counsell you, and, GOD willing, shall my selfe practize, paying my Penny at the first demande to save further Arrearages.

This is as much of that daies passage as the Actours themselves give leave to recompt.

III

EASTER, 1631

Humility and moderation of the Emperor Charles the Fifth—His sister, Mary Queen of Hungary.

IN the like kind were their appointed houres dayly spent till after Easter, when the whole frame of this lower world wherein wee are bounded, seeming to sett itselfe forth with all manner of bravery to entertaine the approaching Sun her Paramour, least the outward glory and pleasure that every way offered it selfe should by ravishment of the senses steale away their hearts from the pursuit of those farre more rich though lesse evident beauties and delights which they were enamoured of, this sober Company resolved, both for a Counterpoyze to the common Jollity of that season and for a wholesome restraint of their weaker Affections (that they might not melt away through too much sweetness in an unparalelled Prosperity, which GOD had every way crowned them with), by the Choyse of more sad and solemne meditations and discourses to allay that lightnes and excesse of Cheerefulnes which too much happines doth unhappily breed in most mens minds, perswading themselves, that in a moderate and temperate enjoyment of their outward Comforts they should both better confirme the fruition of them, and more certainly attaine those Benefitts to which Prosperity, when it is conferred by GODS Love and favour, is intended. Which in their Judgement they determined to bee not the Debauchment of the soule through a dissolute surfetting in those vanities and pleasures which the world sucks out of GODS blessings, but rather the composing of mens minds by the experiment of the Insufficiency of all earthly things to give Content to a right esteeme and use of them, not as things wherein our desires should rest and settle themselves, but whereby they should bee carried up to the Contemplation and pursuit of those true, eternall, and absolute good things whereof all that seems good here below is but as a beame or rather glimpse of light to the body of the sunne itselfe.

These great thoughts working in the minds of this little society, and a necessity of handling some choise subject being occasioned by the presence of certaine Freinds whom dearest Affection enforced to admitt, and worth required to entertaine with more then ordinary preparations, the CHEIFE thus gave vent to their overflowing thoughts.—

The desire of happines is one and the same in all men, but the apprehensions and pursuits thereof are almost as many as the men themselves. Some few select soules agree that it is not else where to be found but in GOD. But the most part, deceived by false appearances or rather shaddows, hope to attaine it in the heaping up of riches, honour, and pleasures. Hence ariseth that continual restlesse toyle of mind and body with which wee find all men overwhelmed whilest they seeke to multiply the store and possession of these things to themselves wherein they conceive happines to be included. And although they find their expectation still frustrated of that Content which they imagined, yet bewitched with the glorious prospective of things which are before them, they are led on, both with unsatiable desires and unwearied attempts in the following of these vanities, ever imputing the want of their Content to the want of some one thing or other. Whereas, in truth, if all whatsoever the world hath from its beginning afforded in matter of riches, Honour, and Pleasure were molded in one Lumpe, and given to any one Man to enjoy, it were not able to satisfy his soule, but he would still find an emptiness or rather an increase of anguish.

Its a well knowne story of Alexander the great, that having conquered the greatest part of this world, and undoubtedly possessed himselfe of all the good in it, hearing talk of more worlds hee fell a weeping. So little was all that which he had able to satisfy his desires, that it could not keepe him from lamenting his miserable Estate. Questionlesse if wee did seriously weigh, as wee must necessarily beleive, the truth of this, wee should not bee so violently and vainely led on to the spending of our selves in the seeking of the things of this world. I suppose, therefore, that there can bee nothing more profitable, either to the disturning of our minds from the over-greedy pursuit of things here below or to inflame them to the endeavour after those things which are above, then to add to the continuall experiment of the insufficiency of these things which every one findeth in their owne soules by dayly tryall, the often refreshment of those illustrious examples which GOD hath continually sett forth before our eies for the full reformation of our understanding touching the Vanity of all earthly things, still making this application to oure owne hearts, that if the mighty men of the world could not attaine Joy nor Content in the right and fulnes of all things that this world affords, it will bee mere madnesse for us to hope to find it in the offalls and scraps of meaner fortunes; and if they were forced at last to goe to GOD, and to seike their happines in his service, how much wisedome and Happines wilbe in us to beginne timely whither they all in the end strive. But because old stories move not so much, either because they have beene often heard formerly, or perhaps are not so fully credited, I shall desire that our instances may bee of later times, and that you, deare PATIENT, would make the enterance by the recompting of that incomparable History touching the Death of the last King of Spaine, Philip the third, then which I have never heard a more convincing proofe both of this worlds Vanity and of the worth of GODS service.

(The Stories of King Philip, Henery the fourth of France, and the two Popes Marcellus and Adrian, being this day told by the PATIENT, CHEEREFULL, and AFFECTIONATE, are here omitted, being brought in afterwards to serve for Innocents Day.

But the conclusion of this day proving the beginning of a large and painefull work to the CHEIFE, I have thought fitt to insert here that passage which it brought on, the rather to enforce the full performance and perfection of the same.)

Both the vehemency of spirits and the abruptnes of the Period with which the AFFECTIONATE closed, made the Company for a while to expect her further proceeding, which by her rising from the Chaire perceiving to be otherwise, one of them smiling, as though hee would make believe that the AFFECTIONATE, whom they prized for a good Historian, was but a bad Herald, stayed her, saying, your Conclusion is not necessary, because your Induction is not full, having left out that which is the cheife, the imperiall Diademe, which perhaps by its transcendent power and Dignity circles in that perfect happines and Content which these lesser Orbs of Kings and Popes Crownes cannot.

The AFFECTIONATE, turning her eies to the CHEIFE as admonishing her of her Cue, That part (sayd the CHEIFE) is imposed on mee for the Conformity of Name, not for the proportionablenes of abilities, for it might have beene performed better by some others. And although in regard of the worth and weight of the subject it requires a more curious hand then mine, yet that I may shew that just obedience to your authority which I shall require in the like kind from you, I shall recount a true and fresh History, which shall serve as a seale to your Confirmation of all which my Sisters by their former stories have endeavored to perswade themselves and us.

Is it possible, sayd the GUARDIAN, that wee should heare any more convincing proofes and examples then those which have already been told?

Yes, verily (sayd the CHEIFE). By how much the excesse of Dignity, the Excellency of personal worth, and the more lively manner of hearing evidence (hee having put in execution those Conceptions which these former recompted Princes uttered onely in word), by so much doe I esteeme Charles the V a more pregnant testimony that all which this world yeelds is nothing but vanity and vexation of spirit.

The name of Charles stilled not onely the tongues, but the thoughts of the whole Company, who, settling themselves with great attention, seemed with much earnestnes to require the CHEIFES performance of her promise and satisfaction of their desires. But she, drawing back from the Chaire to which shee had all this while sett next, The time, sayd shee, is too farre spent at present, nor am I provided as I wish. Besides, the Story itselfe is worthy of an intire Day. The Company, yeelding to the justnes of her excuse, without further reply dissolved that time.

The next Day, meeting at their ordinary Place and Houre, the CHEIFE finding her selfe unfurnished for the discharge of her promise, casting about with witt to solve what indeed proceeded of want, as if it had beene of deliberate Choise what was indeed constreyned by Necessity, beganne thus.—

Least as it happens in royall Bankets, when they come too thick, the greatest dainties are not sett by, so it should prove in our royal stories, I suppose it not amisse, for the better preparing of our minds to receive them with that due attention and affection which they deserve, to give a little respite to the digesting of those which have beene yesterday told, least perhaps else, as hony to a full stomake, they should prove lesse regardfull in our minds. Wherefore, by your good leave, waving for the present the performance of my purpose and your expectation touching Charles the V his relinquishment of this worlds vanity, I shall tell you a particular Act of his which, as it was perhaps a preparation to these excellent resolutions which he at last undertooke, so it shall serve mee for a preface to the recompting of them.

Having overcome John Frederick of Saxony and Maurice of Silessia in a most unexpected manner, when all the world sang the applause of his invincible prowesse, wisedome, and good

Fortune, comparing him to Julius Cæsar in the greatnes of his attempts, and particularly in the happy acheivement of this victory, attributing to him, as of right, that famous Motto which Julius Cæsar used, I came, I saw, and overcame. Hee, striking out the last word as too full of arrogancy, added a Couple of farre more truth and sobriety, making it thus to runne, I saw, and I came, and GOD overcame: by his Humility and wisedome farre more deserving admiration then by his victory.

The CHEIFE having ended her story, the PATIENT thus seconded her.—

There is no Meddow more abundant of sweet and beautifull Flowres then this noble Princes Life was of faire Actions and vertues. Wherefore I desire, since wee are in so rich a Garden for beauty and delight, that wee should not seeke any further to finish this daies worke. Our CHEIFE hath told you a passage of his humility to GOD-ward; I shall tell you one of the monstrations of his mind towards his equalls and enemies. As hee was going to Even-song, News was brought him that his great and potent enemy, Francis the first, was overthrowne and taken prisoner by his Captaines. When his Counsellors and Courtiers attending on him broke out into great rejoycings and Boastings, hee with a severe Countenance, stilling all their unseasonable mirth, kept on his Course to Church, where, commanding Publick thanks to be given in a solemne manner for the victory which hee had obtained, hee did streightly forbid all those expressions of publique mirth which by fires, Bells, and other waies were intended in the Citty, deeming the effusion of so much Christian bloud and the Calamity of so great a Prince to deserve rather teares and Compassion then mirth or insultation. The next morning hee received the sacrament with evident tokens of great devotion, and went, accompanied with the whole Court, in procession. Neither in words or deeds, sayth the Prince of Historians, did hee discover any spice of unfitting mirth or swelling thoughts. To the congratulation of Embassadours and other great Persons about him his answere was, That hee could not but much rejoice by the manifest assistance of the Divine Power to have received a certaine earnest of GODS favour towards him, and to bee made confident, though most unworthy, that hee was in his grace from whom hee had obtained so singular mercy. For the rest hee no further rejoyced then that there was thereby opportunity offered him to settle peace in Christendome to turne their joynt Armes against the common Enemies of our Faith, and together with these greater designes to bee able to benefitt his Freinds, and to pardon his enemyes, and in Confirmation of these intents hee did then receive the Justification of certaine States, which had highly offended him, although as hee professed, their excuses were altogether insufficient, and by this occasion hee had gained much advantage to right himselfe: But he rather chose to follow St. Pauls example, using the Authority which GOD had given him, to edification and not to Destruction.

Yet all this, mee thinkes, seemes little (sayd the AFFECTIONATE) in point of Moderation in regard of that surpassing Patience which this heroycall Emperour shewed, when at the seige of Metz a souldier of base ranke, but baser Condition, after the bitter imputation of their common Miseries to his folly called him to his face the sonne of a madwoman. How great a magnanimity was there in his brest, that could without disquiet passe over such an affront, which, to that Anguish of mind hee then endured in the greatest of all Calamities that ever befell him, must needs bee like the powring of scalding oyle upon smarting wounds. The reproaches against Prosperity and Innocency are but the beating of the garments. That cuts to the soule, that are true and given upon advantage. I commend him of generousnes, that contemneth that Injury which hurts him not. But I admire him that holds his hand, whenas his heart is peirced to the quick, and restraines the power of revenge when hee is offended, out of presumption of weaknesse.

The CHEEREFULLS story at that time being more proper to

another head, and hereafter to bee remembered, in supply take that which was told the next Day as more sutable to the former peices, being of the selfe-same Charles, and Mary the widdow-Queene of Hungary, his Sister in bloud and vertue during life, and his Companion in death and in the selfe-same resolutions of abandoning the world, whilst they lived in it.—

After her husbands the King of Hungarys Death shee returned to her Brother the Emperour, and continued with him, in presence counselling and assisting, and in his Absence governing some of the most noble parts of his large spreading Empire. It so happened that a Gentleman of noble birth and great estate corrupted on of her Maides of honour, which shee tooke so heynously, as the Gentleman was faine to fly to the Emperour, beseeching him to mediate the pardon of his offence, which the Emperour loving the Gentleman very dearely, did in most effectuall manner. But the royall Lady standing constant in her Judgement would by no meanes be entreated. The Emperour, hoping that time and Importunity might perswade her, ceased not with all earnestnes to solicite her reconciliation. Shee, seeming wearied therewith, besought her Brother the Emperour no more to trouble her in that matter, which was unworthy for him to meddle with, who being the fountaine of Justice ought rather to urge the execution thereof then the perversion. But, sayd shee, as it becomes a sister for the supply of what is defective on your part, I vow to GOD and you, that if ever hee come neere mee, though it bee in your owne Company, I will cause him to be hanged on the next tree that can be found. Whether this austere Love of Chastity and undanted Courage in the punishment of vice were greater in this noble Queene, or the Moderation and unpartiall mind of the Emperour, that could both patiently endure the dissappointment of his earnest desires and the generous reproofe of his Sister, I leave to your Judgement. To mee they seeme both worthy of highest praise and Imitation.

IV

CHRISTMASTIDE (1631)—ST. STEPHEN'S DAY

Sapritius — Sisois and his angry Friend — Macarius and his Disciple — John the Almoner — Henry IV. of France — Alphonsus XI. of Castile — Queen Katharine of Arragon — Abbot Apollinus and the two Combatants.

THE story of Charles the Fifts relinquishment of the world being grown already to a volume, and yet not perfected, although as much as is done was recited in the summer, is here omitted, and wee passe on to the setting downe of the Christmas Stories; the occasion whereof is expressed by the CHEIFE in the introduction which shee then made, and here next follows.—

It is a hard task that is imposed on us, most honoured GRANDMOTHER and FOUNDER of our little Academy, that wee should make supply of delights to your Family for those vaine pastimes of Cardes and the like, which you have so Christianly deprived them of. But when it is added that wee must likewise endeavour to profitt them in the way of vertue, as well as to please them, in requiring of two things that scarce stand together, there is made a great surcharge of Difficulty to the work and paines to us.

To make it a merry and true Christmas, both together, to your household by delightfull and vertuous exercises, that they should have no Cause to envy others greater Liberty or better Cheere, is the injunction. But that it should bee our performance were more than wee durst hope; but for the great encouragement of our worthy GUARDIAN, who perswades us that it will be easily and certainly effected by the dayly re-compting of some good Histories, whereof wee ought not in truth to bee unfurnished, considering the opportunity that GOD hath given us to grow rich in these kind of jewells; for Jewells they are indeed, especially when they are well sett by a gracefull delivery and a seasonable application.

With which two Conditions could wee bee sure to have our stories qualified, wee should indeed make no question, by giving most delightfull entertainment to the whole Family, to give full satisfaction to your desires and the command that is imposed on us.

But though wee cannot hope so much touching our stories, yet, since wee have no hope at all by any other meanes then by our stories in any part or manner to discharge ourselves of what wee are bound unto, wee have resolved this way to make Essay, wherein, if your good Acceptations shall give Encouragement, wee shall proceede the rest of this Festivall. Otherwise, if by this daies experiment you find our designes unworthy of your precious houres, or unanswerable to your worthy intentions, you may please, by your intimation of your dislike, to give an end to them, and by the direction of your wisedome to sett us in a better and more acceptable way.

Having thus spoken shee rose and sang the Hymne following, which the Master of their Musique played on the Vyoll.

> Unquenched Love in him appeared to bee,
> When for his murtherous foes hee did entreat;
> A piercing eie made bright by Faith had hee,
> For he beheld thee in thy glory sett;
> And so unmoved his Patience he did keepe,
> He did as if he had but falln asleepe.
>
> Our luke-warme hearts with his hott zeale inflame,
> So constant and so loving let us bee;
> So let us living glorify thy Name,
> So let us dying fix our eies on thee;
> And when the sleepe of Death shall us oertake,
> With him to Life eternall us awake.[1]

[1] This Hymne is one of Mr. Withers "Songs of the Church."

The Hymne being ended shee, with a low Reverence setling herselfe in the Chayre, thus proceeded.

This song, refreshing to the Memories the ground of this Daies solemnity, leades us of Necessity—except wee will make a treble Disproportion to the Festivall, to your Musick, and to your Minds, which I am sure are in expectation of matter answerable both to the time and this preface—to beginne and end our present exercise with stories of such affections, words, and Actions as in and by the example of blessed St. Stephen are recommended to our Imitation by GOD and the Church.

You must not looke to heare from us anything that shall match the height of his perfection. It were hard to find and perhaps would not prove so sutable. Dimme eies see better in a shady Light then in the brightness of the Sunne, and midling Examples and arguments more prevaile with weake and feeble minds then those that are more excellent in all other kinds, so especially in Matter of Vertue. That which must strongly move to imitation must not bee too farre removed from hope of matching in some good proportion. Wonder not, therefore, if now and then you heare that which may seeme but ordinary. Its purposely contrived, as courser dishes are served in greatest Feasts, that there may bee that which is pleasing and proper for every Mans liking and Constitution. But the maine ought to bee Dainties; and that it shoulde bee so in our Banquet you doe justly expect, and wee, as GOD enableth us, shall endeavour. And accordingly I shall first present you with a story full of admirable Actions and events and worthy of everlasting Remembrance.

Its a true Story for the substance and maine passages of it. Every Circumstance I dare not warrant, neither in this nor in most others perhaps that you shall hereafter heare. Thus hee spake, and in this manner hee did, are garnishes which wise Masters doe make supply of when the originalls are perished. Things did not passe nakedly, though they be nakedly recorded to us. It hath beene judged, therefore, no diminution of truth of History to make supply of such kind of particulars, which, when they are rightly fitted, serve not onely to pleasure, by representing the matter as it were in prospective, but to great benefitt by instructing and preparing the hearers minds how to behave themselves comely in the like occasions.

This Apology, sayd the GUARDIAN, is needlesse at all times, now very displeasant, because it hinders the story which wee so much desire. Whereupon the CHEIFE began.—

Sapritius was a Preist of Antioch in Syria, every waies venerable for excellency of Learning, for Sanctity of Life, for indefatigable paines, and happy fruit of his paines and Labours in Christs Church, not only confirming the Beleivers but converting many Infidels to the faith by his Doctrine and Example.

Amongst many that frequented his Divine Sermons there was one Nicephorus, a young man in Age, but old in Wisdome, whose extraordinary zeale and Diligence recommending him at first to Sapritius, his acquaintance afterwards so indeared him in his affections that Sapritius could not forbeare, if Nicephorus came not of himself to seeke him out every day, finding such an excesse of Content in Nicephorus his ready apprehension and carefull practize of highest Mysteries which hee was able to teach, as hee thought no time nor Paynes too much that was thus imployed. But when after two or three yeares space Nicephorus, as well by the eminency of his owne true worth as by the continuall recommendation of Sapritius using to put him for the Instance of holy Conversation, beganne to grow into such reputation as Sapritius thought it did much detract from his the Love and Goodwill which was not truely founded upon the Advancement of CHRIST his honour—howbeit, it had altogether beene exercised in things pertaining thereto—began by little and little through the undermining of envy to sink; and first by a cavillous kind of Demeanour in all things, and afterwards by an affected strangenes, Sapritius gave Nicephorus plaine remonstrance of an alienated mind and Affection, which, seeking occasion to breake of Freindship, quickly found it. Some difference arising betweene them, words were multiplied, and in heat of passions, wrongs and injuries offered on both parts. Nicephorus is scarce gone when, as Men in coole blood begin to feele the smart of those wounds which they felt not in the fray, the consideration of this error and of his Loss being represented in the cleare light of true Judgment, hee finds the Burden of them intolerable. To discharge himself therefore of that which he could not beare, hee hastens to Sapritius, makes Confession of his Fault, offers all amends that could bee, humbly sues for Pardon, but cannot obtaine it. He hopes time shall afford him helpe for what he cannot then effect, and continues by Meekenes, giving of honour and all manner of good offices, to endeavour the regaining of Sapritius Love and Friendship. But in vaine: Sapritius every day gives proofe of more and more displeasure. It was Nicephorus his vertue that he began to feare, and now was given to hate. Goodnesse, that appeaseth all other kind of wickednes, adds to the rage of envy.

Nicephorus, seeing that himselfe was not able to prevaile, imployes his friends to find the cause and mediate the peace between him and Sapritius. But herein hee proves as unhappy as in all his other attempts. Sapritius his obstination encreaseth by the application of the remedies, and Nicephorus, though wearied in body and wounded in mind, yet resolving not to bee overcome by any Faintnes till he had overcome by vertue, enforceth himselfe to make the last experiment. Hee goes home to Sapritius his house, falls downe at his feet, and with his hands lifted up, and teares running downe his Cheeke, beggs forgivenes of what he knew and what hee did not know to have done amisse. But Sapritius answeares were frownes and cruell words, and when they served not to drive him away, hee layes hands on Nicephorous and thrusteth him out of dores, bitterly laying to his charge not onely forepast matters but even his owne present distemper and all those misbeseeming outrages which himselfe had then committed. The Imputation of this guilt and the unexpected issue of

Businesse so amated poore Nicephorus, as he went away fuller of perplexity then he came ; and though many feares and sowre thoughts sett upon him, yet would hee give admission to none, but with meeke and humble Affections addressing himselfe, to GOD, besought equally the pardon both of his owne and Sapritius his errors, and for the rest perceiving all things sort contrary to reason and his owne forecast, hee grew to a firme resolution to committ himself wholly to the direction of GODS good spirit, and no more to disquiet himselfe touching what hee was further to doe or suffer in this matter, but with patience to wayt what the event should bee, assuring himselfe that by GODS mercy all should turne to his good.

Within a short space after the persecution that was begunne at Rome by Valerian and Galienus, whose thirst of Christian blood was so great as every Day three or foure thousand Martyrs were not sufficient to quench, it spred to Antioch. A President is sent armed with much Power, and enforced by a rigorous Commission to destroy all that will not deny CHRIST. He enters, and the same houre beginnes his examination. A light on a Hill cannot bee hidd. The generall voyce of all the Idolaters appeach Sapritius as the cheife upholder of his owne Christian religion, the greatest enemy of theirs. He appeares, confesseth the accusation, and after many cruell torments, wherein hee seemed rather to triumph then to suffer, is adjudged for his constancy in the Christian Faith to have his head strooke off. Nicephorous sees and heares all this, and leaping for joy upon Sapritius his bringing forth from the Tribunall, meets him, falls downe, and being ashamed, not for his owne but for Sapritius his sake, to give any intimation of such unworthines and weakenes as the memory of injuries implies, instead of Pardon craves his Blessing. Sapritius turnes away his Countenance as still retaining the former enmity ; and immediately the concurse of the people, striving to gaze on the condemned Man, forceably carries Nicephorus away and debarres him from all further speech. Hereupon hee makes hast, and running before to another place where hee knew Sapritius must of necessity passe, presents himselfe a second time in a suppliant gesture, and with words of great submission, beseeching him now at last to pardon his forepast errors. The standers by, and the very guard that led him, second the request by making roome, keeping silence and compassionate Lookes, and when they saw these prevailed not, by plaine words willing him to forgive and grant whatever it were that was so earnestly, so humbly, and at such a time desired. But Sapritius persists obstinate, and not able to make a good answere, forbeares to give any at all. Hereupon the Guard grew angry, and drag him away with much more despite then formerly.

And Nicephorus, cast of againe by the Presse, runnes before to the place of execution, where, as soon as Sapritius appeares, casting himselfe on his face, and kissing his feet, hee cries out aloud, the teares trickling downe his face, Martyr of CHRIST, forgive mee for his sake for whom thou givest thy life. These words and tears, that moved all others, moved not Sapritius at all. Hee remaines setled in his former perversnes to part with all things but the enraged Affections that he beares to Nicephorus. This matter was like to have gone on in length, but the Guard, seeming wearied as well with the ones Importunity as with the others Obstinacy, removes Nicephorus, and wills Sapritius to lay downe his head to the Block. At which speach, lifting up his eies like a Man come out of a Trance, he demanded very seriously why hee was to dy. Because thou refusest to offer sacrifice to the immortall gods, replied the executioner, and despisest the Commandment of our most godly Emperors. Then hold thy hand, sayd the wretched old Man. I am ready in all things to doe as our most godly Emperors have and shall appoint. Their gods shall be my god, and for CHRIST JESUS—he was aboute to have added some fearefull blasphemy when Nicephorus starting forth interrupts him. And wilt thou now at last, Sapritius, deny that blessed LORD whom thou hast so long time served, whom thou hast preached, whom thou hast praysed, for whom thou hast done and suffered so much? Why, what evil hath hee done unto thee? Nay, what good hath hee not done unto thee? And how much more and more inestimable is the good and grace which hee yet intends and offers unto thee if thou despise it not? Looke up and see, blind, fainting Soule, that Crowne of Glory that is prepared for thy head as soone as it shall bee stroken of for his sake. Loose not for a little paine that is gone before it bee felt that ineffable happines that shall never have an end. But Sapritius, full of gastly Horror, seeming as deafe to his exhortations as hee was before to his intreaties, without any reply drew back. Which Nicephorus seeing, stepped boldly forth, and presenting himselfe before the Executioner, Strike, Freind (sayd hee), and send mee quickly hence to recover that immortall Inheritance of Blisse in Heaven which this wretched man hath made exchange of for a few daies continuance of his miserable life here on earth. The standers by hearing this, as soone as amazement gave leave, began sharply to reprove Nicephorus, calling him Madman, and threatening that he should indeed undergoe what hee sought and deserved, except hee quickly withdrew and recanted his vaine speeches as they termed them.

They bee not vaine words, sayd Nicephorus, but words of sobriety and truth. Nor am I besides myselfe, as you think, in offering to dy for him that died for mee. But you are besides yourselves in leaving that GOD which made you, to worship gods which yourselves have made. Judge in yourselves. Is it meet that you shoulde bee so diligent and carefull for the satisfaction and Honour of the Emperor, whose perishing bread you eat, and that I should not bee much more zealous for the glory and service of my LORD JESUS CHRIST, who hath redeemed mee with his blood and promised an everlasting Kingdome to them that faithfully believe and confesse his holy Name?

The Ministers of execution, stopping his mouth, presently led him and Sapritius to the President, who, after many flattering curtesies and vaine promises heaped upon the miserable Sapritius, turning him to Nicephorus with marveilous commendations and compassionate esteeme of the many excellencies both of mind and Body which (hee sayd) hee saw and heard to bee in him, began with faire speeches to desire, and with many reasons to perswade him to follow the example which his Master Sapritius had given, swearing that so doing hee should receive many great Favours not onely from himselfe, but from the Emperors, when they should understand the matter.

I have a better Master, replied Nicephorus smilingly, to follow then Sapritius ; and if Sapritius must still bee my Master, it is better that I should follow the good Counsell that hee hath heretofore given mee, then the foolish Course that himselfe hath now taken, in preferring Men before GOD and the Love of a few wretched daies in this world before the enjoyment of œternall blisse in heaven. But if thou refuse to follow his example, foolish young Man, sayd the President, know thou shalt assuredly undergoe the punishment which hee hath escaped. Why, that is it I long for (sayd the blessed Saint) ; thy other guifts and favours keepe for thyselfe and Sapritius. Let him have what thou intendest mee, and lett mee have what thou formerly ordainedst for him. And thou shalt have it double and treble (cried the enraged President). Bring forth the Torments, and let him prove the sweetnes of that which hee entreats for and deserves. Whips and Wracks and iron Combs, Fire and scalding Liquors, and other Instruments of painefull death are instantly presented by the ready Ministers, and when the sight of them could not terrify Nicephorus, they are with all cruelty and force applied to his Body. Thats wounded and torne on every side, but his mind remains firme and cheerfull, singing and praysing GOD, that had made him worthy to suffer such things for CHRISTS sake. At last the President, seeing Nicephorus his strength and courage to goe on encreasing in Torments, thinking it a double Shame to bee foyled in the putting too of greater force, and envious of the Honour which his owne heart told him such incomparable Patience and Magnanimity deserved, resolves to loose the victory in the lightest manner, and so commanding the tormentors to cease, wills his head to be stroken of, which was immediately performed. And in the fall of his Body on the Earth, his soule mounting up to heaven, hath in the example of his Christian meeknes left the way tracked out for us to follow and attaine that œternall Happines which hee now enjoyes. As on the contrary Sapritius his miserable Ruine, like the downefall of a mighty Tower, gives a fearefull warning of that danger that lies wrapped up in envious and emulating thoughts, and a full proofe of certaine Damnation, which at last attends on implacable Dispositions.

Its impossible to retaine joyntly in the same brest the faith of CHRIST and the memory of Injuries, when amends is offered. Hee that denies his Christian Brother pardon when hee sues for it, hath already denied CHRIST in his heart; his owne Conscience tells him as much, and his Tongue will not spare to tell it others; if hee bee putt to the Triall upon the hazard of any great sufferings, you shall see him turne open Renegrade. The shipwrack of his faith must needs follow, the losse of whose charity is gone before by the settled purpose of revenge or the obstinate putting back of reconciliation.

The CHEIFE had no sooner given evidence that she had concluded what shee then ment to say, when the AFFECTIONATE, taking the eccho of her last word:—

Reconciliation (sayd shee) with our Brethren is one of those maine services which GOD hath for ever enjoyned us, when hee made the Reconciliation himselfe with us in our LORD JESUS CHRIST. But revenge is one of those peculiars which hee hath for ever reserved unto himselfe. Wee cannot enter upon the Exercise thereof without incurring a Premunire in the highest degree. You have heard the proofe thereof in miserable Sapritius, you shall know the reason thereof from good Sisois.

I should doe you wrong to deprive you of the Preface with which I was first taught the Story. You shall therefore have it intire, being indeed full of good matter, and much to our present purpose.

A certain holy Father taught his Disciples touching Anger on this wise.

It proceeds from four Causes— { Covetousnesse, Selfe-will, Desire of Honour and Conceit of a Mans own will.

And it workes foure deadly effects in a mans soule towards his Neighbour— { Hatred, Contempt, Envy, and Evill speech.

And it hath foure degrees of working in a Man— { First in the heart, Secondly in the face, Thirdly in the tongue, Fourthly in the Actions.

Let a man therefore seeke to kill it in the Heart, but if it doe forceably arise there, let him restraine it in his Countenance. Iff hee cannot there master it, yet let him be sure to restraine it in his tongue, and most of all keepe it from performance by deeds. And further this good man added, that he that being offended willingly pardons, is after the Nature of CHRIST. Hee that would not bee offended is after the Nature of Adam, but hee that offends and doth wrong is after and of the Nature of the Devill; and to the inducing to the Necessity of forgiving this story is recounted.

One having received a great Injury comes to Father Sisois complaining much and deeply threatening revenge. Sisois willed him to leave vengeance to GOD, to whom it belonged, And doe thou forgive the wrong; thats your part. Nay, sayd the other, I will right myselfe. Sisois, perceiving his obstinacy, before hee would lett him depart, went as his Custome was to prayers, and when the other kneeling downe was ready to second him, hee spake in this manner. LORD

God, henceforth have wee no more need of thee, as farre as I perceive by this my Brother here, who takes upon him to have both Justice and Power enough to right himselfe and to revenge the wrong that he hath received. The other cried out hearing this, and falling on his face, Mercy, Lord, Mercy, Lord, I did not know what I did; but now I doe not onely forgive, but beseech thee likewise to forgive him that hath done mee this wrong.

A word is enough to the wise (sayd the Cheerefull); a little warning setts a good understanding in the right way. So it happened to this good Man, and to another of whom I shall tell you, who by the good odour of this excellent vertue of Love and meeknes was drawn to embrace the Christian Fayth.

Macarius, travailing to Mount Nitra upon some occasion, sent his Disciple before him, a young Man and highly conceited, rather for the fame of his Masters worth then his owne vertue. This disciple meeting one of the idolatrous Preists running in great hast with a heavy piece of timber on his shoulders, scornefully demands where away runs this Bedlam? The Preist flinging downe his Burthen fell upon him, and when he had beaten him almost to death, taking up again the Timber, prosecuted his journey till he met with Macarius, who, being farre of another Temper, with great Affability saluted the Preist. Hee, wondering thereat, asked Macarius whence this Curtesy proceeded. Alas, sayd Macarius, perceiving thee overtoyled I cannot but pitty thee, and therefore was willing by a gentle greeting to give opportunity of breathing, ready likewise to afford the helpe, if in any thing I may steed thee, either for the ease of thy labours or for the mollifying of those other discontents which is evident by your face doe vex thee. It had beene happy for him whom I mett last, sayd the Preist, if he had learned so good language as thou now usest. Oh, mee, sayd Macarius, hast thou perhaps done him any hurt? Sure it was my disciple. I, so I guesse (sayd the Preist) by the conformity of your habitts.

But however you are like, yet assuredly your hearts are farre unlike. Hee reviled mee without Cause, and I have left him sore wounded in my rage. But by thy meekenes and Love I am so farre convinced, that I purpose from henceforth to bee of thy religion, which must undoubtedly bee the best, that hath made thee so full of true goodnesse. Having spoken this, Macarius with teares embraced and baptized him, having first given order for the Cure of his Disciple, whom and all others hee was wont by his example to admonish to the Practize of kindnes, willing them to observe for certaine truth that proud and evill words make even good folkes the worse; but sweet and humble speech induceth them that doe amisse the rather to Amendment.

Well might Macarius teach (sayd the MODERATOUR) that the Love of enemies, the speaking kindly and doing good to them that hate us, is the Cognizance of a Christian. Hee may perhaps bee of another religion, and have some other power, Mars, or Bellona, or some such other Deity for his God, that nobody shall wrong him; but, according to the Proverbe, hee shall carry as good as hee brings. But Christian religion hee cannot bee of, nor have Interest in their GOD, except hee be resolved to overcome evill with good; so farre must hee bee from the requiting it with the like. To which purpose I shall tell you a famous Story, and worthy Imitation.—

John the Almoner being one day with much Company about him, his young Nephew, whose Name was Gregory, entering in with a troubled Cheere and confused manner, made a bitter Complaint to him of a certaine Shopkeeper who, upon the Demande of some arrearages of rent, had not onely loaded him with many opprobrious words before a great Number of people, but otherwise manifoldly abused him. The standers-by, discovering a manifest altercation in the Patriarchs Countenance, esteeming it to proceed from the sence of his Nephews wrongs and teares, thinking to ingratiate themselves into the Patriarchs favour by complying that way which they conceived his Affections to incline, began much to exaggerate the offence, joyntly concluding that it was not to be passed over without sharp and exemplary punishment, that might teach all others with what respect they ought to proceede towards them which have so neere relation to him. You say true, replied the Patriarch, there is no question but my Honour suffers much in this Busines; and that in the Injury of my Nephew, whom every one knows to bee as deare to mee as mine own eies, there was an affront to mee which, since you all agree requires some amends, I will take such order in the matter as all Alexandria shall ring of it. The young Man gave his unkle great thankes for the profession of so much Love and his promise of such full right, and departed very joyfully to call the Steward over those affaires, as his Uncle willed him; who, comming immediately, the Patriarch openly told the Steward that whereas such a Taverner (of that Profession hee was) had very much misbehaved himself by evill words and deeds towards his Nephew Gregory, which in all men's opinion, sayth the good Patriarch, trencheth very deep to my Creditt. I will have you henceforth forbeare to exact any rent or other duties from him, to the intent that by the unexpected Benefitt which hee receives from us hee may the better understand the undeserved Injury which hee hath offered to my Nephew, and on him to mee. And so stepping to his Nephew to prevent the further affliction of shame and greife, both which passions the changing colour of his Face gave remonstrance began to work in his heart, he first embraced and kissed, and afterwards thus bespake him: My Son, that is true kindred which meets in vertue, not Bloud onely. If thou wilt therefore be mine, thou must bee like minded, patient to beare and ready to forgive. That is it which I by GODS grace have resolved touching the requitall of Injuries. If herein thou resolve to follow mee, thou shalt have mee, nay, thou shalt have GOD himselfe for thy Father and Heaven for thine Inheritance; but to repay evill with evill proceeds from the wicked one, and carries the soule headlong to everlasting Death. Let these thoughts, my Son, restraine thee, whenever thine owne or others Instigation putts you on to revenge. He certainly looseth all his owne good that thinkes to gaine by harming others.

Blessed bee GOD (sayd the PATIENT), there have not wanted, even in these last and evill daies of ours, illustrious examples of this Vertue. I have one to tell you, which both for the excellency of the Action and the admirable Conclusion which it inferres, deserves, in my opinion, to weare the crowne of this daies Stories, especially considering that it was a king that did and sayd it, the great Henry of France, the Father of our happy Queene. This noble Prince, lying before Roane, having received certaine Intelligence of an enterprize that was to bee attempted against his life, as hee walked one day with an observant eie, perceived a suspicious person not farre from him, whom by the confrontment of many particular signes that had been given him, hee began strongly to conceit was the Murtherer whom he was advized to beware of. Whereupon hee commanded the Gentleman (such hee was in appearance and indeed by birth) to bee brought unto him. The Palenesse of his guilty face and shaking of his Joynts in his Approach verifying the suspicions, Your countenance, sayd the King, speaks aloud; you know what I have to charge you with. Leaving therefore all fruitlesse denialls, as you tender your owne life, confesse plainly the whole truth of your intendement against mine.

The wretched Man, seeing himselfe taken in the snare that he was laying, began with teares and stretched out hands to beg for mercy. Speake, Freind (sayd the King); did I ever doe thee any wrong or any of thy Freinds, or what may bee the cause that thou goest about my death with the hazard of thine owne? The miserable wretch, as soone as hee could recover his fainting spirits, with a trembling voice made answere that no particular occasion of his owne—having never received any offence from his Majestie—but the Interest of the generall cause of his party had drawne him to these resolutions, having beene perswaded by his ghostly Father that the making away, by what meanes soever, of so great an enemy of their religion was an Act of so high merrit, as a Crowne of eternall happines was but the due reward for it. Well, then, sayd the King, since it is the difference of religion that hath sett you a-work, I will shew you the difference betweene those two religions which you and I professe. Yours perswades you to kill them that never have hurt you, and mine wills mee to pardon them that never so much offend mee. Its a matter of merrit with you to murther them that have done you no Injury; and it is a matter of Necessity with mee to forgive mine enemies, though they seeke my Life. Goe your way, then, and let mee never see you here againe; and judge in yourselfe which of the twaine answeares more to the Doctrine of CHRIST: your religion, that makes you an [assassin], or mine, that makes mee so mercifull, and whether is liker to be the right way to Heaven: That which overrules to spare the guilty soule, or that which teacheth to shed the innocent Bloud.

The Traytors happ that thus scaped (sayd the GUARDIAN) was much better, though the deed farre worse, then of that Moore, who would have slaine Alphonso the Eleventh of Castile, in which point, deare PATIENT, your story, that in everything besides is œquall, is perhaps not a little inferior; the barbarous Kings Justice being no lesse admirable then the Christian Kings Patience.

It is no great Merveile (sayd the MODERATOUR) if there were two kings for one, that your story should in some points exceede. Defraud us not, therefore, I pray, of that delight which the Conjunction of two so different Vertues in one and the selfe same Action must needs breed, especially when they both meet in their hights, as it seemes here they did. Why, since you will not bee denied, sayd the GUARDIAN, take it breifly and plainly as my Author setts it downe.

Alphonsus the Eleventh, having streightly begirt Algezira, one of the beseiged Moores issued forth with intent to kill him before he should carry the Place, which hee was certaine within a few daies to doe. The Moores purpose was discovered, and himselfe brought to the King. When all expected he should bee putt to some cruell death, Alphonsus gave him a rich garment and a good summe of Mony, and caused him to bee conveyed safely to his owne King, whose Name was Belmazin. The other no doubt went full of joy, expecting to receive a double reward from his Master, for whose service hee had so desparately engaged himselfe both soul and body. But Belmazin hearing the matter, after he had with sharp words rebuked and terrified the poore Moore, commanded hee should bee instantly slaine, saying hee was unworthy to live who would have robbed the world of so magnanimous and meeke a King.

A notable Example of royall Justice, sayd the CHEIFE, and an admirable proofe of that universall Grace which Meeknes hath both in heaven and in earth. It is a thing of great price with GOD, sayth St. Peter, and of great power with men. You see by this Instance, when it winnes favours and obtaines Justice from a barbarous King, and he an enemy too in the very height of his owne wrongs. Hee is zealous to doe Meekenes right, though it bee in the cause of his Adversary and on the Person of his Freind. Hee cannot forbeare to give Testimony that it deserves Love above all things, and shall find protection everywhere. Let others, if they list, pride themselves of great Stomach, and seek to ward of Injuries with Power; but let Meeknes of spirit, LORD, bee my Armes against offences and the ornament which my soule desires to bee beautiful with. Let others learne of the world to prevent wrong by doing it first, and to keep peace by making warre. Let mee learne of thee, LORD JESUS, and of thy Saints, to be meeke and lowly. So I am sure I shall find rest unto my soule, and otherwise I am sure I cannot.

The Company was about to rise when the MODERATOUR, staying them with the beckening of the hand to sett downe againe : I should bee sorry (sayd shee), that wee should part without an Example of this Grace of Meekenes in some of our owne sex, to which it seemes more properly, at least more necessarily, to belong then to Mankind.

The SUBMISSES Countenance (sayd the CHEIFE) seemes in mine eye to promise the satisfaction of your desires, most honored MODERATOUR, if shee might bee admitted to beare a part in this exercize. I have beene much troubled, sayd the GUARDIAN, in mine owne Mind, that both she and the OBEDIENT have beene so long left out from that whereunto they ought to have beene compelled. I pray, therefore, let us not loose the Advantage of this occasion to bring them in. And in regard that the first attempt cannot bee so perfect, let them have the Liberty for a while of telling their stories as they can; I meane without the expectation of any Preface or Application from them. So they bee to the purpose it shall suffice. If they cannot truly be cast into the ranke with others, they shall serve apart, as auxiliar supplies upon speciall occasion that may happen.

Whereupon the SUBMISSE told the story following. Katharine, the wife of Henery the Eight of England, was Aunt to Charles the Emperor. After about twenty yeares continuance in wedlock, the King procured a Divorce. The Cause was undoubtedly just, but the affections and courage of the King full of unkindnes and harshnes. Yet could not this Queene bee perswaded by the most earnest Invitation of the Emperor, nor of his Brother Fardinand, King of the Romanes, nor of his Neices, the Queenes of France, Hungary, Portugall, and Denmarke, to leave England, but rather choose in an unhealthfull Place and in a retired Manner to lead a desolate Life in England, then to have Honours and Comforts abroad. Neither was shee ever heard during her life to make any Complaint against the Kings unkindnesse. And on her Death-Bed shee wrott him a letter full of Affection and sweet and profitable Counsell, without any touch of Distast. At the hearing of her cause at Bridewell, before Cardinall Wolsy and Campeggius, shee, refusing to answere her appeale to the Pope, the King, vexed thereat, after shee was departed sent for her againe into the Court; shee, submissively returning, was admonished by her Proctor that if shee appeared againe in the Court shee did ipso facto disannull her appeale, and the Cardinals being made for the King would certainly give sentence against her. Whereupon shee immediately retired to Bainard Castell, the place of her Abode, but always shewing a marveilous perplexity of Mind. As soone as shee was Landed, turning unto her Attendance that stood about her, This is (sayd shee) the first time that ever I disobeyed my Husbands Command, and though the occasion may seeme most just, yet, next time I see him, I will on my knees begg his pardon for this necessary disobedience. This shee delivered with passionate words and accompanied them with many teares, leaving a rare example for all women of wifely Obedience.

This Story (sayd the GUARDIAN) is indeed an Honour to your sex, but a shame to your Age. Its beyond commendation of words. Let us heare what the OBEDIENT hath to say.

Abbot Appollinus happening in fray, sought with many arguments and much earnestnes to sett them at unity. One of the Combatans bad him spare his paines, for hee would not prevaile. As I live, sayd hee, I will have no peace with mine enemy. To which the holy Man with a troubled Cheere made reply, Thou hast refused Peace, and Peace hath forsaken thee. Thou shalt want thyself when thou most needest what thou wilt not give thy Brother. The other made light of the matter, but the next day proved it a heavy and sad doome to him. They that heard him thus threatened found him the next day torne a peices of wild Beasts.

He had his due (sayd the MODERATOUR) and they that follow his example must looke for his reward. And things that belong to GOD are in a joynt Confederacy one with another, and for the maintenance of Peace have sworne a common

League both for offence and Defence. He breakes peace with all that proclaimes warre with any, and makes the whole Creation his Enemy that will needs bee his Brother's Adversary. When any ill therefore comes upon any Man, the first Queere which I should wish him to make is, whether he beare ill-will to any. If hee doe, hee need goe no further for the ground of his Calamity. Nor may hee instantly expect the release till the Cause bee removed. Hee that keeps others faults alive in his memory, refresheth the guilt of his owne before GOD, and in seeking to take vengeance necessarily pulls it upon his own head.

Sapritius lost his Soule, this other his Life, by these Desires. But Meekenes carried up Nicephorus whither St. Steven by the same steps had before ascended; and not onely in Heaven, but here on Earth, crownes all the Possessors thereof with a happy quiet in themselves and an honourable and everlasting remembrance to after Ages.

This is the inference of our Stories; I pray GOD it may bee the practize of our Actions.

V

CHRISTMASTIDE, 1631—ST. JOHN THE EVANGELIST'S DAY

St. John's Fishery—Bishop Troylus—Cosmo de' Medici—Consalvo Ferrantes—Salladine.

THE Remembrance of the former Daies Pleasure having after a quicker dispatch then ordinary, though of extraordinary cheere, carried up most of the Family to the SISTERS Chamber, the GUARDIAN, seeing unusuall Lonelines in the Dining Roome, himselfe onely and one or two more being left, smilingly sayd to his MOTHER that it might well now bee seene that there is as great delight to bee found in good things and profitable as in pernicious Vanities. For I doe not think any Gamesters within twenty Miles more egerly bent upon their Play then our Family on their Stories. I beseech you, therefore, let us put them to no further paine by our longer differing to give them by our presence a beginning to that which their minds are so longingly sett upon.

So going up they found the Company indeed, as the GUARDIAN supposed, with Repetition of what they had heard sharpening their Appetites for that they were to heare. The SISTERS, having notice given them, instantly appeared, and the CHEEREFULL, to whom the Guidance of that Day fell, made an enterance by singing of the Hymne following, as formerly, playd on the Violl.

Teach us by his example, Lord,
For whom we honour Thee to-day;
And grant his witness of Thy word
Thy church enlighten ever may.

And as beloved, O Christ, he was,
And therefore leaned upon Thy breast,
So let us also in Thy grace
And on Thy sacred bosom rest.

Into us breathe that life divine
Whose testimony he commands;
About us cause Thy light to shine,
Light which no darkness comprehends.

And let Thy ever blessed Word
Which all things did create of nought,
Anew create us now, O Lord!
Whose ruin sin hath almost wrought.

Thy holy faith we do profess;
Us to Thy fellowship receive.
Our sins we heartily confess:
Thy pardon therefore let us have.

And as to us Thy servant gives
Occasion thus to honour Thee:
So also let our words and lives
As lights and guides to others be.

The Hymne being ended, shee thus began.

The Light, Life, and Fellowship with the Divine Majesty, which this Hymne so sweetly descants on, and whereunto wee all pretend with such inflamed Affections, are by no other Steps to be ascended unto then by a stedfast Continuance in an holy fellowship with our Brethren through the Light and Life of Love alwaies abiding and working in us. Hee, therefore, that casteth away the last shall bee sure to make forfeiture of the first.

This is that which, as the blessed Apostle, whose Feast wee now celebrate, cheifly insisteth upon; so is it most especially, as I take it, intended by the Collect, when it praies that the Church may bee enlightened by the Doctrine of the blessed Apostle and Evangelist John.

In these Considerations, therefore, wee have agreed first to present you a short epitome of St. Johns transcendent doctrine touching this matter of Love, confirmed and illustrated with the parallell Practize of St. Paul, which however our after Stories prove, cannot but bee of singular benefitt to make us in Love with Peace and Love, and at perpetuall warre with hate and enmity. Hee that loves (sayth St. John) is and abides in the Light, and there is no occasion of stumbling in him. Hee walkes cheerefully, and he walkes securely through this Vale of Misery and Danger. Death lies in waite to swallow him, but hee escapes the snare by this Light, and is carried over into the dwelling of Life. Wee know that wee passed from Death to Life, because wee love the Brethren. Other men and creatures are made by GOD, but hee that loves by a more excellent kind of Generation is borne of GOD. Other men are farre estranged from the Apprehension of GOD, but hee that loves hath a neere acquaintance with GOD. GOD knows him, and hee knows GOD. Every one that loves is born of GOD, and knows GOD. From knowledge hee passeth on to perfect union with him, and so to uneffable Happines. Hee dwells in GOD, and GOD in him.

This is the progresse of Love according to St. Johns Doctrine, whereunto, as Hatred and enmity are opposite, so likewise the paths and issues that they lead unto. Though a Mans sight be never so good, yet they cast a darkenes before them, so that hee that hates knows not whither hee goes. Hee that hates his Brother is in darkenes, and walketh in darkenes, and knoweth not whither hee goeth, because darkenes hath blinded his eies. Hee thinkes his Life, at least the Joy of it, consisteth in the prosecution of his Malice; but hee runs himselfe on his Death thereby. Hee becomes a Murtherer; and no Murtherer hath œternall Life abiding in him. Hee may linger for awhile here in the life of this world, but his perpetuall residence must bee in the habitations of Death.

Hee that loveth not his Brother abideth in Death.

Hee may talke much of GOD, and perhaps offer to teach others, but in truth hee knows him not. Hee that loves not, knows not GOD, for GOD is Love. Hee that departs from Love hath cutt himselfe of from GOD, I, and all reference to him too; he is none of GODS, at least for good. Hee that doth not righteousnes is not of GOD, neither hee that loveth not his Brother, but is the Brother of Caine, and is, as hee was, of that wicked one.

You have heard the Nature of Love and Hatred; compare them together, and the choyse will be as easy as betweene Hell and Heaven for our Portions, GOD and the Devill for our Father. We are all for Love, blessed be GOD. But then, sayth St. John, wee must love in deed and not in Tongue, in truth and not in word onely. Hee that sayth hee loves GOD (and who will not tremble to say otherwise?) must needs love his Brother, otherwise hee proves himselfe a lyar. Its a contradiction to reason not to love GOD in his Image, which wee see, and to love Him in His owne Nature, which wee cannot apprehend. Besides, it is a plaine breach of his Commandments, which absolutely enjoyne that hee which loves GOD should love his Brother also. Wee must love one another for GODS sake, and wee must love after GODS example too. His Proceedings must bee our Patterne. GOD layd downe His Life for us, and wee ought to lay down our lives for the Brethren; and if wee must lay down our Lives, much more must wee impart our goods to them that need. Hee that shutts up the Bowells of Compassion to others shuts out the Love of GOD from his owne heart. How dwelleth the Love of GOD in such an one? sayth John.

You have heard St. Johns Doctrine, and now heare St. Pauls Practize of Love. Not that either John did lesse then himselfe taught, or Paul taught lesse then himselfe performed touching Love. They were both equally perfect in the Knowledge and the Practize of this supreme vertue. But that the unity and excellency of the same truth and Grace might by the variety of witnesses bee the better confirmed and sett of, God hath pleased (as we may conceive) that the Doctrine of one and the example of the other should bee more fully entred in the everlasting rolls of his sacred word, from which, intending to present you with a perfect modell, wee dare not digresse one step to the intent that it might bee of infallible Verity, which is propounded for absolute imitation. St. Paul, therefore, testifieth of himselfe—and you know he durst not ly—that his Love was so ardent that it alwaies sett him on fire when hee was absent. God is my witnesse how greatly I long after you in the Bowells of Christ Jesus, sayth hee to the Philippians. And when he was present with the Thessalonians it was so fervent, as hee melts into tendernesse. Wee were gentle amongst you, even as a Nurse cherisheth her Children, ready to feed them, not with the Milk of his Gospell, but with the Life of his soul.

Being affectionately desirous of you, wee were willing to have imparted unto you, not the Gospel of God onely, but also our owne soul, because you were deare unto us. And no marveil if hee were willing to impart his soul unto them that had the whole possession of his heart. So hee tells the Corinthians, You are in our heart to live and dy with you. Hee neither feeles joy nor sorrow, but in the fellowsence of their Afflictions or Comforts. His Flesh had no rest in Macedonia; without were fightings, within were Feares, but all fly away like Mists before the Sunne when Titus brings him relation of the Corinthians welfare. I am filled with comfort, I am exceeding joyfull in all our tribulation.

The like effect did the same good News that Titus brought him of the Thessalonians worke at Athenes when hee was hard besett on all sides. Hee tells them frankly, Now wee live if you stand fast in the Lord. But if there be any want of good, any suffering of will on any hand, it breeds double the Anguish in St. Paul that it doth in the Patient himselfe. Who is weake, and I am not weake, who is offended and I burne not?

This greater feeling of others Paine then his owne makes him altogether neglect himselfe to give them Content. Even as I please all Men in all things (sayth hee to the Corinthians), not seeking mine owne, but the profitt of many, that they might bee saved.

This greater desire of doing good to others then to himselfe makes him undergoe all things, though never so hard to the sence, never so unfitt to the eie of Mans reason.

Hee is free from all, and yet it makes him servant to all ; he is stronger then any, and yet it makes him as feeble as the weakest. To winne the Jews hee walkes fettered in the legall Cerimonies. Hee seemes to walk in the Liberty of the Gentiles to perswade them to the subjection of the Gospell. Hee is made all things to all Men ; and it is his Joy that it is his owne losse in every thing, so it may be their gaine in any thing. So hee tells the Corinthians, Wee are glad when wee are weake and you are strong. These are Coppies for all to take out, especially those that take upon them the care of the Church, which was putt upon him. But that which hee writes to the Romanes I know not whether it bee for Imitation, so surpassing is it to apprehension ; I could wish that myselfe were accursed from CHRIST for my Brethren, my Kinsmen according to the Flesh. This is a flight that our eies cannot follow, much lesse our discourse. Weele now come downe to the representment of some of those things in Actions which you have heard of in the Abstract, and my story shall be as well of the Person as of the vertue that this day more especially recommends to our Consideration.

St. John the Evangelist having in his Fishery for soules gained a young Man to the Faith, accomplished in all perfection of Mind and Body, upon his necessary departure from that place committed his rich prize to the Guardianship of the Bishop of the Citty, that by his care and paines hee might bee fitted for the service of GOD, which the Bishop for a while did with great Diligence and happy successe. The young man making great progresse in vertue, but afterwards relenting the strict tuition with which he at first began, the young man grew from remissenes to negligence in good things, and from thence by little and little descended through the Inticement of evill company to all manner of debauchnes, giving himselfe to riott, gaming, and the like, and (as excellent dispositions of Nature if they be corrupted prove most pernicious) became a Captaine of certaine outlaws about the Citty. St. John, after some yeares space returning, after the accompt of other Businesse from the Bishop, publickly demanded of him the redelivery of that Jewell which hee had consigned. The Bishop at first amazed what the Apostle ment, was suddainly in plaine termes demanded touching the young man committed to his charge, to which with teares he answeared hee was dead. How and when? sayd the glorious Apostle. In his soul to GOD, sayd the Bishop, and breifly with many teares, both of his owne and St. Johns, recompted the miscarriages of the young Man; which St. John had scarce heard when, tearing his garment, and crying out, Oh, what a good Guardian I have found thee to bee of thy Brothers Soule! commanded a horse and guide to be given, by whom being conducted to the passage which the outlaws had besett, hee was immediately by them carried before their Captaine, who no sooner saw him but, surprized with shame and sorrow, casting downe his weapons, hee began to fly in hast from the presence of St. John, who, perceiving that he could not overtake by running, sent his cries and teares after him to stay him. Wherefore dost thou fly, my Sonne? sayd hee, From thy father —a young man from an old—clad with Armes from him that hath no weapons? But if it bee not scare, but shame and sorrow that makes thee shunne mee for thy misdeeds, behold mee here the messenger of peace and pardon. There is yet abundance of mercy, there is yet certainty of saluation for thee. What doubtest thou? See, I am ready to go with thee to my Master, JESUS CHRIST; ready, if need were, to give my Life for thy soule, as CHRIST gave his for us all. The young man, overtaken with these sweet and unexpected Comforts, staies till the Apostle overtooke him, and then falls downe at his feet, weeping and sobbing, holding up his left hand by way of supplication, his right hand reeking with blood hee kept hid under his garment. St. John, perceiving his thoughts, laies hold on that hand, the Instrument of much wickednes, and for the confirmation of his promises washed it with teares, and kissed it with his mouth, that hee might bee confident that nothing should remaine uncleared when the guilt of that guilty member should be quitted. From thence hee led him home, and so to the Church, where hee continued with him some daies in fasting and praiers. Hee left him so confirmed in grace and all manner of vertue as he left him Bishop of the same Place which he had some few daies before beene a Captaine of Theeves, and now faithfully taking care of their soules, who a little before was the greatest enemy to their lives and estates.

The good hope that wee have touching sinners, how farre soever they may seeme to wander, and the diligence that wee ought to use for their conversion, especially when they have any more particular reference unto us, are two plaine and easy Collections out of your excellent Story, sayd the CHEIFE. I pray GOD that they may bee as carefully practized by everyone as I see them by everyones Countenance with Admiration approved in St. John. I cannot say my story shall œquall, but sure it will second yours. A charitable prevention of Sinne is next to a charitable redemption from sinne in our Brethren, and great cost is next of value to great care and paines. Herein our Stories well suit, and so they doe for the Realty of the Acts and the Excellency of the Persons. Hee was not an Apostle, but next the Apostles wee may place him, his memory being more honourable and precious to a very great part of Christendome then of any other Saint whatsoever. It is St. Nicholas of whom I have to speak. And since I have spoken so much of him, give mee leave to tell you a little of his former life, which I hope will bee neither lesse pleasant nor beneficial then the particular Action itselfe. Besides, I should perhaps bee

I H S

longer in contriving how to unloose it handsomely from that whereto it is already woven then in recompting both together. (The story of St. Nicholas is omitted.)

The Beauty of faire Actions inflames generous minds (sayd the MODERATOUR), but the greater sort of men are of a lower pitch, and except there bee an evidency of reward, are hardly wonne to the exercise of any costly or painfull vertue. I shall therefore tell you a story setting forth the great and infallible gaine that in the end accrues by trafficking a Mans estate this way.

Troylus was a Bishop of great Learning and integrity of Life, but carried away with the tyde of evill example, somewhat more addicted to the love of money and to the maintenance of pompe then benefitts that holy profession which receives more foyle then grace by setting forth itselfe to those vaine and boisterous desires of state and Magnificence which the world admires, and is never comely exercised about mony but in the giving it away for GODS sake. But Troylus, that had not yet learned these Mysteries, thinking (as men usually teach one another) no harme to bee in keeping of a Mans owne, and much good in spending it to his honour, taking a great summe of mony which had beene long in getting, comes to Alexandria to lay it all out at once in Plate, Hangings, and other rich furniture and Abiliments for himselfe and his house.

Love and Duty leads him at his first repaire to the Patriarch, who not onely offers, but enforceth him to become his guest during his abode in Alexandria. For his comming to and his stay there Troylus wanted not faire pretences to the Patriarch. But the Servants boastings disclose what the Masters wisedome seeks to hide. Each plays his owne game. Troylus thinks it most to his creditt to conceale the matter, his followers think it makes to theirs to lett their Masters wealth and noble disposition bee knowne, and so the Patriarch comes to bee informed of the truth ; at which, being not a little greived, he bethinkes himselfe of a way if not absolutely to cure his freinds disease, yet at least to controule the exorbitant working thereof. To this end hee takes occasion next morning somewhat early to lead Troylus forth to the view of a great Hospitall, wherein this good man had gathered a Number of poore people, and according to the distinction of sexes, Ages, Abilities, and Inabilities sorted them in severall apartments and for severall Imployments. Hee tells Troylus what hee had already done, and what hee further intends; and demands his advice in many particulars. But Troylus, his mind sett upon the pursuit of his owne honours and Contents, finds much distast in the enforced vein of others Miseries; and though hee strive to dissemble it, yet his carelesse behaviour and cold Answeares to everything gave such remonstrance thereof as the good Patriarch, halfe ashamed at his slothfull demeanour in that which hee ought to be most zealous for, taking him by the hand, I perceive, Brother, sayd hee, that your thoughts are otherwise; I will therefore take a fitter time for your good counsell in these matters. Onely now, before you depart, I pray give a testimony of your Love both to GOD and mee in your bounty to these poore members of CHRIST and my LORDS. That was the name by which this holy man used to style the poore when hee spake of them. Troylus being thus surprized when hee least thought, put on by feare of shame and offence if hee should deale sparingly, willed his Steward to bestow crowns apeice on the poore of that Hospitall. Well done, good and faithfull servant, sayd the joyfull Patriarch, thou hast honored thy Master by this liberall distribution, and hee shall make his Blessings to abound to thee. Having so sayd and embraced him, hee carries him away, full of confidence for the good that hee had done, and for the honour which hee had and hoped to receive thereby. But when his steward coming some houres after rounded him in the eare that hee had layd out about £200—so great was the number of poore that belonged to that house—the poore Bishop, overcome with greife and anguish of mind for so unmeasurable a wast of his mony, which hee loved so dearely, and so unexpected a disappointment of those longing desires which his heart was sett upon, faining that a suddaine qualme had ceazed on him, craves leave to goe to his Chamber, which the compassionate Patriarch gladly condescends unto, willing some of the Company to attend him and see that all things were carefully ministered both for ease and health. They that went along for that purpose immediately returne to the Patriarch and tell him smilingly that the Bishops sicknes lies in his Vertue. The largenes of his bounty was that which pained his narrow heart, and the weight which hee had disburdened his purse of in the morning is that which now lies so heavy upon his mind. Hee was no sooner out of the roome but he began to complaine that hee was undone, and to blame himselfe for a foole, his steward as unfaithfull to him, and us all as plotters of his ruine. His intent was to give to those onely whom hee saw, and to stretch his words to the uttermost was neither œquity nor freindship. These and the like passionate speeches, sayd they, did he utter in our conducting him to his Chamber, where, seeing that our presence was offensive, wee have left him to himselfe.

The Distemper is farre worse, answered the good Patriarch, then I conceived, and above that which our helpe can reach unto. To repent of good deeds and to bee afflicted for a mans happines, why this is a malady indeed, and such as no Physitian but hee that sitts in heaven can remedy; but in what wee are able wee must not be wanting. If wee cannot heale the sore yet may wee not forbeare to swage the paine; that perhaps may easily, though not without cost, bee effected. Goe therefore, and keepe the poore man cheerefull as you may till I come and bring the Medicine, which about an houre in the night hee accordingly did, entring Troylus his Chamber, whom hee found layd on his bed. And after the ordinary questions touching his indisposition were asked and answered, Brother Troylus (sayd the good Patriarch in a pleasant manner), doe you think in the discharge of my duty to carry away my reward ? Nay, verily, you come not, I hope, to Alexandria to robb mee of that which you cannot give mee. The releife of the poore, especially those of this Hospitall, is my charge, and the benefitt whatsoever shall arise thereby belongs to mee alone. No man shall stop mee of this boasting. I pray, therefore, take againe your two hundred pound which you layd out this morning, and contenting yourselfe with your goodwill leave to mee the blessing, whatever it bee, which GODS mercifull acceptation shall give for the recompence of the deed itself. Let your good intent suffice you, for nothing but the worke itselfe will suffice mee. The poore Man, not able to resist the temptation, perceiving in the restitution of money the accomplishment of his former designes, and yet a good saving of his Creditt in seeing it forced by the Patriarchs Importunity, yeelds his Consent to the Match, and setts his hand to a certaine kind of acquittance which the Patriarch had brought ready drawne to this effect. Which being done hee goes down to supper with the Patriarch, passeth the time cherefully, returned to bed full of Content, and sleeps quietly till about midnight, when hee thinks himselfe wrapt up into heaven, and there sees a very stately Palace, passing the conceit of mans Imagination for excellency both of matter and workmanship, and in the forefront thereof he reads ingraven :—

The Mansion of Bishop Troylus.

Whilst he stands thus ravished in the contemplation of his happines, hee perceives a yong man of great majestie in his face and habitt, waited upon by divers Artificers with their severall Instruments of building, comming towards him. The yong man, in his passage by the house lifting up his eies and perceiving the engravement, turnes him to the company, and stretching out a golden rod which he carried in his hand, Blott out, sayd hee, the writing which you see there engraven, and put instead thereof

*The Mansion of John the Almoner,
which he bought of Bishop Troylus for two hundred pound.*

The tenor of these words and the apprehension of his unestimable losse waked Troylus full of greif and affrightment, and though hee found it in the end to bee a dreame, yet finding it agreable to that which our SAVIOUR hath promised, that hee that sows Almes on Earth shall reape Treasures in heaven, it made such an impression in his mind that hee never after could bee persuaded either to keep mony or bestow it otherwise then in this kind and way.

The repayment of charitable deeds in Heaven to worldly-minded men (sayd the CHEIFE) is like the improvement of rents after many yeares to spendthrift Gallants, a matter however most certaine in itselfe, yet of little satisfaction to them who prize (as they say) a little in hand before a great deal farre of. They will not deny the truth of what your story inferres, most honoured MODERATOUR, because they will not bee thought bad Christians, but because they are indeed flesh and bloud (as they terme themselves) they cannot be without the contents of this world, and therefore think it better to lay out their mony for that which will certainely benefitt and delight them on earth then to greater advantage hereafter in heaven, where the happines is so compleat that hee which hath the least part cannot find any cause of greife or envy. Why, then, should they loose the pleasures which they take in this vale of misery, where they are so needfull, for covetousnes of having more in the Land of blisse, where all manner of desirable things so runne over as the first step into it takes a man over head with joy and happines? What need they therefore trouble themselves to swimme in the deepe when the shallowest place is past sounding?

But how they should come there at all with this mind, at least how they should stay there, except they bee well furnished with good works of this kind, if it were in their power to performe them (sayd the GUARDIAN), I know not, considering the triall lies mainly on this point, if charitable workes bear witnesse to the Christian profession which is alledged on their behalfe. Come you blessed directs them into everlasting joy; but otherwise, Goe you cursed damnes them to eternall torments. The world would count him but a shallow-headed fellow that, standing for some office or degree, being certainly informed what questions would bee made for triall of his sufficiency would not have the right and full answeres provided beforehand; and yet they will passe for Masters of wisedome that, pretending to œternal happines, and knowing from the Examiners owne mouth the arguments of opposition, come no better prepared then either to stand silent, or at best to shew forth hounds and horses, and idle droanes fatt cramm'd with continuall surfeets in the Hall when the question shall bee of feeding the hungry. Will the bringing forth of Liveries for Pages and Footmen, and costly hangings for the very walls, or the dayly visit of Ladies and great men bee accepted for answeres touching the clothing of the Naked and visiting the sick? I need not goe over the other particulars. You know what GOD will ask; you see what men can say. If you venter yourselves upon such answeares with them so will not I. My simplenes, I confesse, reacheth not to understand how these Allegations will serve their turne. I meane, therefore, by GODS grace, to keep on the plaine way, fulfilling the letter as much as may bee; and both mine owne body and my children must excuse mee if I take lesse pleasure to myselfe, or leave lesse wealth to them by this meanes. Its Admission or Exclusion from heaven that depends upon this point. It is best, therefore, to be of the surer hand, especially considering that the pleasures which are here foreborne shall be recompenced at the last an hundredfold, and GODS blessing, which I am certaine through His infallible promise thus to obtaine for my children, is a surer and better portion then any great riches which my thrift and care might bequeath them. Your resolution is the more wise and the more noble, worthy GUARDIAN (sayd the CHEIFE), by how much the more absolute; though it should bee with losse of comforts and lessening of your estate, youl bee sure to bring this part of your accompts in such forme as shall not bee refused at the great Auditt. For mee not to bee of the same mind were double folly, inasmuch as my virgin-estate œqually excludes the care both of worldly pleasures and children, and I am over and above perswaded that a man cannot bee either the poorer or lesse full of comfort by that which hee gives to the poore. I have a good ground in reason for it, since the fruit is alwaies answerable to the seed. Hee that sows joy must needs reape it; and doing good must needs turne to good. But I have an obligation in CHRISTS words, where hee tells the Apostles that hee that parts with anything for his sake shall receive the selfsame an hundredfold, even, that is, if himselfe desire it. GOD will bee no mans Debitor. Hee that brings in his Accompt shall instantly have it cleared. I hold it much the wiser course not to make offer of it till GOD himselfe call. But I am sure it cannot bee so soone offered as discharged. This have I beene taught, and beleive, and the truth I doubt not may easily bee confirmed by instanting many Saints whose riches and prosperity have gone on multiplying by the distribution of them in pious uses; so that by their owne confession they have still had the more by that which they have thus given away. The maintaining of this point was that which I intended to invite the PATIENT and AFFECTIONATE unto when I beganne this digression, which now, by that which hath thereupon happened, I much more earnestly entreat them to performe. The Examples of Saints (sayd the MODERATOUR) works little but upon those that endeavour to become Saints, or find themselves plaine sinners. The first are taken with the Conformity of that profession which themselves long after, and the last are troubled with the deformity of their owne vices in the light of others vertues. But wordly men that think themselves Christians good enough for heaven, whilst none can touch them with open enormities, make but a jest of the Authority or Examples of holy men, when they are alledged either to prove or perswade that which they please not to beleive or follow. I would rather, therefore, wish to heare, if it might bee, the confirmation of this new Doctrine (for so it will be counted) by the Testimony of some such persons as there lies no exception of partiality against by reason of any great eminency of Holinesse.

And wee shall fit you (sayd the PATIENT, having a little conferred with the AFFECTIONATE) with a couple of such witnesses as the world cannot refuse; having, as it were, by an extraordinary kind of Patent imposed on them the surname of Great, gives them a Testimony of irrefragable Authority touching those things which they deliver on their creditt and experience. Hee that I shall tell you of was but a private man, but such a one as, by the Absoluteness of his Authority, which hee had in a free Estate, the excellency of his Actions, and the unparalleldnes of wealth, merited the Name of Great. The great Cosimo de Medicis, from him in a lineall descent sprang many famous Personages, and some such as wore the greatest and noblest Crownes on Earth; and from him by a collaterall succession is the Greatnes of that great Family of the Medicis descended, which, besides the soveraignty of almost all Tuscany, have now mingled their bloud with all the royall Families in Christendome. Hee was but a Merchant by Profession, and gott his excessive wealth by trading, as others thought; as himselfe was of opinion, by bounty and Almesdeeds. I doe not remember the just Number, but I think it was not under thirty severall Churches, Colleges, Hospitalls, schooles, and religious houses that he founded and indowed. His house was the generall refuge of all that were in distresse; they came to him as to a common Father, and no lesse indeed they found him in effect, not onely releiving them according to their severall Necessities, but with that Love and tendernes as the very manner of bestowing made the Benefitts double of that which they were in their owne Nature, and yet were they in their owne Nature of that height and worth as is scant to bee credited, much lesse to be paralelled. He gave ten and twenty thousand Duckets at a time (sayth mine Author); and that you may not think it was but once or twice that hee used this princely Bounty, hee adds that when his Bookes of Accompts came to perusuall after his death, there was not found in Florentz, however great and populous a Citty it bee, any Man of Name or esteeme whosoever, whether

Gentleman or Commoner, that ought him not a good summe of Mony. When some would reason with him touching these unreasonable Almes, as they conceived them, hee would shutt up all with these words: With all the Almes that I bestow for GOD I cannot ballance the Accompt, but still remaine his Debitor. For however much it be that I give to him, yet it is still much more that which hee gives mee.

You have cleared this first point, deare PATIENT, beyond all exception, sayd the CHEIFE. His words are rather short then over in this matter, that sayd GOD multiplies Riches and temporall good things in the very selfe same Act whereby they are distributed to the poore.

Who was hee, I pray (sayd the GUARDIAN), that went so farre and spake so boldly in such a Paradox?

It was Gregory the great, sayd the CHEIFE; and so you have the Doctrine, both in Theory and Practize, verified by the seales of two such Personages as by their excellency above all others of their professions have merited the Name of Great by a joynt suffrage of the whole world. Whether the peevish Contradictions of some petty Doctors or pedling Merchants of our Times have weight enough to beare downe the scales in this Matter, judge you. But it cannot bee that the AFFECTIONATE should as happily acquitt herselfe of the second part, —that content and comforts are multiplied, as well as riches, by Almes-deeds.

How a Man should gett content or comfort I have now to dispute (sayd the AFFECTIONATE); but for to obtaine that which a Man desires and the accomplishment of that which hee intends, in which two things most Men, I am sure, hold content to ly, theres no readier nor surer way, by the Testimony of Consalvo Ferrantes, whose matchlesse Exploits in warre gained him that paragon title of Great Captaine. Though there bee but one Pheenix in the world, yet there is alwaies one. A new one ever springs from the Ashes of the old, but this transcendent title rose and died with him. Neither before nor since his time hath the world judged any worthy of such grace. The same envy that removed him from the Government of Naples, prosecuting him to Spaine, hee is commanded by the King to give an Accompt of the revenues of that kingdome, and the other summes which he had received in above twenty yeares space. Hee makes answere that it is just it should bee so; and great reason likewise that whether hee or the King proved indebted should make to the other. A longer time would no doubt have been given, but hee requires no further respitt than the next Day. When hee appeares before the Officers of the Chequer with a Booke of Accompts in his hand, out of which, being willed to speake for himselfe, hee reads the first parcell. Item—To the poore and to Monasteries, that they might make praiers to GOD to give mee Victory, given in ready mony, two hundred seventy thousand thirty-six Ducketts of gold, nine royall. The next parcell was six hundred thousand foure hundred ninety-foure duckets, layd out on private spies. The King advising himselfe of his error by an absolute Injunction not further to mention the Busines, gives the great Captaine, though a silent, yet a sufficient Quietus est. But the great Captaine by this manner of Accompt gave the world an everlasting direction, how in his Judgement and from whom they ought to seek the Attainement of their desires and the good successe of their Affaires. Others attributed his victorie to his valour; hee himselfe to GODS Blessing, and that cheifly procured, according to his Computation, by the means of Almsdeeds.

If any one should think this but a false entry devised to cleare himselfe of the busines, by how much hee detracts from the great Captaines worth by making him a silly Cheater in the upshott of so many heroicall Actions; by so much hee enforceth the Necessity of the Argument itselfe.

Let not our thoughts (sayd the GUARDIAN), much lesse our mouth, be soyled with the refutation of such absurd suspicions. Wee beleive he spake truth, both what hee had formerly done and what hee then thought, and must conclude that the proofe is incontroulable. If Almesdeeds march in the Van of all meanes for the settlement of Estates in warre and Peace, how much more advantageable must they needs bee for other lesser and more able designes. It cannot, therefore, bee to losse of Content that is so laid out; not more then it is to lessening of meanes. But I hope wee shall have further occasion to prosecute this matter. Now let us hear the SUBMISSE.

The SUBMISSE her story for this day being that which wee call the Lady of the Lights, is formerly entered and therefore here omitted.

The OBEDIENT follows.

The famous Salladine, that drove the Christians out of Asia, being incomparable in the excellency of all princely vertues and happines had hee not beene miserable in the Profession of a false religion, having conceived a singular Affection to a French Gentleman, whom hee had taken Prisoner in the warres, seeing him one day stand very pensive in his presence, demanded earnestly the reason of his sadnes, which the other not daring to conceale acknowledgeth to bee the remembrance of his native Country and freinds. If that company like you better then my favour (sayd the noble Prince), with my good grace thou mayst returne, and in reward of thy service and the Testimony of my Love, turning to his Treasurer, Give this Christian (sayd hee) a thousand Markes in gold. The Treasurer, according to his Custome, writing downe immediately his Majesties Command, instead of one made three thousand, which being about to blott out, What dost thou, sayd Salladine? Mending my error, sayd the Treasurer, who have sett downe three thousand markes for one. Now GOD forbid, sayd Salladine, thy penne should be more liberall then Salladines heart. Let him have it all. The French gentleman returning to the Christian Prince was a meanes of truce between them and Salladine, in which time, upon often meeting, it happened that the Christian Princes perswaded Salladine to leave his religion for theirs, which hee, confessing himselfe not well satisfied in his owne, was somewhat inclined to doe. But first, hee sayd, hee would advise himselfe and fully understand their customes, before hee left his owne. Whereupon being solemnely invited to a great Feast by the Kings of France and other Christian Princes, having curiously observed the Kings state in which he satt at meat, his servants attendance, the furniture of his house, the manner of his Lodging, and all other Customes and Usages, he confessed they were much to bee preferred before those of his owne country and people. But seeing certaine poore Men in meane rayment sitting in the Hall on the ground feeding with the broken meat that was left of his servants table, hee demanded who those were. They are, sayd the King of France, the children and freinds of GOD, who hath promised to accept that which is bestowed on them as given to himselfe. The next Day Salladine invited the Christians to his Campe, where was a tent royally furnished, the pavement being all spred with Turkey Carpets, all woven thick with crosses. Into which the Christians entering without any respect, not onely trod on them with their feet, but as occasion was, spitt upon them continually.

The Feast being ended, and the motions of turning Christian being againe renewed, hee with great semblance of gravity made answere : Why perswade you mee to the embracement of that religion which yourselves so much contemne ? At home you entertaine those whom you say are GODS Children and Freinds more vilely than the basest of your owne servants, and here abroad you trample on and defile with spitting those Crosses which you would have mee to doe reverence unto. I cannot bee perswaded yourselves beleive what you say, seeing your practize so contrarie to your words.

VI

CHRISTMASTIDE, 1631—HOLY INNOCENTS' DAY

Philip II. of Spain—Death of Henry IV. of France—Pope Adrian VI. and Pope Marcellus II.—The Shirt of the Happy Woman's making—Maurice, Prince of Orange—Queen Elizabeth—The Dying Man that smiled—Gillimer and Bellizarius.

THE guidance of this dayes exercise befalling the PATIENT, she rose and sung the hymne following :—

>That rage, whereof the psalm doth say,
>   Why are the Gentiles grown so vaine?
>Appeared in part upon this day,
>   When Herod had the infants slaine.
>Yet, as it saith, they raged in vaine,
>   Though many innocents they slew,
>For Christ they purposed to have slaine,
>   Who all their counsels overthrew.
>
>Thus still vouchsafe thou to restraine
>   All Tyrants, Lord, pursuing thee;
>Thus let our vast desires be slaine,
>   That thou mayst living in us bee.
>So whilst wee shall enjoy our breath,
>   Wee of thy Love our songs will frame,
>And with those Innocents our death
>   Shall also glorify thy Name.
>
>In Type those many died for one,
>   That One for many more was slaine;
>And what they felt in Act alone,
>   Hee did in will and Act sustaine.

> Lord, grant that what thou hast decreed
> In will and Act wee may fulfill,
> And though wee reach not to the deed,
> From us, oh Lord, accept the will.

The Hymne being ended, she took the Chaire and thus began.

This solemne Festivall seemes, in my Apprehension, to bee answerable to the Deaths Heads which the Aegyptians of old were wont in greatest Banquets to have served up amongst their Dainties, a counterpoize to the many delights and satisfactions that this good time useth to afford the Flesh. Least they might perhaps steal away the heart by their too much lushiousness, heres a public Caveat entered, the Imagination of our owne Deaths being necessarily represented in the solemn Commemoration that wee make of so many Innocents slaughter.

You cannot sever the thoughts of our owne and others deaths, and wee can no sooner think of our Deaths, but wee begin to bee weary of our Lives.

A handful of dust cast amongst Bees stilleth their greatest tumults.

Theres no pleasure that can delight, nor strong Passion that canne worke in a Mans mind, where the consideration of Death comes in place.

The Slaughter of those vast desires which our Hymne praies for cannot by any reasons bee better furthered then by that continuall application of this corrosive Plaster, which certainely eating out the dead flesh of all worldly desires and delights from the soul of Man, they that think happines consists in a licentious enjoyment of such trash as can never bee brought to forgive the wrong that they imagine to be done them by this solemne Festivall interposing itselfe, with sad considerations, to the utter overthrow of all merry thoughts and pastimes, but that they are so wise as to give no entertainment to such sowre considerations as this day presseth upon them. But that injury was intended, and therefore shall be requited. Not onely the present Day itselfe, but the returne of it every week for the whole yeare following is branded with a mark of unhappines.

But that which worldly minds dislike this day for ought to make it more precious in our eies. That it serves by admonishing us of our necessary Departure out of this world, to abate or our Love to the things thereof, is a double benefitt in truth, and I hope in all our Apprehensions. Wee have therefore resolved not to wave the proper subject of this Day for satisfaction of carnall minds, but according to the practize of all holy men which have ever made the Meditation of Death a necessary Ingredient in all Compositions of Joy, and despising of this worlds happines, a necessary preparation for the attainement of that true happines which wee pretend unto, to make our Histories of this day suit to these Intents, by representing Death on the stage in his owne dreadfulnes, to perswade you to make timely provision for his entertainment; and by representing the world on the other side in its owne Nakednes to withdraw you from further lose of Time and paines in the pursuit thereof: since, however largely the world promiseth, you shall clearely see it is not able to performe anything touching that content which you seek after.

And to this Intent I shall tell you one of the most famous passages that have beene ever acted in this worlds stage; and had it beene putt into a better hand, I doubt not but it would have beene so judged by all the hearers thereof. But as it can receive no grace by my weak delivery, so that it may not suffer prejudice by any unskillfull variation of mine, I shall endeavour to declare it in the same words, as neare as my memory will serve me, in which the true and authoreticall History hath related it according as it hath beene delivered unto mee by them, who I am sure deceived me not.

When King Phillip lay desperately sick, hee caused Florentius, his Confessor and Preacher of his Court, to bee thrice sent for at midnight, who presently came unto him with the Provinciall of Castile, and bringing with him Father Ignatius his Chirograph, who discoursed with the King of his approaching death, exhorted him to submit himselfe to the Divine Pleasure of GOD. The King gave Florentius, his Confessor, great thankes for such comforts, and turning towards him, Truely (sayd hee) my Florents, I am much obliged unto thee for those wholesome admonitions which thou hast continually raysed up and refreshed my soul in thy sermons. Florents made answere, that hee had nothing more in his wishes, if GOD prolonged his life, then that hee should now vow that hee would build a chappell in the honour of the Holy and Immaculate Conception of the Virgin Mary, and perswade the Pope that he should at last decide the Controversy which had beene so long debated thereabout.

To whom the King, Doe not you remember (sayd hee) in your sermon on Ashwednesday, that one of your Auditours should finish his last Day this present Lent? That touched me, and now the fatall houre is upon mee. But shall I bee partaker of everlasting Felicity?—and then great heavines and Anxiety supprized his mind, and then hee presently sayd to his Confessor, Thou hast not hitherto used the right course of healing mee. Which when the Confessor understood of the medicining for the body, the King added, I am not solicitous of my body and temporall disease, but to my soul. To whom the Confessor, I have done what I could. That which remaines is to be left to GODS Providence. And upon this occasion Florentius did largely discourse of the mercies of GOD, and brought unto his remembrance those things which hee had laudably performed for Christian religion. But the King answered, Ah, how happy had I beene if I had lived in a Desert these three and twenty yeares wherein I have held this kingdome. To whom FLORENTIUS sayd that his Majestie might performe even now also an acceptable duty to GOD, if hee would cast downe all earthly things, his kingdome, dignity, Life and salvation at the feet of his crucified Saviour JESUS CHRIST, and committ all to his will. Then the King sayd, Very willingly will I doe this, and even in this very moment; whatever GOD hath given mee, my Principalities, my Power, and my Life itselfe, I lay downe at the feet of JESUS CHRIST, the Saviour crucified for mee; whose Image he did kisse with singular affection, and further sayd to Florentius: Now, truly thou hast ministered egregious Comforts to my soul, and shall henceforth endeavour that it may bee openly signified to the people that I, at the point of death, have acknowledged all things that are in this world to bee but vaine things, and this very kingly Dignity which, during Life may be splendent and pleasant, but in the point of death it is very bitter and troublesome; and so hee did joyfully render up his spirit to GOD the heavenly Father as became a Christian King. Before his death hee did likewise exhort his sonnes to all Piety, and in especiall his eldest borne. Hee admonished that hee should well weigh that hee also was mortall, and therefore should so institute both his Life and the administration of his kingdome that it might not repent him at his end of his kingly power and Dignity as it now befell him, breathing out his soul. That hee should bee a Father of the poore and of the Common-wealth, that hee should be enflamed with the zeal of GODS glory, and that hee should account the dishonor done to the Divine Majesty to be put upon himselfe. Then hee gave him a sealed Codicill, and charged him exactly to observe all that which was therein contained; and presenting him likewise the Image of CHRIST crucified, hee sayd, This Image thy great Grandfather Charles the Fift gave my Father, which I now doe, as it were by will, bequeath unto thee. Thou shalt reverence it as a Christian Catholick King, and by the beholding thereof remember thine owne Mortality.

As concerning his will, he bequeathed nothing else therein than Admonitions belonging to Piety, and diligently recommended to his Sonne the Monastery at Madrill built by his Mother, and the Colledge of the Jesuites which is at Salamantica, and gave Commandment that his Body should bee buried with slender Pompe or without many or magnificent Ceremonies, and that it should not bee prepared with spices. For being so great a sinner I accompte myselfe unworthy of Buriall at all, sayd he.

This was the end of that great Monarch, whose Devotion that it was not righter sett in many Particulars deserves, meethinks, rather Teares than Censures; but ever where hee went most wrong himselfe, there perhaps hee may most confirme us in the truth. But leaving him to GODS mercy, touching his soules estate, I wish that the remembrance of his Acknowledgment touching this worlds vanities may ever remaine fresh in mine owne and all your minds.

The PATIENT having ended, after a good Pause allowed for Consideration of this wonderfull History, the CHEEREFULL began.

A Concurrent to King Phillip of Spaine was Henry the Fourth in France, the Father of our Royall Queen Mary. How his tragicall end made proofe of the misery of humane Condition is too well understood to be repeated in this Companie. But that which went before his death is not perhaps so generally knowne, though farre more observable in my Judgement, and most suitable to the Theme propounded by the PATIENT.

Whatever on Earth could be devised for the affording of Content and Joy might justly seeme to bee united in the Person and prosperity of this Prince: a large, faire, flourishing Kingdome, more honour from abroad, more Love at home of his subjects then ever any of his predecessors had. A strong Body, a faire Issue, abundance of treasure, a setled peace, and what could bee imagined to give Content that hee wanted? Besides a Festivall time, the Queenes Coronation being then solemnized, debarred out all Cares and businesses, and in a thousand kind of vanities brought in mirth and Jollity into the Court.

How full of joy and Comfort may wee deeme this Prince; and yet, alas, it is all otherwise. His heart is swallowed up with greife and Melancholy, though hee knows not why. Hee riseth early from his wearied bed, and goes to masse. That hee heares devoutly; at his returne they bring him his Children, and, amongst others, the Duke of ———, whom he loved dearely, and in whom hee tooke great delight; but then very pensively hee bid carry the Child to breakfast, and turning himselfe away sadly, casteth himselfe upon his Bed to sleepe, if he might. But rest forsakes through anguish of mind, which makes him rise and fall on his knees in prayer to GOD, from him to find Comfort, which no where else he could. Then againe hee lies downe, and againe riseth to praier. This he did three times. In the end, to shift by change of Place the wearisomenes of his owne thoughts, hee goes to walk in the gallery till dinner. Costly victualls restore his body, but they refresh not his mind. Thats still encombred with perplexity, which the noble men perceiving and pittying, strive by divers merry passages to allay, themselves mutually laughing to draw him on to mirth. With much adoe they force a fained smile or two from him, though naturally of a most pleasant disposition. In the end hee breakes of all with a French Proverb: Wee have laughed enough for Friday, wee may well weepe on Sunday. And so they did indeed. But of his death I meane not to speake at this time. Its the insufficiency of all worldly things to breed comfort that I have told this story for. In proofe of which I suppose wee may read, as it were in text Letters, and withall where indeed true happines is to be found. Which hee, seeking it in GODS service, and particularly in praise, directeth us unto.

The CHEIFE seeing the Story ended, and by the fixed eies of all the Auditours perceiving that they esteemed silence the fittest Descant on so sad a Tragedy, conforming her Demeanour to their solemne Countenances and stillnes, did by a gentle Invitation of her hand direct the AFFECTIONATE to the Chaire, who, with great reverence to her and all the rest, thus began and proceeded.

My Sisters have severally told you of two Kings. I shall bring two Popes to serve on this Jury, Adrian the Sixt, and Marcellus the Second. It is not much above a hundred years agoe that the first, and little above halfe the time that the other lived; both of them for Wisedome, Learning, and Integrity passing any of that Rank that went before them many hundreds of yeares, and both of them advanced from low degree, which should have made their happines seeme the greater to themselves, which to all others seemed the very Crowne of humane Felicity. But heare the Evidence that themselves give. Adrian wills it to be graven on his Tombe, that hee esteemed nothing to have befallen him more unhappily then that hee had raigned, and Marcellus, even in the heat of the Congratulation which all the world offered him, grows into so deepe displeasure with that which others terme soveraign happines, that repeating Pope Adrian his Epitaph, hee brake of his dinner, and smiting his hand on the Table hee cries out, I see not how they that hold such high dignities can bee saved.

Goe now and seeke for Content and happines in the propriety of a few acres of Land, or in the Command of a few silly people, or in the wantonnes of a few vaine pleasures, which neither Kings nor Popes could find in all what their royall Estate afford. Is hee not a mad man that hopes to fill himselfe in the shallow pitts of civill or ecclesiasticall Dignity, when hee sees that the overflowing Rivers of Crownes and triple Mitres leave their possessors soules as dry and thirsty of Content as the sands of Arabia are of Moysture? If neither Kings nor Popes can find Joy or Happines, who can hope to doe it in this world?

The AFFECTIONATE having concluded, least the height of examples should lesse move those of lower rank, the MODERATOUR thought good by a more familiar Instance to sette forth the Matter.

A great Lady of Naples having in the prime of her youth lost her husband, and being left with only one sonne, grew so distasted with the uncertainty of this worlds happines, which had deceived her in its fairest blomings, and so in Love with vertue and godlynes, wherein alone shee saw true Content was to be found, as utterly shutting of all other designes, she makes it her onely end to become good, and to make her sonne such; which, as these desires, when they are reall, never want effect, shee did by Gods grace so accomplish, as shee became in that great Citty the cheife Example of vertue in herselfe, and of happines in her sonne.

Her son comming to Mans Estate, was desirous to travail for the perfecting by experience of that wisedome which hee had learned by precepts; to which his Mother, that more tendred his improvement in good qualities then the satisfaction of her owne Affections, gave a willing though a sad Consent. And so hee proceeds from one famous Citty to another, every where giving such proofes of excellent vertue and abilities as his Mothers heart melts with joy and desires upon the continuall reports which on all hands are made unto her of his noble demeanours. At last, comming to Bologna, a Feaver ceazeth him, which hee finding to bee mortall, calls for Pen and Ink, and having writt and sealed a Letter, hee sweares all his servants that they should not give any manner of Intimation of his death to his Mother till they received the answeare of that Packett which hee delivered unto them; the tenor whereof was, that hee was well, and hoped to bee better, and shortly to attaine the uttermost in all good things, which shee and hee sought for; that as shee was his good Mother and loved him, she would procure a shirt to bee immediately made up for him by the hands of a happy woman.

The carefull Mother, upon the receit of these Letters, assembling all her kinred at a feast—the last that shee ever made after her husbands death—served up for the last course her sonnes letter, and besought them of all Love to help her in the accomplishment thereof. Everyone (though they were very many) began to excuse themselves, alledging so many misfortunes, as shee herself could not but grant they had reason to deny her that which they could not really and truely performe. Whereupon some of her wiser freinds advised without more adoe to cause a shirt to bee made up, by whom she thought good, and to lett it be sent to her son, adding that it was undoubtedly but a youthful Conceit, which would bee much easier perhaps deluded then accomplished. Neither is it fitt for me, replied that good Lady, to delude whom I so much love, and who hath so much affiance in mee. Nor can I think it a light matter which my son so earnestly desires; besides, the very stile of the letter speakes it is a desire of Judgement, and not of fancy. I will not therefore be wanting in what I may. With this resolution shee riseth next day, and first goes amongst her acquaintances and afterwards amongst strangers, as shee heard of any whose prosperous estate gave her hope to attaine by their meanes what shee desired. But all in vaine; upon the first opening of her request everyone starts back, and not onely tell her, but make it evident by recompting their particular afflictions, that shee was not the woman that was sought for. The good Lady, after fourty daies spent in this search, and many hundreds of persons spoken unto, returnes her sonne answere that hee should quiet his mind by wisdome, for to give satisfaction to his desire was impossible. I have sought, sayd shee, all Naples over as it were with a Candle, and find nothing but misery in all Mens and Womens Condition. Most have their Calamities hang upon the rappers of their dores; and they that have no greife without to others have two within.

Upon the receit of these letters his servants returne to Naples, and presenting themselves unexpectedly, shee instantly reads in the mourning habits the sad Message which their tongues could not utter. The noble Lady having wept awhile, and payd Nature her due, at last gives place to reason, and drying her teares, comforts both her selfe and her servantes, telling them that since the common position of this world was nothing but Misery, as shee by particular survey had found, it was great unreasonablenes for her not to undergoe that part thereof which befell her by Gods appointment.

It was a witty Invention (sayd the CHEIFE) if it were not a truth, which you have recompted, most honoured MODERATOUR, and sensibly leading our Imaginations to the veiw of this worlds wretchednes. In which respects it may very well serve, as statues doe, though not for upholding, yet for ornament of royall Buildings, a gracefull setting of, if not a supporting argument to that Conclusion which this daies stories all of them inferre: That the best and fairest Happines of this world is begun in vanity, grows up with vexation, and even ends in repentance.

That Difference of religion may not derogate from this truth, GOD makes the greatest Opposites in this Age to agree therein, that there may bee no place for Cavill, where there is no liberty of appeale or controule of what part soever a man bee, Papist or Protestant, hee hath an over-ruling example. Maurice, Prince of Orange, that in everything was so averse was in his last end so answerable to Phillip, as we must needs say whatever els may be disputable, yet this is plaine and certaine.

All tyme is lost but what is bestowed in GODS service When hee find his sicknes mortall, hee forbidds the mentioning of any worldly Affaires. When the Minister tells him that GOD had made him an incomparable Prince, so that the whole world admires his Actions, hee keeps silence, as if it were nothing appertaining to him. But when hee beginnes to speak of the breach of GODS Commandments, hee opens his mouth, and sayth, I have sinned; and instantly doubles it with greater vehemency, his teares bearing wittnesse how it afflicted him at the heart, I have sinned grossely. When hee is exhorted to putt himselfe on GODS disposall, hee answeres, So I doe.

When Comforts are propounded hee closed his hands, confesseth his faith, and shutts up all. I take my refuge unto the great Mercy of GOD, and I beleive that JESUS CHRIST died for mee on the Crosse, wherein I putt all my trust. I need not goe over all the particulars, the booke being extant; the summe of all is, all his Greife was that hee had not served GOD better. All his care and feare was, least his repentance shoulde not bee sufficient. The best comfort in this world that hee could find, was GODS word read or repeated to him. The most wellcome Persons were the Ministers. The most acceptable discourse was touching GODS mercy. The onely thing he longed for was true repentance. I shall not need to make the application of these things, they speake so effectually themselves. If wisdome and happines lie in this kind of disposition, and these kinds of Practizes at the time of sicknes and at the approach of Death, to steare our Lives a contrary Course in the time of health must needs bee extreame madnes and the height of Misery.

To the testimony of so many men give mee Leave (sayd the GUARDIAN) to read the evidence of a woman, that the proofe of the thing may bee compleat on all hands, and both sexes may have their proper witnesses to informe them.

In the yeare 1586 Queene Elizabeth told this whole state in the representative body of the Parliament, that Happines was so farre estranged from this world that the first steppe towards it was to bee quickly gone out of the world. Heare her owne words. I am not ignorant of all kinds of Lives: for I have obeyed, and I have governed: I have had good Neighbours and also evill: I have found trechery where I trusted: I have evill bestowed benefitts, and I have beene evill reported of when I have done well. When I call these things past to mind, see and behold the things present, and expect future things, I think them most happy who dy soone. I think them most happy who dy soone: this is her censure, which addeth to that you have heard. Meethinks wee may boldly conclude that what is thus jointly ratified by the Defender of the Faith, the Christian and Catholick Kings, must needs bee an orthodox Christian, Catholick verity, that this world is a vale of misery, and that there is no true and solid Comfort to bee found, whilst wee are here on earth, but in the faithfull service of GOD.

This is that which you propounded at the first and have clearly proved by these Examples. GOD grant that our assents to this truth may appeare as well in our Lives as it doth now in our faces.

The GUARDIAN having ended, the SUBMISSE told the story following: A holy Man having closed his eies to dy, hearing the standers by making great moane for him, and to talke of death with evidence of much affrightment and perplexity, smiled three severall times. Whereat they amazedly demanding the reason, hee thus made answere :

I smiled first to see you so much afraid of Death, which you can by no meanes escape. Next I smiled to see you unprepared for that which you are so much afrayd of; and lastly, I smiled to see you mistake touching my death, which is the entrance into everlasting happinesse.

The OBEDIENT concluded the day with the story following :

The famous Gillimer, being first overcome by Bellizarus and afterwards streightly beseiged, upon the yielding himselfe to mercy desired a Loafe of Bread, a spunge, and a harpe to bee given him : the first to satisfy his hunger, having tasted no food in many daies ; the next to dry his teares, the continuall streames whereof had perished one of his eies ; and the last to vent his greif by, which through concealment broke his heart. Being afterwards lead to Constantinople and brought before the Emperor, considering the strange successe of humane condition, that of a mighty King hee was now become a servant, hee cryed out aloud : Vanity of vanities, all is vanity.

The Emperor, moved with compassion, gave him certaine lands in France, where hee ended his Life.

VII

CHRISTMASTIDE, 1631, DECEMBER 29TH

*Brother Genadius—Cinesius and Enagrius—Bishop Sidonius—
The Forty Martyrs—Michael Mercatus.*

Song by the Submisse

O happy you, that have subdued
    The force o th worlds desire !
And into th fort of solitude
    For safety do retire.

You fled from freedome so supposed,
    In straitnes freedome find,
Because true freedome is inclosed
    I th circuit of the mind.

The world and fortune that deprive
    From doing you despite ;
Dead unto Men, to God alive,
    Which gives Life true delight.

That soule, sayth God, which I affect,
    I will withdraw apart ;
And tell unto it in effect
    The secrets of my heart.

Think then you that retirèd live
    For Gods dear Love and dread,
His Love your soules desire doth give
    Retirèd Lives to lead.

So that with him you may conferre,
    When sole your selves you deeme ;
And so alone lesse never are
    Then when alone you seeme.

Faith of your Fort is Governor ;
  Love is Leiftennant there ;
Hope is ordainèd Officer
  The Ensigne for to beare.

Contempt of wealth is Treasurer,
  Which workes no guile for gaine ;
Within whose coffers never there
  Corrupting drosse remaines.

Pure Chastity the Charge doth take
  The Cloyster cleane to keepe,
And of her thoughts the brome doth make,
  Wherewith shee doth it sweepe.

Obedience, then, with sacrifice
  In value worth exceeds,
Is ready for each exercize
  As Duty deemeth neede.

Persèverance is Centinell ;
  The watch-word, Watch and Pray.
Whose due observance doing well
  The Heavens will repay.

Though earthly things (sayd the Cheife) to them that are unexperienced seeme full of happines, yet to those that have made any small triall they are found so full of insufficiency that most men perhaps would bee easily persuaded to call back their Affections if they knew where else to place them ; but now because Love cannot but work, and desire pursue something, there seemes to most Men a kind of Necessity imposed on them to follow that which they see heere below, because those things that are above, being farre removed out of sight, they can scearce bee perswaded that they are at all. The Inevidency of the things after this Life breeds a doubt in most Mens minds of the certainty whether they bee or no. And the Affections, that, like the Conclusion, follow the weaker part, thinking it ground enough to be cold in the Love of what they have not knowne ; and in the feare of what they have not seene, spend all their strength in the embracing or avoyding of the good or evill that falls under their sences. Further then they reach few Men will adventure; holding it great folly to leave the hold of what wee have in our hands for the apprehension of that which is represented unto us in hope.

It will be, therefore, in my opinion, sweet Companions, most profitable to carry up our thoughts, that are amated with the wretchednes of this world, to the meditation of those better things in Heaven by the recompting of some such story as may tend to the Confirmation of our mutual vows touching the despising of all which the world tenders unto us now, for the Love of that which faith promiseth us hereafter to enjoy.

What an Absurdity seemes it to flesh and Blood to put a Mans selfe to certaine paine here in expectation of future Joy, or to defy present for the dread of after Torment.

To take away this perplexity theres nothing more effectuall then the remembrance of those proofes which GOD hath sometimes extraordinarily given of the certainty and largenes both of the rewards and punishments that shall crowne good or evill Actions. I pray, therefore, let this daies Stories bee to this effect. But let them bee such as may suit with the excellency and dignity of our former discourses. And because that all Mens minds, when they enter into these meditations, doe first stumble at the very entrance of the other world; that is, how it can bee that there should bee any sensible apprehension of things when the senses are dissolved with the bodies corruption in the grave; I pray you, dear PATIENT, to remove this block by the recompting of that admirable passage which our VISITOUR lately told us out of St. Augustine, if I mistake not.

You mistake not at all (replied the PATIENT), for it was St. Augustine that recounts it in a certaine Letter which hee wrott to one Euodius. This Particular I afterwards learned, for the excellency of the matter made me curious to informe myselfe more fully of it.

You did therein (replied the AFFECTIONATE) answerably to that good discretion which you use in all other matters. The knowledge of these circumstances not onely gives much satisfaction to the hearers, but adds Authority to the relation itselfe.

But, I pray you, proceed, for our desires brooke no delay. You shall have it (sayd the PATIENT), neither of mine, nor of any others composing, but in the very words of St. Augustine himselfe, for so did our VISITOUR, giving mee the story in writing, advise, if ever Occasion were, I should recompt it.

Our brother Gennadius, famous amongst all and very deare to us, that now lives a physitian at Carthage, and was highly esteemed for his skill at Rome, is, as thou knowest, a very devout Man, most bountifull in the free disposition of his mind, and of unwearied Mercifullness touching the care of the poore. Neverthelesse, as himselfe lately related, when hee was a young man and very fervent in those kind of almesdeeds, hee fell into a doubtfulnes whether there were indeed any other life after Death. Now GOD no way purposing to desert this mind or his and these workes of mercy, there appeared unto him in sleepe a yong man very conspicuous and regardfull, and sayd unto him: Follow me. Whom whilest Gennadius followed, hee came unto a certaine citty, from the right hand part whereof hee beganne to heare the sound of Musique most delectable beyond all usuall or knowne sweetnesse. And whilest hee was musing what it might bee, the other told him that they were the Hymnes of blessed Men and Saints. What he reported to have seene on the left hand I now remember not. In the end Gennadius awaketh and his dreame departed, and hee thought no more of the Person then of the dreame. But behold another Night the same yong Man comes to him againe, and demands whether hee knew him. Gennadius made answere, hee knew him full well. The other asked him where hee had known him. Gennadius his memory was not wanting what to answere, but, with as great facility as things freshly done, remembered both all the vision and those hymnes of the Saints which hee came to the hearing by his guidance. Whereupon the other asked whether hee had seen those things which hee now related in sleep or waking. Gennadius answered, In sleepe. You say right, replied the other; you saw them in your sleep; but know that what thou now seest thou likewise seest in thy sleepe. Gennadius hearing this beleived it to bee so, and by his acknowledgement confirmed it. Then hee that taught the Man added further, saying, Where is now thy Body? In my chamber, sayd hee. And dost thou know, replied the other, that those eies in thy body are now bound up, shutt and silent, and thou seest nothing at all with them? To which Gennadius, not knowing what to answere, became mute. Whereupon the other in this perplexity tooke the hint to open unto him that which hee had intended to reach by these former questions, and immediately sayd: And those eies of thy flesh are now altogether still in this sleepe on thy bed without any manner of operation, and yet, neverthelesse, are the selfe same with which thou now lookest on mee and usest in this vision.

So likewise, when thou shalt bee dead, the eies of thy flesh ceasing from all worke, there shall yet remaine a Life to thee whereby thou shalt live, and a sence by which thou shalt be sensible. Take heed, therefore, that thou doubt no more whether there bee any life after death. By this meanes, that faithfull Man affirmes, his doubtfulnes was removed. Who, instructing him about the Providence and mercy of GOD (for he was so taught by a naturall Instance), yet his mind being illuminated by the brightnes of heavenly Grace, hee was changed, as the Apostle speaketh, from Glory to Glory, even as by the Spirit of the Lord.

The PATIENT having finished her Story, the CHEEREFULL beganne.—

If the Creditt of my Author were equall to St. Augustines my story would be in no whitt inferior to that which you have heard. I cannot deliver it upon so bold warranty. No. Sophronius, that relates it in his Spirituall Middow, is not so authentick a wittnesse. If any refuse it I will not contend. Let him have his opinion, so he will allow me mine. The approbation of many excellent Men hath in my Judgement sett the seale of truth to it. None can deny it in the morall: I believe it is so in the Fact. The famous Cinesius, chosen a Bishop almost as soone as baptized, laboured earnestly to bring Enagrius, his Companion in Philosophy, to the fellowship of the same true relligion which he had himselfe by GODS mercy attained, was by him still answered that hee could not condescend thereto, cheifly because of the Impossibility of the resurrection and the unlikelyhood of that great repayment which our holy Faith promiseth to them that bestow their substance on the Poore for CHRISTS sake, that they should receive treasure in heaven for that which they had parted with on earth, a hundredfold, and everlasting life for vantage. This to him, as hee professed, seemed but a fancy in them that beleived it, and a subtilty, if not worse, in them that perswade it. Cinesius, like a true freind to Enagrius and a faithful Servant to his Master, ceased not with all diligence to instruct, exhort, and intreat him, till in the end the light of GOD shining into his heart, he gained him to become as strong in true faith as before he was obstinate in the errors of corrupt reason. Shortly after hee was baptized, intending to free himselfe of all worldly superfluities, that hee might the more expeditely runne the race that hee had beganne, hee brought unto the Bishop a great summe of mony, saying, Take this here, and dispose as thou knowest best amongst the poore, and give me a bill under thy hand, that I may receive proportionably, as thou hast told mee I should hereafter doe in heaven from the hand of CHRIST. Cinesius gladly received the Mony, immediately bestowed it, and under his hand gave the writing that the other required.

Enagrius, after some yeares spent in holines, comming to dy, called his sonnes, and delivering the obligation which hee had received from Cinesius unto them without acquainting them how it was. When you bury me, sayd he, put this deed into my hands; which they accordingly with all care performed. The Bishop, that knew nothing of the obligation, early in the morning sending for Enagrius his children, demanded of them whether that they had put anything in the grave with their Father.

They, doubting he might suspect the burying of some Mony, answered, Nothing, my Lord, but the usuall Gravecloths.

Nothing at all, sayd the Bishop—no writing, nor Paper; are you sure?

Yes, sayd they, remembring themselves. Our Father, indeed, at his death gave us a certaine writing, and charged us to put it into his hands when wee put him into the grave. But what the contents thereof may bee wee are altogether ignorant; for, he not pleasing to reveale it himselfe, wee durst not presume to open it. Whereupon the Bishop declared unto them his Vision, and sending for the Clergy and the Cheife Magistrates of the Citty, went immediately to the grave, which, after they had opened, perceiving the writing in his hand, the Bishop tooke it and read it, and found, newly written by Enagrius his owne hand: I, Enagrius the Philosopher, send greeting to the most holy Lord Cinesius the Bishop. I have received the debt specified under thy hand in this writing, and acknowledge myself to be contented, neither have I any right against thee touching that gold which I gave to thee, and by thee to CHRIST, our Lord God and Saviour.

They that were present, hearing this, brake out into great outcries of prayer and thankesgiving to GOD that of his infinite mercy was pleased for the satisfaction of our weaknes to give such evidency of proofes touching the Infallibility of his promises.

This is a Story which I the more boldly report unto you, because I have heard it to have been publickly delivered by a famous Divine in a very solemne Assembly. But however the Action passed, wee have a sure word concerning the truth of the Doctrine itselfe, even the Testimony of that great Doctor of the Gentiles, That every Man shall receive according to the things which hee hath done in his body, whether they bee good or bad.

Undoubtedly they did (sayd the AFFECTIONATE), and in confirmation of this latter pointe, that strict Judgement and severe punishment shall follow wicked deeds after this Life, I shall tell you a story every way admirable as being of most famous Persons, conteining rare passages, and of unquestionable Verity.

I pray you of whom is your story (sayd the CHEIFE), and by whom is it written?

It is written by Gregory Turonensis (sayd the AFFECTIONATE), and is of that most renowned Man, both for learning and holines, Sidonius, the Bishop of Arverene in France, who being, as my Author sayth, wholly given over to the service of GOD, so that he lead the life of heaven here on earth.

Two Preists of his, rising up against him by dispoyling him of his Authority and stripping him of his meanes, brought him both to great Necessity and Shame.

But the Judgement of GOD was quicker to punish then their Malice to performe the uttermost of their evill Intendments.

One of these sonnes of Belial, having threatened over Night to drag the holy Bishop out of the Church upon the first sound to Morning Prayers ; but before hee could go out, the necessity of Nature urging him, hee withdraws apart, willing his servant to attend, which, whilst he doth, a Messenger comes posting from his Companion in Evill, upbraiding his sluggishnes : That it was now broad day-light and they had yet done nothing.

The long stay of the Master, and the importunity of the Messenger, forced the servant to call first ; and, receiving no answere, goes into the Place where his Master was, whom hee found dead, his bowells having gushed out below. The fearefulnes of this Judgement abated both the courage and power of his companion ; so that the Bishop was immediately, by the helpe of good Men, restored to all that which hee had beene deprived of by these wicked ones. But being too good for earth, GOD shortly after, by a Fever, sent for him to heaven ; which, the holy man perceiving, caused himselfe in his sick bed to bee carried into the Church, whither instantly by troupes resorted not onely Men and Women, but the very Children also, with one mournfull voice crying : Why dost thou forsake us, thou good Pastor ? To whom dost thou leave us all Orphanes ? What a Life shall wee have when thine is departed ? Who shall henceforth season us with the salt of heavenly wisdom ? Or who shall by prudent reproofe inforce us to the Feare of GODS Name? These and the like things spake the Multitude in a confused Manner, and mixed Expressions of words and Teares ; whom, the holy man having a good while accompanied in their weeping, at last the Spirit of Courage and Comfort descending downe upon him, hee began to courage and comfort them, saying, Feare not, my Children ; behold, Apeunculus my Brother liveth, and hee shall bee your Preist and Pastor. They, not understanding him, thought that what they heard was not intended to them, but spoken by him in Exstasy. Hee had scarce surrendered his faithfulle Soule to Heaven, when that cursed Preist, left alive to a more fearefull vengance, ceazed upon all that Sidonius had left behind on earth, and flattering himselfe in his abominable sinne to wipe out the Terror which his fellows horrible Confusion had bred, insults upon the Saints livelesse Corps.

At last (sayd hee) GOD hath looked downe upon my wrong and hath revenged mee of myne Enemy, having taken him from that Dignity which hee unworthily usurped, and hath bestowed it on me, whom hee hath found more faithfull.

In these and the like Conceits hee proudly hurries up and downe the Citty. And on the Sunday following invites the whole people to a solemne Feast, where, contemning all others, hee setts downe in the cheife seat, and takes that honour to himselfe which no man ought to take but hee that is called of GOD. Having begun to eat without feare, hee calls for wine to encrease his Mirth ; which the Cup-bearer, with a low obeisance delivering unto him : I saw, my Lord (sayd hee) a vision to Night which, if you give leave, I will declare.

The sadness of the relatours countenance affrighted the unhappy Man, so that hee could not tell what readily to answere. Whereupon the other proceeded thus :

This Sunday Night I saw a stately Pallace, and therein was a throne placed, wherein a Judge satt seeming to excell all others in Power. Many Preists in white vestiments attended neere, and an innumerable Company of all other sorts of people round about him. Whilest with great amazement

I beheld these things, I perceived blessed Sidonius earnestly contending with that Preist, once so deare unto thee, and so ever unhappy in his most wretched death. After some whiles pleading, Sidonius having convicted him, immediately the King commanded that the other should be cast into the innermost dungeon. Hee was scarce removed when Sidonius, rising up againe, began to accuse thee also, saying that thou likewise was a partner in that wickednes for which this other was condemned. Whereupon the Judge, beginning to enquire whom he might send to warne thy appearance, I fearefully drew back doubting with my selfe, least peradventure, if I were knowne to bee there, it might bee imposed on mee. Whilest I silently cast these things in my heart, lo! I find my selfe on a suddaine left alone with the Judge, who, beckoning unto mee, I, not able to endure the brightnes of his countenance, mine eies became dimme and all my Joynts fell a-quaking. But hee cherefully sayd unto mee, Feare not, yong-man, but goe thy way to that Preist and will him immediately to come to his triall, for Sidonius hath desired to have him summoned.

Take heed, therefore (sayd the Cup-bearer to the Preist), that thou make no delay; for with a vehement protestation the King charged mee to tell thee all this, saying unto mee, If thou forbeare to speake what I have commanded, thou shalt dy surely a cursed death.

Hee had no sooner ended these words then the affrighted Preist, letting the cup fall out of his hand, fell downe likewise eternally dead.

Thus (sayth my author) were the Judgements of GOD upon these two rebellious Preists, the first perishing with the destruction of Arrius, and the other condemned after the example of Simon Magus, falling downe from the high soarings of Pride into the lowest pitt of Condemnation. And the like end shall in the end befall those that, swelling with Pride and envy, oppose and persecute that goodnes which they cannot, or will not, themselves reach unto.

The AFFECTIONATE having ended, the MODERATOUR began.

I will warrant the truth of my story ; touching the excellency of it, yourselves shall bee Judge. And so, having before obtained the priviledge for that once to read her story, which shortnes of time and other occasions had not given leave fully to finish, much lesse to committ to memory, she proceeded.

Licinius, Brother-in-Law to Constantine the great, and partner with him in the Empire, upon the Breach of Friendship betweene them, casting away Feare and all other respects which had formerly caused him to dissemble, makes open profession of his secret Enmity against CHRIST himselfe, and against all that called upon his holy Name, and were called by it. Fire long-smothered breakes forth with greater violence, and suppressed Malice fiercer when it comes to uncontrouled vent. A publick Edict is made that the fading worship of Idols shall bee revived, the encreasing worship of CHRIST shalbe abolished. Fire and sword and gibbetts, sacks and wheeles and scourges, and all other Instruments that cruelty could invent, are sett forth every where to open view, first by their sight to terrify, and, if that prevaile not, by the bitter sence of torment to enforce the gainesayers. Barbarous minded Judges, bloudy-handed Ministers, are picked out for execution of these laws. Spies are suborned, Accusers are rewarded. Curious inquisition to find out Christians is the best service that can be done the State. There is no possibility of Concealment; there is no mercy in discovery. Many fly and keep their Faith safe, with the losse of all other things. Others stay for the Love of other things, and loose themselves. Some beginne well, but fainting in their tryalls, like ships driven from their Anchor-hold, make shipwrack in the Haven. In the Emperors Campe, which was then in Armenia, there was one company of souldiers, small in Number, being onely 40, but great in reputation for many notable Exploits which they had performed ; Cappodocians by their country and Christians by their religion, and that they so openly professed as the whole Army takes Notice of it. The Judge deputed in this Commission, whose Name was Agricola, resolves to beginne here, hoping that, as in Conquest of warre, the great Citties and holds being taken lesser Forts come in of themselves, upon this famous bands deniall of CHRIST there would be no other of inferior Quality dare to confesse him for their God. The first Battery that he laies is faire words, magnifying their approved valour, their mutual Love, and sober Conversation, for which things sake they might assure themselves, as they all well deserved, to find great reward from the Emperors bounty and Justice if now they overthrow not all by an obstinate disobedience of absolute Commande, which was that they should offer incense to the Gods upon the Altar there prepared.

They joyntly made answere the demand was unjust, and the Conditions unequall. They hoped for better Crownes then the Emperor himselfe wore by serving JESUS CHRIST, the true and onely Lord of heaven and earth, and therefore by this double right to be much rather obeyed and served then Licininius.

The angry Judge advised them to bethink themselves well what they lost, and what they were like to incurre, and to bring him a better resolution, in the meane time committing them to safe ward.

The next day they appeared, and the unchangablenes of their Answeres breeds a change of Agricolas proceedings. Fierce words, base Tants, bitter Threats, are heaped on them, which they answere, though mildly, yet boldly and plainly, telling him that what he thinks to fright them with is that which they above all other things long after, to dy a speedy, a painefull, and a shamefull death for CHRISTS sake. Agricolas incensed rage was desirous to have satisfied their strange request; but divers good respects perswaded him to forbeare till their Captains comming, which was not till seven daies, when suddenly they are sent for, and that with such terrors of words and other frightfull circumstances as a chill paleness of their faces manifested some fearefull apprehensions to have ceazed their hearts. Which one of them named Grion perceiving, he began to cheare them up by the remembrance of former dangers. Wee have, through GODS power strengthening us, withstood (sayd he), my Brethren, with undaunted courage, as ye well know, thousands of Enemies that have assaulted us, and come of victorious, where the whole Army fled ; and now theres no more at most than the Judge, our Captaine, and the Devill that assault us, and shall wee faint in so great odds as fourty hath of these ? Or shall GOD now at last abandon us in the laying downe of our Lives for his Honour, that hath ever heretofore so strongly and faithfully assisted, when it was but the Emperors pleasure and service that wee went upon and hazarded ourselves for ? Let us lift up our eies whence our help cometh, and carry up our thoughts to those Joyes whither wee are going. Having thus spoken, they joyntly repeated that Psalme of David which beginnes, Save mee o God, for thy Names sake, and avenge mee in thy strength.

Thus armed, they presented themselves at the Tribunall, and by wise answeres to what was objected, constant profession of what they believed, and patient enduring of the Injuries which were done to them, leave their enemies so confounded and enraged, as taking time to bethink themselves of torments answerable to the excesse of malice which they had conceived, they for that Night returne the blessed Saints to their former prison, where continuing in prayers, as some relate, they heard a voice with greater Majesty of sound then can proceed from mans brest, saying, Your beginnings are good, but happy is hee that perseveres unto the end. But that which is certain, by St. Basils relation, is, that the next day towards evening they were adjudged to bee put into a great Lake neere unto the walls of Sebast, and there to freize to death, except they would deny CHRIST JESUS ; on which condition they might, when they desired, be taken out of the cold water and put into a warme bath, which was ready prepared and at hand for the enforcement of the Temptation and doubling of their torment, as well by the sight of comfort as by the sence of paine. The sentence that others trembled to heare, these blessed souldiers of CHRIST JESUS received with gladnes. As soone as they come to the place they made hast to strip themselves, and entering manfully up to their very chins, beseech GOD with a joynt cry that as they went in so they might come out, fourty Martyrs for his holy Names sake.

God heares and grants their Petitions (sayth St. Basil) although hee made it good after an unexpected manner.

The Guard walk trembling on the shore, and the Martyrs stand cheerefully in the water, encouraging themselves and one another with thousand the like words as St. Basil reports. It is a happy thing to enjoy the delights of Paradise.

Heaven shall restore with endlesse joy the momentary Torments that wee now suffer. This bitter Night shall be changed into an everlasting day of Happines.

But the tender pitty of GOD, that cannot endure their greife so long as themselves are content to endure it, setts about a shorter period to their sufferings then themselves had appointed, not by taking away of the praise, but by supply of such comfort as mans heart is not able to conceive. The Angels descend from Heaven, and by putting crowns on their heads give them the recompence of their present Misery, the earnest of their future happines. Onely one of the fourty is omitted. The Bath-keeper that stood to watch sees this, and whilest he sees and wonders at what hee sees, hee heares that miserable wretch who was left uncrowned by the Angells, and uncomforted, calling to bee taken out of the cold water, and to bee put into the warm Bath, which is instantly performed by the willing Guard, but with greater anguish to the noble Martyrs, his companions, then all their own sufferings had caused. A sharper cold ceazeth their soules then before pinched their Bodies. Their hearts quake and their spirits groane in evidency of their fellows Backsliding, in the doubtfulnes of their owne Continuance.

But having received the first fruits of Glory there was no residence for greife in their soules. GOD comforts and confirmes them without delay in a double manner. Hee that would not continue in the cold water for CHRISTS sake dies when hee comes out of it; he no sooner setts foot in the warme bath but his life departs, for which hee had lost his soule.

The Bath-keeper, that had before seene the vision, and now fully understood the Mystery, cries out to his companions, See, I am a Christian; and instantly dispoyling himselfe of his clothes steps naked into the water, joyning himselfe in sufferings to them with whom hee desired to bee partner in glory.

It came to passe here (sayth St. Basil), as it did in the Case of Judas, hee lost his office and another tooke it to make up the Number of the Apostles, and it came to passe, as it did with St. Paul, hee that stood to seduce others becomes himselfe the Martyr of CHRIST.

The MODERATOURS longsome Pause gave evidency that she was come to the end of what shee then ment to say.

The Company was about to dissolve, when the GUARDIAN staying them with the signe of his hand, spake thus:

The least of these foure services might have sufficed for a Kings entertainment, and therefore wee cannot exact more that have already had overmeasure. But to refuse the banquet which I know is prepared, answerable to the richnes of the former messes, were not the wisdome of Temperance, but the excesse of folly. Theres no surfeiting in this kind of feast. Let us therefore, I beseech you, sitt downe again, and receive those further dainties which the CHEIFES bounty intendeth to the perfecting of this Daies worke, that it may every waies bee a compleat peice!

I understand (sayd the CHEIFE), most honoured GUARDIAN, and hope to satisfy your desires. You expect that, according to the wise householders practize in the Gospell, bringing out both new and old things out of his treasure, these elder miracles should he confirmed and sett forth by some further examples of later times.

You so well know my thoughts, dearest CHEIFE (sayd the GUARDIAN), that you have much better expressed them then I myself could have done.

IHS 87

The proofe of having taken so right Aime (sayd the CHEIFE) at your Intention makes mee the rather hope to hitt the mark which you desire. If you doe but beleive it true, you cannot esteeme it lesse wonderfull then any you have yet heard. And that you may beleive it to bee true, you shall know that it is not onely confidently written in serious workes of most famous Men, but hath beene often by very discret and religious Persons delivered in the Pulpits of Italy as an undoubted truth received at first from the relation of those whose Fidelity and wisedome was above all suspicion, either of deceiving others or being deceived themselves.

Marsilius Ficinius, the Oracle of his times for Learning, had a deare Freind and Companion in the selfsame studies of Philosophy, named Michael Mercatus, to whom, amongst his workes, there is extant an Epistle full of excellent Matter touching the Æternity of GOD and the immortality of Mens soules. One time, amongst their philosophicall discourses happening to fall upon the consideration of those things which follow after the determination of this Life, finding a greater perplexity according to the principles of Philosophy (though they both followed that which is farre the best, Platos schoole) then they could well explicate, and perhaps even in this regard the rather by GODS just award intangled in this Labarinth of human Reason, because they had attributed too much thereunto, they in the end grew to a covenant, and confirmed it with solemne Oath, that hee that first should dy of them two would, if it might bee, give the other Notice of his Estate.

A long time past after this, and a large separation by distance of place betweene them. But in the end, as Michaell Mercatus one Morning very early was deepe in his philosophicall speculations hee heares afarre of the Noise of a horse running very swiftly, and at last upon a stopping under his window, the wel knowne voice of freind Marsilius calling out aloud, Oh Michael, Michael, those things are true, they are true indeed! At this, with much astonishment, Michael starts up, but his speed was farre slower than Marsilius, who before the other could thrust his head out of the window, had turned about his horse, and was now upon a swift pace departing. But though hee saw not his face, yet by that which hee saw, hee knew him perfectly to bee the Man whose voice hee heard, onely his habitt was farre different, all white, and of the same colour was his horse. Michael followed him with his voice, doubling the Name of Marsilius. But hee answered not. Hee followed him with his eies, but those were immediately likewise disappointed by the others vanishing. When wonderment had given way to other thoughts, hee gave present order to enquire touching Marsilius, whom in the end hee understood the very selfe same houre that hee appeared unto him to have departed this Life at Florentz. You desire to know, Ile tell you what followed, and with that, as it will bee to the confirmation of the Truth of this Fact, so it may bee to the impression of the like affections and resolutions in our Minds.

Though Michael was a Man of that goodnes which, because wee cannot find in our present times, wee attribute to the Old World, though he had led a Life not onely full of innocency, but of much Benefitt to others, as a true Philosopher should doe, yet from that day sending a Bill of divorce to all his former studies of Learning, hee applied himselfe onely to learne CHRIST JESUS crucified; and the remainder of his daies was altogether spent in the preparation for that better Life which is to succeed the short and miserable Ages on Earth, and hee dies more famous for devotion then he lived ever honoured for Learning, and yet therein, by the common Vote of this world, hee was not second to any.

This was the conclusion of this daies stories, the song before excusing the SUBMISSE, and this following the OBEDIENT, for those stories which they otherwise were bound to have told.

> Why doth this world contend
> For glorious vanity?
> Whose wealth so subject is
> To mutability.

As earthly vessels fail
Through their fragility :
So standeth worldly force
Unsure and slippery.

Charàcters rased in Ice
Think rather permanent
Then earthly vanities
Wasting incontinent.

Shaddowd with vertue pure,
But false in recompense ;
At no time yielding us
True trust or Confidence.

To Men more Credit give,
That want Fidelity,
Then trust to worldly wealth,
Whose end is Misery.

Falsehood in Good delights,
Pleasures in Franticknes,
Desirèd vanities
Of fleeting Ficklenes.

Where now is Solomon
Sometimes in Royalty ;
Or Sampson with his great
Invincibility ;

Or gentle Jonathan,
So praysd for Freindliness ;
Or fairest Absolom,
So rare in Comelines ?

Where now is Cæsar gone,
Highst in Authority ;
Or Dives, with his fare
And sumptuosity ?

Tell now where Tully is,
Clearest in Eloquence ;
Or Aristotle fled
With his intelligence.

O silly vermins food,
O Mass of Dustines,
O Dew, o Vanity,
Whence is thy loftines?

To-morrow for to live
Thou hast no certainty;
Doe good therefore to all
Whilst thou hast Liberty.

This worldly Glory great
How short a Feast it is,
And like a shaddow here,
Lo, how it vanishes,

Taking rewards away
Of long Continuance,
And leads us in the way
Of erring Ignorance.

This earthly Glory most
Which here is magnified,
In Scripture termèd is
As Grasse that witherèd.

And as the lightest leafe
The wind away doth blow,
So light is life of Man
For death to overthrow.

Think that which thou mayst loose
Is not thine certainly.
This worlde will take againe
Her guifts of vanity.

Think, then, on heaven above,
Thereon thy mind addresse,
Contemne all worldly wealth
For endlesse Blessednesse.

VIII

CHRISTMASTIDE, 1631

*St. Antoine's Vision—The Devil's Confession—The Dying Lamp
—The Self-righteous Hermit—The Accuser of Himself.*

THE delight that these former Daies had bred in the Auditours more swaying then the Compassion of the Sisters excessive paines, it was resolved that this storying should be proceeded in till the full Number of twelve daies were made up; whereupon they, being the Daughters of Obedience, casting away all desires of Ease till they had performed the work that they were tasked at, the Company meeting at the appointed place and time, the CHEIFE began.—

Theres little Constancy in humane desires, and much unsufficiency in the things of this world that a Man is almost a weary of having what hee most longs for. Wee were solicitous (most honoured Grandmother) for your approbation of our Exercizes, and now we can hardly keep ourselves from wishing it had beene lesse. Without it wee had lost our Labour, and by it wee are forced to loose our Ease, whilest wee are enjoyned to begin afresh for the continuance of your satisfaction, that worke which with no small Content wee supposed to have beene at an end. But though the issue of a Mans own choise bee so uncertaine, as is most what proves to his Dammage, yet the fruit of Obedience being alwaies in the end most delightfull and advantageable, wee have resolved, in hope of future pleasure, gladly to goe forward, though it bee to present trouble in the exercize, till the full Number of these Festivall twelve daies bee made up with stories of so many severall subjects. Concluded every day must handle a new matter; thats your Injunction, and because the daies themselves afford not, as those that are already passed, to any especiall occasion, wee have thought good to raise the Persons. Those particular surnames which you have imposed on us shall successively be the subjects of our severall Exercizes. My Sisters happy Names, like fruitfull plants, speak wine and oyle and all manner of sweetnes; but this ambitious title of CHEIFE which I am burdened with put you, I am perswaded, as it hath done mee, to a stand how to find good entertainment for you. Theres neither vertue nor profitt to bee extracted out of it that I can see, and yet I have sought it diligently. As for honour, which is the proper fruit of preeminence, its indeede the Daintiest and most pleasing to Mans Pallate of all other dishes whatsoever, but so perilous as my heart serves mee not to invite my Freinds thereunto. I know not how it fares with others, for myselfe I solemnely avow every little tast that I willingly make of it distempers mee. Looke not therefore by the setting forth of the excellency of Dignityes and high Matters in this daies discourse to have your Affections enflamed to the pursuite of them, but give us leave by the remonstrance of the Necessity, the safety, the acceptablenes with GOD and Men, and the incestimable benefitt that accrues to the soule by Humility, to perswade you and to confirme ourselves in this opinion:—That it is the cheife of all vertues, and that which most belongs to them that are by GOD and Man appointed Cheife amongst others.

.
    Like the grasse thats newly sprung,
    Or like a Tale thats new begun,
    Or like the Bird thats here to-day,
    Or like the pearlèd dew of May,
    Or like an houre, or like a span,
    Or like the singing of a swan :
    Even such is Man, that lives by breath,
    Hes here, now there, so Life and death.

The grasse witherth, the tale is ended,
The Birds flowne, the dews ascended,
The houre is short, the span not long,
The Swan neere death, Mans life is done

Like to the Buble in the Brooke,
Or in a Glasse much like a Looke,
Or like a shuttle in weavers hand,
Or like a writing on the sand,
Or like a thought or like a dreame,
Or like the gliding of the streame,
Even such is Man that lives by breath,
Its here, now there, so Life and Death.
The Bubles cut, the Looke forgott,
The Shuttles flung, the writing blott,
The thought is past, the Dreame is gone,
The water glides, Mans Life is done.

Like to an Arrow from the Bow,
Or like swift course of watry flow,
Or like the Time twixt floud and ebbe,
Or like the Spiders tender webbe,
Or like a Race, or like a Goale,
Or like the dealing of a Dole ;
Even such is Man, whose brittle state
Is alwaies subject unto Fate,
The arrow shott, the flouds soone spent,
The Time no Time, the webbe soone rent,
The race soone run, the Goale soone wonne,
The dole soone dealt, Mans Life first done.

Like to the Lightning from the sky,
Or like a Post that quick doth hy,
Or like a quaver in short song,
Or like a Journey three daies long,
Or like the snow when Summers come,
Or like a Pare, or like a Plumme ;
Even such is Man, that heapes up sorrow,
Lives but this day, and dies to Morrow.
The Lightning past, the Post must goe,
The song is short, the Journeys so,
The Peare doth rott, the Plumme doth fall,
The snow dissolves, and so must all.

> Then why should men thats borne to dy
> Live here below and looke so high ?
> Or why should hee oppresse the Poore
> Or drive the Needy from his dore ?
> Or why should hee goe feast and play
> When hee, alas ! should fast and pray ?
> Harke, I will tell thee what to do—
> Rend thy proud heart and Garments, too ;
> And think on this, thou art but dust ;
> For Earth thou art, to Earth thou must.
> And after Death 'twill be too late
> To call for Grace or mend thy state.

Other vertues have their particular Masters, the Ant to teach Industry, the Serpent Wisedome, and the dove simplicity, but Humility is the joynt Lesson of the whole Creation. They tell a man, and truely they tell him, hee is a farre more perfect Epitome of their weaknesses then of their Excellencies. Hee can find no ground of Contempt in any Creature, but hee shall find it double in himselfe to that which hee sees in them.

And how then can a Man without sending a divorce to reason seperate himselfe from Humility, for the embracement whereof every thing that hee can think of makes a concluding Argument ? But this is one but of the weakest motives that you shall heare.—A great desire having entered into St. Antonies heart to understand the Nature and Condition of the way to heaven, wherein so little progresse is made by many that seeme to pretend nothing else but how they may walk therein, hee was one day wrapt in spirit, and looking round about saw the whole world overspread with snares and Gins. Whereupon he cried out amazedly, If such, LORD, bee the passage to heaven, who can ever attaine thereunto ? It was answered, Humility walkes free through all the Toyles which thou seest.

And verily let a Man search well, and hee shall find that there is no entanglement of the soule in any sin whatsoever but the fastening of the Corde is alwaies in some kind of pride or other. Humility is a Universall Medicine for all diseases whatsoever. Hee that alwaies keeps his mind low and his Body under can by no meanes through the continuance in sinne become himselfe a Castaway.

You have heard St. Antonies vision, now heare his practize of humility from the selfesame relation of Athanasius. Though he were mighty in Miracles, and, which is farre more, the spirituall Father of many thousands of Men admirable in holines, though the whole would seeke to him for his Blessing, and Emperors lay up his letters to them amongst their most esteemed Jewells, yet hee himselfe disdaines not to submitt his head to the Bishops and Preists hands wheresoever hee mett them, craving their Blessing, thereby giving an equall Testimony both to the Excellency of their Dignity and to the Eminency of humility above all other graces and priviledges whatsoever, whilst for the exercize and attainment of it he waves all other respects. My Story (sayd the AFFECTIONATE), worthy CHEIFE, suits every way so well to you that, being afrayd not to fitt it otherwise, I desire, without breach of that humility which wee are now commending, to have leave now to tell first, though mine own place be the last. And although a Liars Testimony bee not to bee credited, yet when the truth is manifest before hand it may serve as Black doth to sett of white the better to appearance, though not in substance. The Devills Confession, which I shall tell you of, though it adds no Authority, yet it may add perhaps Illustration to that truth which St. Antonies Divine vision taught us.

A holy Virgin having from her youth up beene combated with noysome thoughts, perceiving an enforcement of them in her mind when through Age, whereinto she was now well stepped, and weakenes of Body by continuall Mortifications, she expected an utter extinguishment of them, grew much amazed, both through shame and sorrow, at so strange a Case, whereof she had neither heard Example nor could conceive the reason. Walking thus perplexedly one day, when she least expected, finding a suddaine and furious charge of wicked Imaginations to be given to her Fancy, leaving her wonted

Hymnes of Psalmes, wherewith she used to defeat herselfe in this kind of skirmish, shee starts and runnes with a strong but holy kind of Impatience to the window of her Chamber, where, lifting up her right hand, and fixing her eies on the sun, that shone out with great Brightnes, she cryed out amaine, as her teares and sighs gave leave, How long, how long, thou Sun of Righteousness, shall the beames of thy grace be restrained from my soule? Rise up like a Giant in thy might, LORD JESUS, and chase away these workes of darknes never more to returne. It is enough, Lord, it is enough; comfort thy handmayd againe for the yeares (and many yeares they have beene) wherein she hath suffered adversity.

She had no sooner ended her short praier but shee had obtained the grace which shee had so long sought for. Faith and zeale, when they joyne strongly together, carry all things in the Court of heaven, not onely without deniall but delay. The spirit of Fornication was rebuked, and makes hast to depart visibly in a loathsome forme, presenting himselfe to her eies, and with an enraged murmure tells her that shee had at last overcome him. But shee quickly replied with a loud and cheerefull voice, doubling her words, Not I, Satan, but my Lord and Saviour JESUS CHRIST is hee that hath overcome thee; his bee the praise altogether from whom the power is derived. My forepast weaknes of so many yeares continuance shows plainely that the new supply of strength is none of mine.

Thy Abstinence, thy watching and wearines, have hindered mee from prevailing. But this humility debarres mee from henceforth for ever approaching nigh unto thee.

Other vertues keepe us safe, but lowlines of mind makes us victorious in all encounters of our Enemies. Hee that is well armed with true mortification can hardly bee wounded, but hee that is cloathed with humility can hardly bee assaulted. GOD dwells so plentifully by his grace in an humble heart that the Devill hath no power to come neere with his Temptations. Hee cannot come neere with his Temptations, indeed (sayd the PATIENT), nor can hee hurt farre of by meanes of wicked men. GOD keeps the humble safe as well from shame and sorrow as from sinne. It is a sure defence against the injuries both of hand and tongue. Humility is an Armour of proofe against all manner of Evill. To which purpose I shall tell you a story, if not of undoubted truth for the fact, yet of excellent use for the morall of it.—

There were two Brethren, the one of great Age and long exercized, the other yonger and but a Novice in true and pure Religion, who being late together one Night at their Devotion, the Lampe which hung betweene them went out suddenly. Whereupon the yonger rose and lighted it againe, but in vaine. Hee was scarce well settled in his place when it went out againe, and a third time; at which the elder, being much troubled for the interruption of his better thoughts, gave his Brother not onely with sharp words, but by a sore Blow, that chastisement which, hee told him, was due for his negligent or unskilfull trimming of the Lampe. The yonger, though he knew the Imputation wrong, and knew not how to mend the fault, yet seing plainly a fault, was content to take it upon himselfe; and not finding the immediate Cause, either in himselfe or in the Lampe, not onely began to think, but to say, that it was guilt of his former errors that now without cause made the light faile, and bred disturbance in those holy Exercizes, whereof (sayth hee, turning to his Brother and kissing the hand that strooke him) by how much I am the more unworthy to partake, by so much I beseech your fervent praiers may bee the more intended for mee, that the Light and fire of grace which GOD hath kindled in my heart may never bee quenched by mine owne sinnes or any devises of the evill one. The remembrance of my greivous Crimes would perswade mee so to interpret this strange accident, but GODS Mercy assures me the contrary, and that hee will never faile to give new Illuminations to my soule when ever darknes over shaddows it, as I will still supply fresh light to this extinguished Lampe. Having so sayd, and stepping to the fire to do what hee had sayd, the Lampe burst out of itselfe with an unusual Flame and brightnes. At which, whilest they both stood amazed, and the old Man began a little to swell in the Conceit of his Holines to which the spirit of vainglory perswaded him to attribute this admirable effect, they heard a voice, which was of greater Majesty of sound then can proceed from Mans Brest, told the elder that as the lighting, so the putting out of the Lampe was miraculous. This last by the Devills Malice to Cause diversion in their good Imployments and to raise Contention between them; but the lighting it again was by GOD's appointment and the Ministry of an Angell; Not in regard of thy holines (sayd the voice), which, both by Error and Impatiency hath manifested itselfe to bee much more imperfect then thou perhaps esteemedst it, but in approbation of thy Brothers Patience and Humility, which in GODS account is of farre greater worth then all thine Innocency with the least taint of selfe conceit thereunto annexed. Not hee that doth most, but hee that thinkes least of himselfe, gaines the Prize in well doing; and he that in suffering of Evill laies the Blame on himselfe getts the soonest cleare. Hee that meekely condemnes himselfe as worthy of what hee undergoes makes GOD to plead his Cause, and getts certain pardon, though hee bee in fault. But if innocent, the wrong that he thus takes and beares turnes to a Crown both of Glory and Content.

The PATIENT having ended, the MODERATOUR succeeded, recompting this story following:

There was an ancient Hermite, whose Austerity of Life sealing the opinion of perfect holines attained here on Earth, gave assurance in his owne and all others Judgments of eternall happines to bee hereafter by him enjoyed in heaven. At last incurable sicknes layes him on his Death-bed, which is no sooner noysed abroad, but instantly from all parts good and bad run to his little sell to minister in what they were able to his Necessity, and to receive his Blessing, which they esteemed advantageable to all things. Amongst others there came to these intents a grave Father, accompanied with a young Man that had newly entered into the profession, but made greater progresse than most others in the truth of Christian religion. In the midst of their Journey there overtakes them a famous Malefactor, who tells them the trouble and terror of a guilty Conscience leads him to the same place and person whither they were going, if happily by the meanes of his holy Counsell hee might receive Comfort in his wounded soul, and directions how to serve GOD, whom he had so infinitely offended. They encouraging him in these good thoughts, hee proceeds full of Confidence till hee comes to the Hermites Cell, where shame of his unworthines forbidding him to enter, and dread of loosing the remedy of Misery forbidding him to depart, he stands perplexedly without the dore. As hee stands, hee heares the old Hermite make relation of his forepast Life full of holines, and of his present hopes to bee immediately crowned with Glory for those great things which hee had done and suffered for GODS sake and in his service. The poore man having heard all, burst into teares, and striking his hand to his Brest, cries out aloud, Wretched Man that I am, such a Life as this ought I to have lead. To which the sick Man, having been formerly informed of him, made instant reply, Thou oughtest indeed to have so done, if so bee thou hadst any care at all of thy Salvation. With the conclusion of these words the sick man breathed out his soule, and the elder of the two that came to visit him remained much comforted in so quiet, glorious, and happy an end. But the younger began to weepe sore and make bitter mourning, as if some great and fearefull accident had befallen. Upon their departure the Malefactor followed them, greviously lamenting his forepast Life, confessing aloud his sins, and calling upon the mercy of GOD in and through CHRIST JESUS, in whom (hee sayd) he would trust, and on whom (he sayd) hee would rely for the making answere and giving satisfaction to GOD for all his sinnes, and for the obtaining of eternall life for him. Theres ransome enough in CHRISTS Obedience to quitt all my guilt and to purchase mee grace.

Whilest hee goes along so full and fixed in these meditations, as hee neither sees nor heares anything besides, comming to a dangerous passage hee stumbles and falls, and in his fall breakes his Neck; at which, whilest the elder of the two made shew of much greife, the younger cherefully began to praise GOD with Davids words, Precious in the sight of the LORD is the Death of his Saints.

The elder, being much scandalised at these proceedings, sharply demands, What meanes this double contradiction not onely to my affections, but to my reason? Thou bewaylest the just Mans happy decease, and rejoycest in the sinners unhappy death. To which the young Man mildly answered, The Ignorance of GODS Judgements makes you erre both in your pitty and your comfort touching these two. I saw his soule, whom you so much admire for outward holines of Life, dragged into hell by many Devills for that Pride and Confidence which hee had in his owne righteousnes, which, when it came to triall, was found nothing but sinne and wickednes, however fairely guilded it appeared not onely in ours, but in his owne eies and imaginations. But that poore Man, who could find no good in himselfe, by the putting on of CHRISTS righteousnes through faith, was found righteous in GODS approbation, and as such was by the hands of Angells carried up into everlasting happines.

It so fares alwaies in CHRISTS Kingdome; the last are made first, and the first become last. Hee thats great in his owne Conceit is nothing in GODS esteeme, and hee thats truely great in GODS esteeme is alwaies nothing in his owne. This is a faythfull saying, CHRIST came into the world to save sinners, whereof I am the cheife, sayth St. Paul.

Theres no sin so incompetible with GODS grace as Pride; theres no kind of Pride as that which perswades itselfe to deserve GODS grace. Grace of what kind soever it bee, is alwaies freely given on GODS part; and good workes, of what value soever they bee, are alwaies insufficient on ours. When wee have done all, wee must say Wee are unprofitable servants. Our good workes are at the best but like those tickets whereby Men gett admission unto Princes royall Festivals.

Its the Mediation of CHRISTS righteousnes that obtaines the favour that wee may bee thought worthy to enter into GODS presence and Joyes.

Well have you observed, most honoured MODERATOUR (sayd the CHEEREFULL) that they which are high in GODS grace are alwaies low in their owne esteeme, and desire rather by publishing of their Infirmities to give glory to GOD, whose strength is perfected in weaknes, then by Manifestation of their vertues to gett prayse to themselves.

To which purpose my Story is. GOD grant my Practize may be answerable.

The Fame of an holy Man being very great, a certain devout Person came from farre to visite and bee instructed of him. Drawing neere to the Citty it was his Chance to meet with the old Man himselfe, who by discourse perceiving the strangers Businesse, began seriously to reprehend so much Labour and time needlessly spent and imployed, telling him, that instead of a Saint hee should find a great Sinner, and thereupon recompted unto him many Errors and Crimes which hee solemnely affirmed hee knew this good Man (as hee was commonly called) guilty of. The stranger, much troubled, held on his voyage unto some of the principall of the Citty, to whom hee was of kin, began after the first salutation to declare why hee came, and what had happened unto him. They, jealous of the holy Mans reputation, sending for divers others, began seriously to advise of the finding out and punishing of this Slanderer, who durst thus traduce and revile the Man of GOD. Whereupon requiring the signs to know the Person, they then perceived by all tokens, both of features, gesture, speach, and habitt, that it was the holy Man himselfe that had disgraced and accused himselfe, and perceiving that he had indeed refreshed the Memory of divers errors which were long agoe buried in all other Mens remembrance, and that he had published some which never before were knowne, they remained the more confirmed by this proofe in the opinion of his holines then all his other Actions that hee had done.

IX

CHRISTMASTIDE, 1631

Discussion on Patience—Chivalrous Tales—Christopher and the President of Samos—Patience a Miracle—A Noble Woman of Alexandria—A Young Man and his Master—Eulogies of Alexandria and the Leper—Didimus of Alexandria—Cazimere, Prince of Sendomiria—St. Gregory the Great and the Emperor Mauritius—The Story of the Oil—Agaton—Anub and the Idol.

THE next Day falling to the PATIENTS turne, the Absence of the MASTER and the removall of the provisions necessary for the Musick giving notice that it was not that Day to bee expected, shee began to the excuse thereof in this manner :

The want of your wonted Musique, whilst I am so poore not onely in skill, but in good happe, as I cannot find a song any wares answerable to your present Action, gives you opportunity (most honoured Grandmother and worthy Company) by the gentle passing over this wrongfull disappointment of your justly expected Pleasure through my defect, to exercize that vertue of Patience which falls to be the matter of this daies consideration.

The happy agreement of your Practize in this thing to your Name, deare PATIENT (sayd the CHEIFE), causeth sweeter Melody than any voice or instrument could doe. Wee want not Musick therefore, though wee have it not in the Eare, that have so much delight in our hearts through the Harmony that is made by the sweet Concent of your Disposition and Actions to that which is the subject of our intended discourse. Yourselfe are an Example of that Patience which you are to speake of. This is the noblest Musick that can sound in mine, and I am sure in all others opinions.

What I am (sayd the PATIENT) in this respect is GODS Grace; and what I want (and that is infinitely more then what I have attained touching this Vertue) is my owne Fault.

Well (sayd the GUARDIAN), in the Country of the blind hee that hath but halfe an Eie is King. Our generall Imperfections make us all think you are proceeded farre in the grace, for which wee as truely blesse GOD as wee heartily desire to bee partakers of the same. But I hope, that though you are not furnished with Musick, yet you have in supply thereof provided some other kind of Antepast for us. If wee cannot have a song, let us have (as the old proverbe is) some good saying, I pray, to beginne with, touching this matter of Patience, in knowledge whereof I confesse myselfe to bee a stranger, as well as in the Practize, having all my lifelong till of late beene perswaded that Patience was not a vertue to bee sought for, but only for Necessity to bee accepted when a Man could not choose; not to bee desired when a Man might shift it.

You say very true (sayd the CHIEFE), thats the worlds Doctrine and Language; when a Man cannot put away sufferings in any kind, then he is advised to put on Patience. You must bee content to have Patience, say the wise Freinds of this world. But to bee so in Love with Patience as a Man should gladly undergoe grief and Evill when it comes, for the exercize thereof, is an argument of a crazed Braine and of a cowardly heart in most Mens Judgements, and yet is the plaine and constant doctrine of the Blessed LORD by whose Name wee are honoured, and of all his Holy Apostles, that there is more Excellency both of strength and happines in patient enduring of Evill then in the prosperous enjoyment of all the good things in the world. And therefore St. James wills to count it when wee fall into divers Temptations, onely for this reason, because it workes Patience, which, if it may have its ree and full operation, will worke us perfect and compleat both in Grace and Glory, so that there shall be nothing wanting either in body or in soule even in this life on Earth, not onely in that which is to come in heaven. Let Patience have her perfect worke, that yee may bee perfect and intire, wanting Nothing.

Oh, the wretched mistake of my blind affections, that in the pursuite of Vertue and happines have ever avoyded and impugned that which would have given the greatest furtherance to what they pretended unto!

I thought the exercise of Patience a Burden that would tyre out my strength, a Block that encombred the way, and made mee stumble, and made mee fall, and therefore thought even Impatience itselfe in removing of that which was offensive to have beene a piece of wisedome, a practize of Goodnes. That no body should crosse mee, that nothing should bee contrary to my mind, was that which I supposed most just to desire, most profitable to endeavour. I see mine errour, I feele my losse. I thank my GOD, that hath given mee this timely warning. By his grace henceforward Patience shall bee my study, the attainement of it in my praiers, the exercize of it my Joy, mine Honour, and my Happines. Say, LORD, Amen, to these purposes, to these protestations, which thou hast now put into my mouth and heart.

Wee second you with our Prayers (sayd the CHEEREFULL) and hope wee shall second you with the like resolutions and endeavour not to seeke so much for an uncontrolled satisfaction of our Desires, as for a patient sufferance of what shall happen contrary to them. The last is farre the more easy Condition to bee attained, and surely the more excellent, the patient Man being every way better and more happy then the prosperous, a Mystery which I confess with you to have beene long ignorant of, and now with you comming to the knowledge, I hope I shall, by GODS assistance, with you proceed in the carefull Practize thereof. The great offences which my erring Judgement had conceived against this heavenly grace having beene by GODS Mercy not onely removed out of my mind, but turned into so many arguments of Love. Now, by your Love to it and mee, I beseech you, deare CHEEREFULL, to let us understand the particular more fully (sayd the CHEIFE).

You have so put on your request (sayd the CHEEREFULL) as it would not bee onely unkindnes, but sinne, to deny you. Though it bee therefore to my shame I will freely confesse that I know not how, whether by false Information from the world, or false apprehension in mine owne mind, or both, inward Corruption being attracted by outward infection, I was growne to a strong and manifold prejudice against the Divine Vertue of Patience, as an effect of weaknes, the Mother of Contempt, and an invitation to further Injuries. And thus and no otherwise it appeared to mee a feeble disposition, alwaies disrespected, many times oppressed. Evill Affections instantly followed wrong opinions. Meethought it was unlovely, uncomely, prejudiciall in others, in myselfe it should bee most odious, disgracefull, dangerous.

Its no small happiness, beloved CHEEREFULL (sayd the GUARDIAN) that you have so good an opportunity of making amends for so great Errors, and you improve it wisely by making so large and cleare a declaration of them. The searching of a wound to the quick, though it bee painfull, yet it is a sure preparation to the Cure; in which regard I should perhaps envy you, but that I hope I may become a partner of the Benefitt by application of the selfe same remedy, appeaching myselfe to bee guilty of all that you have made Confession of, and much more in regard of the bad effects which have

. . . . . .

affections. Well had it beene with mee had I stayed there. Many a Mischeife had been avoyded, and many a good busines had been accomplished which hath cheifly ruined by my want of Patience. And I had not, it may bee, wanted it, if I had knowne it so well as I have done of late. I had all your mistake in opinions, and I had more. I perswaded myselfe there was a strong taint of injustice in Patience, that a Man did wrong when hee did not right himselfe, and that hee was cruell to himselfe in being in such a Manner gentle to others. I went further in the misapprehension, and the evil Consequences have beene much worse on my part. But I doubt not but by GODS mercy all is cancelled. What is past is past. How to bee sincere, constant, and perfect in the Exercise of Patience, wherein I have been hitherto so unsound, unstable, and defective, is now all my Care. Let us therefore know, I pray, what it was that helped you, which cannot surely but doe us good. The remedy must needs bee proper since the disease is common.

Pennance alwaies follows Confession, you know (sayd the MODERATOUR to the CHEEREFULL). Let it not therefore trouble you to bee put now to little paines for so many freinds sake in a matter of such Consequence.

Good resolutions, except they bee confirmed in the mind by good reason, runne more hazard of extinguishing the lights sett in open plans without Coverts. The weightiest ships float with every puft of wind, if they bee not well [anchored]. And the firmest inventions of Mans heart for good are easily shaken if they bee not stabilished by good Arguments.

However faire the world seeme to comply in most things with the Letter, yet surely it beares deadly feud to the spirit and power of religion in all points; in none more then in this matter of Patience, which, as it is one of the greatest Buttresses of Christian Faith, so it is mainely and maliciously, however subtilly, undermigned by the world, even when it seemes most to promote and sett it forth. Since it is certaine, therefore, that wee shall meet with much and violent opposition, I would bee glad that every one might bee furnished with some solid arguments both to maintaine the truth and to convince gainsayers.

I beseech you, most honoured MODERATOUR (sayd the CHIEFE), that you would make us understand this Mystery a little plainlyer touching the worlds proceedings with such semblance of Love, and yet with such effects of hatred to this Vertue of Patience, which I am perswaded will rather give light and furtherance then bee of diversion to that which wee hope to learne from the CHEEREFULL.

Why, verily (sayd the MODERATOUR), if you well observe, the wisedome of this world gives no allowance, much lesse applause, to Patience, but onely in two Cases: the first of Necessity, which you before observed; the second of advantage, when either honours or some other gaine is to be made by the exercize thereof, in this last Case making it but a matter of Merchandize; in the first giving it but the honour of a stupifying Medicine, but on the selfe same ground hating the true and perfect, for which they give approbation to this imperfect and counterfeit Patience of their owne devising. This kind and degree of Patience, because it gives furtherance to carnall Affections in the abatements of greifs and procurement of gaine and honour, hath a free and commendable entertainment. But true and Christian Patience, which voluntarily undergoes sufferings and makes Damage and disgrace the subject of her embracements, dissolving the whole frame of their Content, which lies altogether in fleshly and worldly satisfaction, suits onely in their Judgement to the Condition of an Asse, on this ground become the vilest of all other Beasts, for otherwise, undoubtedly, if wee make the Comparison by shape or serviceablenes, there are very few Creatures to bee preferred before the Asse.

But the proportionablenes of his naturall Temper to that disposition and those affections which Patience causeth, is the misery that hath made him the scorne and byword of Mankind; and yet for this very Cause did the Lord of Glory single him out for his owne use amongst all other Creatures. Think not that it was for Contempts sake, for neither was an asse in those times and places contemptible, and it was Act of triumph which was intended, to which a contemptible Carriage had beene altogether dissonant. But it was in regard that an

Asse is an Embleme or meekenesse and Patience, that our blessed Saviour made choise to ride upon an Asse, a Colt the foole of an Asse, when he went to shew himselfe the King of Israell, to comfort the Daughter of Sion.

And undoubtedly as it then passed, so it still fares in these daies, and with us he hath not changed his bodily residence. Our blessed Lord sitts not as a King in any Mans soule, nor ministers the saving Comforts of his grace and spirit in any great measure or sweetnes, but to them which by their Love and exercise of Patience are become in the worlds opinion very Asses.

Christ, for the resemblance that an Asses Nature hath with Meekness and Patience, gave him the preheminence of honour amongst all Beasts, and Man for the same cause gives his Name as the highest title of Infamy to them that are truely patient.

A patient Man is an Asse by the common Vote of the world. Hee that for wisedome, as perhaps many doe, forbeares to express this Conceit of others, yet by enforcement of truth cannot forbeare to instant it in himselfe if hee bee putt hard to it. Doe you think me an Asse? or Would you have mee an Asse? is the last refuge which the wisest of this world betake themselves unto when they purpose to shutt of Patience. But God forfend that such a word of death should bee found henceforward amongst us. To which intent I have beene willing to give you a tast of the Malignity that this kind of Language containes. As for the Contradiction it beares to Christian religion, you may read it, as it were, in text Letters, and yet is this but the least and weakest of many engines wherewith the world batters the fort of true Patience. That generally received opinion that Impatiency is an effect, at least a Consequence, of great spirits and great fortunes is a farre more strong and more pernicious argument of Error in this Matter.

The profession of valour and the ostentation of Dignity in the common Judgement of this world are by no meanes thought possible to bee sett better of then by an absolute kind of Impatiency in all kinds.

Not to bee able to endure Labour in business; not to bee able to endure paines in sicknes; not to bee able to endure the Distemper of the weather, nor the restraint of appetites, nor to be able to bear Contradiction in words nor opposition in deeds, nor to be able to endure Concurrence in Honour nor Comparison in worth; not to be able to endure Instruction in Ignorance or Correction in errors; not to bee able to indure losse in Estate nor disappointment in pleasures: in summe, these and all other the like kinds of Impatiencies, whereby a Man is disabled either to doe or suffer anything but as fond affections lead the minde, are not onely by the bold usurpation of all that pretend to Eminency, but by the flattering approbation of many good men made such necessary allowances to Greatnes, as they are become, if not matters of goodnes and vertue, yet of grace and reputation. And herein chiefly, as I suppose, lies the bane of true Patience. They, therefore, that would not bee guilty of so heynous a Crime as to bee found enemies of Gods Kingdome in the opposition and hinderance of the growth of Patience, must carefully beware of giving any manner of abettment to this cursed doctrine of the world, well informing themselves and carefully instructing others, when occasion happens, that Impatiency, of what kind soever it bee, is a signe and Effect of Pride or weaknes, not of strength or worth, either in mind or body. Thus must every Man doe that will please God and promote his service, although by so doing hee shall bee sure to pull many sufferings on his owne head, the world resenting nothing more impatiently then the Affronts which are offered unto Impatiency, in making it that which it is indeed, a peice and a Master-peice of the Devills Excellency.

Malice, pride, and impotency force an œternall and uninterrupted working of this Passion in Hell. Theres the springhead and thither is the returne of this bitter streame. Theres no manner of sinne that makes a Man more conformable, either in active disposition or passive torment, to the damned then Impatiency doth, and yet it is the worlds boasting; and to perswade men to love of it they perswade them that theres both safety and benefitt in it.

Hee that takes an injury patiently. . . . hee that makes himselfe a worme shall bee trod on, hee that makes himselfe a sheepe the wolf will eat him, are maine Articles of the worlds Creed, and hold invincible arguments to prove the damage and danger of Patience. Thats the third slander whereby the world manifesteth the cankered Malice that it beares against Patience, as well as the Contradiction of its owne Doctrine to that which Christ hath taught in this Matter.

You have made it evident beyond exception (sayd the GUARDIAN) that the world is no Friend, much lesse a good Master to teach Patience. We therefore so much the more desire to understand by whose recommendation and instruction our CHEEREFULL is become so enamored of it that these horrible maimes and deformities with which the wise Masters of the Earth have sett forth Patience, are turned into matters of Beauty and Lovelines in her eies. Sure there must bee some great Sorcery on the worlds part, or some extreme Blindnes in Mens eies, that they should bee thus deluded.

Theres both (sayd the CHEEREFULL), as I have wofully proved in myselfe. The world hath made false spectacles, and Men that have a mind to be deceived gladly put them on.

Corrupt Affections and purblind reason, with which the world hath made false views of this matter, are those deceitfull glasses which cause this monstrous transformation that streight is made crooked, white is made black, and that which is great appeares little. So it fares in this particular. Take it into the true light of GODS word, and you shall see (whatever the world says to the contrary) that there is nothing more strong, more honorable, more beneficiall, more just, and, in a word, more excellent then true Patience is.

The Word of GOD indeed (sayd the GUARDIAN) is a cleare and certaine Light, whereby all Impostures are discovered.

True (sayd the CHEEREFULL). As Metalls are tryed in the Fining Pott, so are all things manifested by the Scriptures of what nature and worth they be. But Patience is one of those things which a Man cannot come to the knowledge of by any other meanes then by the Scriptures. Depraved reason leads cleane away. That which is most rectified falls so short of the truth that it rather confounds the understanding then perswades the heart to the Love and exercize of true Patience.

Undoubtedly it is so (sayd the GUARDIAN), and a manifest proofe hereof is the Stoicks fayling in this Attempt, who are justly taxed by other Philosophers not onely to root up all affections, but to damme up the very senses, whilest they goe about to introduce by force of reason Patience.

A stupid sencelessnes or a wretched Carelessnes may perhaps (sayd the CHEEREFULL) be wrought by arguments and exercize, by long Custome and by firme resolution. But these dispositions are but the Carkesses of Patience ; and, like Mens Bodies deprived of Life, are not onely unprofitable, but offensive to reason and to sence.

True Patience is a most powerfull, active Vertue, full of sweete fruits of Comfort in itselfe, of Benefitt to others, and the Knowledge of it so proper to the Scripture as St. Paul makes it one of the cheife.

Whatsoever things were written aforetime were written for our Learning, that wee through Patience and Comfort in the Scriptures might have Hope.

You have brought us to the Schoole-dore, and to the Mine (sayd the AFFECTIONATE). If wee goe not away rich in this Learning it is our owne Default.

But for our better encouragement and direction by a say taken and Patterne given how wee ought to proceed in this search, wee desire you should shew unto us some of those veines wherein the rich oare lies most easy and abundantly, by telling us some of those maine and most effectuall arguments whereby the Scriptures have informed and convinced your erring Judgement.

That which of all others, in my apprehension, carries the greatest weight in this Businesse (sayd the CHEEREFULL), is that Patience is one of those Attributes which the Scripture gives to the Divine Majesty. St. Paul calls GOD the GOD of Patience, and joynes it with Consolation, to which adde what David sayth, GOD is a righteous Judge, strong and patient, and you have at once the utter overthrow of all the worlds cavillous opposition against Patience.

It is an Honour to GOD, and that as hee is a Judge. It flows from his might. Hee is strong and patient, and is unseparably matcht with Consolation. And how then can it bee matter of disgrace to weaknes, or Injustice, or an Occasion of greife in Man?

It cannot possibly (sayd the GUARDIAN) bee thought, much lesse spoken without Blasphemy, either of preferring Man before GOD or in denying that Patience is in GOD, which not onely the Scriptures, but Experience teacheth, and all men, as I suppose, naturally agree unto. Then is my naturall Disposition most reprobate of all others (sayd the CHEIFE), for till I was instructed by GODS word I could by no means believe that Patience was in God. Your naturall Disposition must have beene better then all others, had you thought otherwise (sayd the MODERATOUR). That all the world partakes of the same Error is evident by the Heathens fashioning their Gods, both in their Conceits and in their writings, full of all Manner of Impatiency, of which Temper even our Christian Poets in these Times faine the blessed Saints and Angels of Heaven to bee, when in their Compositions they bring them on the Stage of this world. Such an unanswerable Contradiction is there in Mans apprehension betweene Meaknes and greatnes, Long-suffering and power, Patience and Happines. Your skill in these studies makes you an absolute Judge (sayd the GUARDIAN).

My many precious houres wasted in these vanities (replied

the MODERATOUR) have given mee too much and too certaine a knowledge of this malignous Error in Poets which, had not my Affections and Opinions complied with, I could never with such delight and approbation have continued in the reading of them.

The Inference which you intend is plaine (sayd the GUARDIAN) and undeniable. The universall applause that these Conceits are entertained with, shew that they are really beleived in the world, however, not so willingly perhaps confessed as by you. But though I was in the wrong touching this particular, yet surely not in that other, which yet the CHEIFE seems equally to oppose, by a precise limitting of her Credence touching GODS Patience to the Authority of the Scriptures, with the rejecting of all other Meanes.

Doth not Experience itselfe convince that there must needs bee an infinite Patience in GOD, whilst he dayly comports such a numberlesse, measurelesse world of Offences and Impieties as are dayly committed?

They that looked upon this matter by the Light of reason in elder times extract a farre more different Conclusion then you doe (sayd the CHEIFE).

This is the very ground which brought over divers Philosophers absolutely to deny GODS providence, and the wisest of them, as I have heard, to speake very doubtfully of it. That either GOD knows not, or cared not, for the things done on Earth are Inferences so necessary, in the eie of reason, upon the observation of GODS forbearance of presumptuous sinners, as the best and holyest Men in the world have beene strongly tempted this way. David confesseth of himselfe that hee could not by any meanes find the solution of this matter untill hee went into the Sanctuary; then hee understood what before and otherwise was too hard for him. I am no whitt, therefore, discouraged at my naturall uncapablenes, wherein I have so great Partners. But I blesse GOD for the revelation of this Mystery, and my assent unto it.

That there is an infinite Patience in GOD, and that this

Patience hath Mans salvation for its End, and repentance for the Meanes to lead him unto it, is a truth which, by the authority of the Scripture and the operation of the holy spirit, I believe ; but, through the violence of the Devill and the fraylty of humane reason, doe continually labour under the defence and Maintenance thereof. I tell you my weaknes, that you may helpe mee with your prayers. Theres no Temptation that I am sorer pressed with by the Enemy of our soules, upon the remembrance and refreshment of my sinnes, then to interpret the long suffering and Patience of GOD to mee ward, that most wretched of all sinners, but a treasuring up of wrath against the day of vengeance; wherein Reason for the most part, although it be infinitely to our Prejudice, takes part against mee. I cannot, therefore, bee perswaded to attribute anything to reason touching my knowledge or Beliefe of this saving Truth. A saving truth, I call it, in regard that the hope of salvation fayles not in any Man till his assent thereunto be overthrown. He that feeles the loving Effects of GODS Patience in the continuance of this life on earth and the affording of meanes for attainement of heaven, can never give entrance to dispaire till hee have inverted this truth as the Devill perswades, construing, with the Devill, that the long suffering of GOD is for the encrease of sin and torment, whereas, in truth, as St. Peter teacheth, wee ought to account it salvation.

I cannot but rejoyce in mine Error, at least in the manifestation (sayd the GUARDIAN), that hath given occasion to come to the knowledge of so important a truth as this is, whereby I not onely understand the soveraigne excellency of GODS Patience but the conditions that wee must have if wee desire it should bee perfect as GODS is :

That Patience is often the Example of GODS which sincerely intends the benefitt of him to whom it is exercized, and that forbearance in Error which workes to amendement is conformable to that Long-suffering which GOD useth. But Patience that emboldens to sinne, or that dissembles a while onely to repay double vengance at the last, as they are contrary both in their Intentions and effects to GODS long sufferings and Patience, so must they needs proceed from a contrary spirit. And yet the last of these is counted a peice of singular wisedome, the first a point of great goodnes; and in the practize thereof lies all the evidenes that the world can produce for its Love to Patience. They can willingly comport all manner of impiety that is not to their owne prejudice. To this end they think Patience to be necessary, and in this way the exercize of it to bee holy; otherwise its sin and folly. Tell a Man that hee should have Patience when his goods are wasted or his good Name impayred, and hee will turne with great Anger and tell you that a Man neither can nor ought to have Patience in such cases; and yet the selfe-same Person will tell another, when he sees him angry against sinne in those who are so under his charge as hee shall give an accompt for them, that he must have Patience; and if hee make answere, as hee ought to doe, that hee neither can nor ought to have Patience in this case, they perswade themselves, and others too, that theres as great a fault in his zeale as in the wickednes which he reprehends and goes about to punish. But let the world say and judge what it please, since I now, by GODS mercy, have attained the true Coppy of Patience, Ile follow it, by his blessed Assistance, as neere as I may. Theres no suffering in temporall respects that I will not endeavour to beare patiently. There shalbe no sinne, especially in those whom I must answere for, which I will not redresse. As long as Patience workes to this effect I shall esteeme it a vertue, and further not. Where Long-suffering mends not, chastizement must follow, and is a part of Charity as well as of Necessity. No Man shall henceforth perswade mee that that Patience which, by abetting or occasioning of Obstinacy in Evill [leads] to destruction, can bee a branch of GODS Patience, which, by inducement of repentance, leads on to salvation.

Your conclusion seemes so right and necessary in my Judgement (sayd the CHEIFE), as I cannot but earnestly beseech GOD that I may bee your partner in the execution as well as I now am in the assent thereunto.

And now, I pray you, deare CHEEREFULL, to proceede, the richnes of this veine having encreased our desires to the further opening of this Myne.

The second great proofe of the excellency of Patience (sayd the CHEEREFULL) is the Scriptures instancing it as a vertue and Honour in all the Saints of GOD. Other Graces seeme to bee parcelled out amongst them; very few have all, at least in any eminency. But Patience, like a joynt Inheritance, appeares equally, as it were, divided amongst them. Every one is compleat in the habitt and perfect in the working of Patience. Begin the examination from Abell to Zacharias, in the Old Testament: There's no one just man to be found that beares not wittnes to this truth by the patient undergoing of Labour, the patient enduring of afflictions, and the patient expectation of the reward which GOD hath promised to them who, by patient Continuance in well-doing, seek for glory and honour and immortality.

As for the New Testament, this Vertue seemes, both by the Injunction and Example of our Blessed Lord and Saviour JESUS CHRIST, to be so farre advanced above all others that St. Paul makes it both the cheife proofe for Eminency of dignity and office amongst GODS Servants and the surest measure of their proficiency in his grace.

Hee preferres it before signes and wonders for Confirmation of his Apostleship, and when he is forced to make comparison with others that boasted themselves for great ones, waving the Excellency of all other guifts, he putts the Issue of the tryall mainely upon the exercize of this vertue. The abundance of his sufferings is that whereby he would have the Aboundance of GODS grace and favour to him to bee estimated, and the Evidency of his exceeding Patience, beyond all others, to bee the unanswereable Argument of his Advantage over them touching spirituall priviledges. And verily, sett Charity aside, which is not one, but the perfection of all vertues and graces, and there is not anything whatsoever whereby our Conformity to CHRIST and his Doctrine is so absolutely evinced and made manifest as by long-suffering and Patience. Its the prime Lesson that CHRIST sett us if wee desire to become like him. Learne of me, I am meeke and lowly; and our carefull taking out is the best testimony that wee can have ourselves, or give others, to bee really his scholars. Other vertues may be learned by his ushers, but Patience is that which our great Master reserves to his owne teaching. Learne of me directs us not onely to the perfect, but to the onely Master of this Profession.

The worlde it selfe confirmes this truth by putting all manner of claime to Patience, which to other vertues it will by no meanes doe. Patience onely hath of all vertues the surname of Christian imposed on it, and those people onely in common Language termed good Christians that are conspicuously endued therewith.

Patience and Christianity are such Relatives as they cannot, in the worlds esteeme, be separated, neither in their being nor in their growth. They enter joyntly into the heart, and run on parallell in the Lives of those that are truely CHRISTS disciples. Hee that by other vertues goes after CHRIST follows him in the way; but hee that goes after him by Patience follows him (as sayth St. Peter) in his very steps, which must needs lead on to eternall happines, whither hee is ascended.

This is that second argument that enforced mee to the Love and admiration of Patience: That our LORD gave it, and all his Saints have accepted it, as the proper Armes of Christian Religion. Not onely the distinction, but the honour of GODS Children lies in it. Hee that refuseth to beare Patience for his Coat must passe over into some other Family. Hee may bee a Gallant, a martiall Man, a great Man of this world; a Saynt of Heaven, a good Christian hee cannot bee. True Patience is ever the inseparable Consort of Christian religion, when it is sincerely professed; and Christian religion is the onely Profession that gives admittance to true Patience.

Verily (sayd the GUARDIAN) it must needs bee as you say; and now I see the reason why not onely Virgill and Homere, but Ariosto and Spencer and all other bookes of Chevalry, bring in their fayned worthies so defective in Patience. Mans witt can well enough, I perceive, fitt all other weapons of Christian Religion to serve the worlds turnes, even against religion; but onely Patience thats too weighty to bee put on a Counterfeit. Hee must bee a Christian in earnest and not in appearance that weares this peice of Armour, which, because these famous Devises want, however compleat in the height of all other vertues they bee made, I cannot allow them to passe for good examples of vertue amongst Christians.

Your Censure is very favourable (sayd the CHEIFE) in Comparison of his that is of opinion that Orlando and the rest of those renowned Palladines through the recompting of their worthy Action have beene made the destroyers of more Christian soules than ever they killed pagane Bodies, and yet he doubts not (as hee sayth) of that Battle wherein above three hundred thousand Moores are, by good and authenticall Historians, reported to have beene slaine by Orlando in one day. The full proofe of this Charge I shall leave to bee made at the Light of that Bone-fire which is resolved, as soone as Conveniency permitts, to be made of all these kinds of Bookes by our VISITOUR. But that which is proper to this subject wee are on, and perhaps not of so common Observation, though of much greater Consequence to the disclosing of that Mystery of Iniquity which lies wrapped up in them, I should doe wrong, mee thinks, to overpasse.

You should, indeed (sayd the GUARDIAN), both to the matter wee have in hand, and to the Company, some of whom, it may bee, through an habituated delight in these vanities from their Cradle almost, have need of all the Antidotes that can bee ministered to keepe them from relapse into a tolerable Opinion, at least of that which they have so clearely loved and prized.

That, then (sayd the CHEIFE), which I have by way of

Minister to present unto you, is that the world and the Devill owe to these Histories of Chivalry the making of that Match betweene Christianity and revenge, which could never, though diligently laboured from the very first, bee brought to passe till these last and perilous times of ours.

If I were not a Christian I would strike thee again, sayd the invincible Christopher, when he received a Blow in the face from the President of Samos; but because I am a Christian I put it up without repayment. Antiquity knew not how, though, in the representation of an Hercules, to fayne a Composition between Christian Profession and requittall of evill, though it were but one for another. Whence, then, comes it now, that a sevenfold returne of Injuries passeth for an honour amongst them that not onely prize themselves, but are honoured by others with the Name of good Christian Professors of the Gospell?

Undoubtedly, from the lying Patternes of Orlando and Rogero, from the counterfeit approbation of Carloman and Gotgride touching these practizes, there lies the springhead of these poysonous [Histories], and thence are those wretched opinions first taken, which afterwards, by fond reason and ungodly examples of eminent Personages, take eternall rooting in carnall Minds.

Theres nothing, questionlesse, more pleasing to Mans corrupt Nature than Revenge. The Allowance that Mahomets religion gives hereunto is one of the great inducements which procured him at the first, and still maintaines him so many Followers.

False Christians loth to turne open Turkes, and yet as eagerly bent to the prosecution of this Affection, have at last found the salve of this by coyning such new patterns as might serve their owne turne. Champions in the Fayth are produced compleat in all manner of Vertues, Patience excepted. That which is left out in the example is that which is cheifly intended for Imitation. All the rest is but a Flourish, and serves onely to make this deformity the more lovely, whilest it is accompanied with such abundance of excellenceyes. But painted Fire warmes not, however lively it bee sett forth, nor was ever any man made truely better by meanes of these Devises. Who dare truely say that either Temperance, Justice, Charity, or any other Vertue ever tooke rise or heate in his mind or desires from Orlando his Examples, or any of the rest of those Chimeras ? And who can truely deny but that, on the contrary, through the faire appearances and encouragements of such uncontrolled Presidents, as they are made, the Impatiency of Offences, the requitall of Injuries, the shedding of Bloud, as if it were but shedding of water, have beene bred and nourished in his heart as Dispositions necessary and comely in worldly respects tolerable enough with Christian religion ? The plausible entertainment of these Opinions in the world is that which cheifly is intended in these bookes ; if not in the Authors designes, yet certainly in the Devills application, without the Assistance of whose spirit they are never contentedly read, and what hand may wee think hee had in the composing of them! Let no man be deceived by the faire, goodly pourtraitures of the vertue which appeareth engraven to the life in them. They are but like the matrone Dresses and modest behaviour wherewith wicked strumpets enflame evill Affections.

In the removall of Patience they sappe the groundworke, and manifest to them that well observe, that all their pretence of building up the walls is but the more [designed] to colour their undermining the foundation of Christian Religion, the life and power whereof, in many wise and good Mens Judgements, hath in these last times beene [more endangered] by these kind of Bookes then by any other engine of Hell whatsoever, insomuch as the allowing of them in a Family professing GODS service is, by Men, very great both in learning and Devotion, thought and written to be sinne enough to cause the burning of the House, or the unnaturall Death of the heire, or any other such greviously calamity, and they think it may justly be imputed to this when other guiltines appeares not evidently to have drawen them on.

But I put my sickle into anothers Harvest. The danger of some weaker minds relapse, which you intimated, hath carried me further then I intended, touching the discovery of the Mystery of Iniquity, which, I told you, lay wrapped up in the kind of Bookes and Composures. To reduce, therefore, the discourse where it begunne, and shutt up all:

As the reconciling of the Difference betweene Mans naturall Temper and true Patience is one of the great Miracles which our Saviour hath wrought, so the League betweene Christian Religion and unpatiency, which hath so openly and solemnly been concluded in these latter Ages of the world, deserves justly to bee esteemed one of the cheife of those lying wonders whereby the comming and power of Antichrist is to be made famous, wherein (to reserve all other parallels to further opportunity) pray observe, that both God and the Devill worke their Miracles after the same Manner. The proposall of true Examples in the Scripture is that whereby God leades his Saints on to Patience, and the proposall of lying examples in Bookes of Chivalry is that whereby the Devill cheifly seduceth carnall and worldly Minds then to the Love and practize of Impatiency in the highest kind and degree.

Since wee have your Assurance, dearest Cheife (sayd the Guardian), that this ere long shall come not onely to fuller handling but finall determination, I think it just for the present to restraine my desires, though they bee very earnest. Onely one thing, which I know not whether I shall have the like opportunity for, I pray now make mee understand a little better. That Patience is a greater guift then Miracles I have often heard from many and believe, and that it is a greater proofe of Gods grace then Miracles seemes undeniable, St. Paul making it plainly the first and maine proofe of our dependance on Christ as Servants, in all things approving ourselves as the Ministers of God in much Patience and in Afflictions; but that it should bee a Miracle itselfe, as you say, I doe not so well [comprehend].

I shall tell you (sayd the CHEIFE) a short story out of Cassianus, which will perhaps better satisfy you touching this matter then a long discourse of mine owne.—

A venerable old Man, walking the streets of Alexandria in time of persecution, upon Notice given that he was a Christian, is suddenly enclosed by an unruly Multitude of Idolaters, who, after all manner of despitefull usage, both in words and deeds, began joyntly with much scorne to demande of him What great Miracles hath this CHRIST of thine done, whom thou makest to bee GOD? to which the blessed Saint cheerefully made answer, That I can patiently endure all those wrongs which you doe mee, and more and greater, if need bee, without any disquiet in my selfe or Offence towards you.

Oh, now I perceive my former dulnes (sayd the GUARDIAN). The fire burnes not the body either more naturally or more feircely then Injuries doe the mind. It must, therefore, bee alike miraculous to comport wrong without offence as to walke through the flame without scortching; and now, there being no more to bee expected touching this point, I desire you, deare CHEEREFULL, to goe on to the next.

The wonderfull gaine that accrues by Patience is the third argument which, mee thinks, ought to compell every one, as it did mee, to the pursuite thereof above all other things. The time would faile to recount all. I will onely therefore instance three Benefitts proper to Patience, and exceeding all others in my Apprehension.

First, it resettles a man in the possession of himselfe, from whence sin and other Passions have ejected him. In your Patience (sayth our Saviour to his Disciples) possesse your soules.

Secondly, it entitles him to the Kingdome of heaven. Blessed are the poore in spirit, and blessed are those that suffer persecution, for theirs is the Kingdom of Heaven.

And thirdly, it invests him in the fruition of all the good things of this Life.

The meeke spirited shall possesse the Earth, and shalbe

refreshed in the Multitude of Peace. Other vertues regaine by little and little one Parcell after another what wee have lost, but Patience makes an intire, absolute re-entry at once into heaven, earth, and ourselves. And what thing then can wee find answerable to Patience for advantage and Beneficialnes?

That Patience makes a Man Owner of himselfe (sayd the GUARDIAN) the world cannot well deny, seeing it is one of the first prayers that Men commonly make upon any great distresse, That GOD would give them Patience to keepe themselves in their right witts; and, on the other side, of impatient Men they say they are out of their witts and beside themselves. As for the Kingdome of heaven, they will not much contend but that the interest that Patience hath thereunto may be as great as CHRIST promiseth, but that it should bee such a seed of content here on Earth, and such a way to purchase honour and Happines in this Life, they will never bee brought to beleive, how many texts of scripture soever bee brought in proofe thereof.

Now, although Proverbs have no Creditt with mee against truth it selfe, whose Authority I have alledged, yet, because they have perhaps with many others, who will by no meanes bee perswaded to understand CHRISTS and Davids words as [applying], I would bee glad to bee furnished with some good answere touching these which you have already recompted, and all other those proverbiall sentences whereof the world is full, to sett forth the Damage that Patience brings to him that useth it.

It is true (sayd the CHEEREFULL). If they be well sought up, there will perhaps bee more common by-words found to the prejudice of Meeknes and Patience then of all the other vertues besides. Such is the worlds Malice to Patience. But Malice never speakes the truth. Lets come to the Touchstone, and you shall see they are all false peices, however currant they passe in the world. Peruse the Bible, which is the onely uncontrollable record of Mens Actions, and you shall find that Prosperity and Patience have ever gone together, and that the mightiest, the most honorable, and the happiest of Mankind have ever beene the Meekest and most Patient in their generation. What was then must needs bee now. Patience cannot loose her vertue, but must still bee a promoter, even in temporall respects, of them that are endued therewith. The Evidency is so great as needs no Instance of Particulars.

What answere shall wee then give (sayd the GUARDIAN) to those Millions of Examples which the world produceth to the contrary, every Man almost lamenting that his Patience turnes to his damage, and the more he beares the more is put upon him?

Patience perforce and Patience for advantage are those onely kinds of Patience which the world knows, at least practizeth (sayd the PATIENT). And as neither of these are thankworthy at GODS [hand] (as St. Peter speakes), so neither have they any certainety or greatnes of reward annexed to them. It is no marveill, therefore, if the world judge them more burdensome in the performance then profitable in the fruit and consequence. But true Patience, that, out of obedience to GODS will and conformity to our Saviours example, willingly undergoes greife by the effecting of good, hath an undefeazable obligation of GODS owne hand for such reward as it selfe desires. Let them produce but one that will say he hath lost by this kind of Patience; either the encrease or continuance of his sufferings have been thought thereby beyond that which otherwise they had beene, and they have indeed brought in a Traverse to that which Scripture sayth. But otherwise all the proofes that are alledged fall besides the cause. They speake home to the Danger and unprofittablenes that is in necessitated Patience, that suffers onely because it cannot choose and dares not resist. They speake home likewise to voluntary Patience, that is intended onely for honour and advantage.

But these fall as short both of the Nature and perfection of true Christian Patience as the cold watery Light of the Moone doth of the warme and Life producing influence of the Sunne.

Wee may well enough perhaps allow the worlds maximes to bee true while they keepe them in their owne Bounds. But if from the defects of worldly Patience, which they make sometimes tryall of, they goe about to inferre the like and greater Inconveniences in Christian Patience, which they are not at all acquainted with, they deale no fairer then some willfull men now adaies doe, who, by the Observation of many Cousenages in base Empericks and some evill consequences from unskilfull Practitioners of Physick, grow absolutely to condemne that Divine Art as the overthrow of Life and health, to the maintenance whereof it is by GODS ordinance instituted, and, being rightly exercized, doth most excellently conduce.

The remembrance of that ancient Commendation of Patience making it the Medicine of Greife setts your comparison of it more lively in mine eye (sayd the GUARDIAN), and by it and that which you have sayd I begin to see the Light. This œquivocall Acceptation of Patience must needs breed a diversity of Conclusions, and so that which the world sayth may in some sort bee true, and that which the Scripture teacheth must needs bee in all regards infallible.

But for the saving of the worlds Creditt I am nothing at all carefull. Let Baal plead for himselfe and for his Proverbs, which, however in sense of words they may perhaps bee made good, yet I am sure in common apprehension are most maliciously false.

But touching the Doctrine of the Scripture I would bee glad to bee a little better informed. I pray, therefore, tell mee whether you so conceive that true Patience ever works to ease of the sufferings and returne of Comfort.

Alwaies (sayd the PATIENT) at the last to them that desire Ease and Deliverance. Many examples, I doubt not, in all Ages may bee brought of longsome sufferings in good men, and some, perchance, which a little Impatiency would have much speedlier ridd them of then Patience did; but none can be brought, as I suppose, where Patience wrought not deliverance in the end, and that of a farre better kind then

Impaciency could have done if they had followed the perswasions thereof.

If David had tooke away Sauls Life upon those faire opportunityes which were offered him, hee might have beene the sooner free perchance from that dread and Anguish wherein he lived by Sauls Persecution, but assuredly hee had never come to that Glory and happines whereunto in the end hee attained. The workings of Patience are oftimes slow, but they are ever sure and abundant. The delay is manifoldly repayed by the Plenty of the retribution which Patience brings to them that desire retribution in this Life, which many have refused, as St. Paul testifieth, to the Intent they might bee partakers of a greater reward in Heaven. Himselfe and most of the just and perfect men since our Saviours appearance in the Flesh have beene of the same mind to think Affliction their happines and the exercize of Patience a better and greater Content then the enjoyment of any though never so lawfull delights in this world. Wee ought not, therefore, to be pressed with Examples of their sufferings who would not bee eased, as giving any Cheque to the truth of this Doctrine which Truth it selfe hath spoken, That blessed are the meeke, for they shall inherit the Earth. That alwaies they doe in the end, if themselves desire it.

The patient abiding of the meeke shall not perish for ever, sayth David. It may bee long put of, but in the end it shalbe fully satisfied according to his own expectation. For the LORD is very pittifull and of great Mercy, as St. James sayth, and for proofe thereof hee brings Job, willing us to looke on his Example, and by it to make this conclusion, That they are happy which endure, not in their owne present sufferings, but in the happy End that the LORD shall give unto them, as hee did unto Job, sending a double portion of very Comforts and good things, the Loose and Depravation whereof he patiently underwent out of Obedience to GOD's holy will and pleasure.

You have fully cleared the matter in my apprehension (sayd the GUARDIAN), and to say something in confirmation, since there is nothing to say in opposition, Davids Impatiency against Abishai for his intended kindnesse to take of Shemeis rayling head, and the reason that hee gives shews plainly that hee thought nothing more profitable then Patience, whilst hee makes the opportunity that GOD offered him to exercize it an Argument of his hope to bee restored againe to his prosperity. It may bee that the LORD will looke upon my Affliction, and that my LORD will requite good for his cursing; not for the Malice, from whence it proceeded in Shemei, but for the Meekenes, wherewith it was entertained by David. That's the meaning, and the may bee which David puts was onely in regard of his owne guiltines, that made himselfe as unworthy to receive those favours which otherwise Patience would undoubtedly procure at GODS hand. Hee is much more offended, therefore, with his freinds Love then with his enemies Injuries, and more jealous to keepe matter of Patience afoot then to ward his head from Shemeis stones. Let him curse (sayth David), deprive mee not of that happy Comfort which the patient enduring of this present greif shall in the end bring unto mee. You know the Issue was answerable to Davids expectation, and ought to bee an incouragement to us to follow his example in the like occasions, which GOD grant mee as happily to performe as now I earnestly desire. And now, deare CHEEREFULL, I pray goe on to that which is remaining, for that there is something yet behind, your Countenance shews as well as the matter it selfe seemes to crave.

There is one thing more indeed (sayd the CHEEREFULL) with which I will conclude, and that is, Since Man's Nature stands so much upon right, that there is nothing more right and equall then that wee should with Patience undergoe those sufferings which befall us, whatever they bee: first, because they come from GODS hand; and secondly, because they come by our owne deserts. David and Job hold the first reason enough to bee content. The LORD hath taken, sayth Job, and sitts him downe patiently in the Dust. And the LORD hath bid him curse, sayth David, and goes on his way weeping indeed, but quietly. Jacobs sonnes use the second as an argument to appease the swellings of greife when unexpected Calamity had overtaken them : Wee are verily guilty concerning our Brother, therefore is this Distresse come upon us. Micah put both together : I will beare the Judgement of the LORD, because I have sinned against him, until hee plead my Cause and execute judgement for mee. Weigh his reasons well, and however too it be with us, wee cannot in Justice make any other resolution then Micah did, to waite patiently and constantly in all our Afflictions upon GOD till hee himselfe give deliverance. And by the same reasons wee shall find that those murmurings, those helpings and rightings our selves which Impatiency perswades us unto, involve a double Impiety of justifying ourselves and condemning GOD, as though wee suffered more Evill then wee deserve, or hee exercized less justice or kindnes then hee ought to doe.

Verily (sayd the GUARDIAN) the heart thinks no lesse whatever the mouth sayth, when Men grudge to beare, or goe about to helpe and right themselves in their sufferings; if they thought not better of themselves then of GOD, they would be content to stay his Leasure for the taking of that Burden which hee layes upon them. And therein perhaps they should take the wiser Course to their own ends, for commonly it fares with them as it doth with untowards Beasts. The Burden that is impatiently cast off is layd on againe with many stripes to both.

This is indeed one of those good services (sayd the AFFECTIONATE) for which Solomon gives it the prize of Madnes above all over vices when he sayth that it exalts Folly.

Truly (sayd the GUARDIAN) other vices proceed much more warily in this matter, though perhaps their good-will they beare to Folly bee never a whitt lesse. They alledge reason, such as it is, and pretend to bee under the Obedience of wisedome, which Impatiency stands not at all upon when it grows to any height. Take an enraged Man, and hee makes no scruple to sett folly out to shew, nor to lett all the world know that hee is guided by it. Heel tell you himselfe that hee is mad, and will bee mad. In this sence, therefore, very truly may Impatiency be sayd, it exalts Folly when it gives it such preheminency of Authority and Honour as to professe itself subject to the Guidance and Government thereof.

Your Interpretation is surely right (sayd the AFFECTIONATE), but very short of that which I have lately beene taught touching the meaning of these words which, because it suits much to the present occasion I shall, if you please, acquaint you with.

Its well you have voluntarily offered (sayd the CHEIFE) that which otherwise wee should have by Course of Law exacted, that you should likewise bring in your Dish to the feast, as every Body else hath done, was intended to have beene demanded, I, and destrained for, too, if you had not done it freely.

I shall bee glad (said the AFFECTIONATE) if it prove as acceptable as expected.

Well, then, I pray (sayd the GUARDIAN), what may that bee which, either out of these words, or by occasion of these words, you have learned so much to the matter wee are now in hand with.

That Impatiency is the Cause of all the Imperfections in Mens works and Actions (sayd the AFFECTIONATE), and that on the other side Patience is the Nurse, if not the Mother, of all Perfection, not onely in Divine, but also in humane respects and things of this world.

Indeed (sayd the GUARDIAN) this is a transcendent exaltation of folly on Impatiencys behalfe, as on the contrary it must needs enforce a great preheminence of Wisedome belonging to Patience if it be such a maine Cause of Perfection. But how can you make proofe of these things by Scripture?

What need wee seeke for proofe in Scripture (sayd the AFFECTIONATE) of that which dayley Experience gives evident demonstration of in all things?

Looke well and you shall see that all that bungling in Trades, that unskillfulnes in Arts, that errour in Sciences, and in a word, all that Insufficiency in professions which deformes and ruines the world, proceeds mainly from Impatiency, either in learning or in practizing their severall workes. Naturall Abilities in most Men serve well enough, fitting instruments and all other opportunities abound to know all things aright and to doe them well. Onely Patience is wanting, and that marres all.

Bee the witt never so good, the Instruments never so apt, the Advantage never so great for learning and performance of any skill, and yet give mee an impatient minded Man that cannot hold him close and constant to the Businesse, and you shall find him upon the Test but shallow in what he understands and a slubberer in what he doth.

The hasty Bitch brings forth blind whelps, is a Proverb truely appliable to all humane Actions. That which through Impatiency is dispatched with speed comes forth alwaies like Chickens artificially hatched in Egypt, some way or other monstreous, either by defect, or excesse in some one part or other, and therefore Solomon sayth, That there is more hope of a foole then of a man that is hasty in his matters. A right simple witt by Patience and Perseverance overcomes all manner of difficulties, and brings forth whatever it undertakes compleat. Whereas the most excellent abilities with all the helps that can bee, if Patience be away foyle themselves instantly in their owne apprehension of things, in the expression of them to others, and in the performance of that which comes to execution. Their conceits runne cleane away; their words are now short, now over, never hitting the Marke; their Actions alwaies full of Errour and Incongruity, all merely through Impatiency, that in contemplation hastens them away before they fully understand the matter, that in deliberation puts them on to speake before they well know what, and, when they come to put things in execution, makes them give over or turne to other meanes when they find any rubbe in that way which they have begunne. These are the fruits of Impatiency, and the predominancy of it and them in our weaker sex the onely ground of the flightines and insufficiency wherewith not onely all womens words and workes, but even their naturall Constitution is taxed. I say not but there bee some few things perhaps whereunto neither the Capacity of womens minds nor the Abilities of their bodies doe generally serve, such as are the depth of Learning and the Labours of warre. But that in all things, I, even in those things which seeme properly our owne, wee should be so farre outrunne by men when they sett themselves to vy with us, cannot proceed from any thing but from the Impatiency of our Minds, which suffers us not to bee seriously intentive to that which wee desire to learne, nor steedily imployed in that wee undertake to performe. So that wee both know and say and doe all good things but by halfes at the best, which questionlesse might be throughly in all perfection accomplished, if we would let Patience have her perfect working; for even to this sence doe St. James his words extend themselves, and all those other many Commendations which Solomon gives unto Patience as including much wisedome and understanding, whereof hee seemes to make Patience the rule and measure, as it were, when hee saith That a mans Learning is knowne by his Patience, whether wee understand by Learning that knowledge which a Man professeth to teach others, or that measure of knowledge which himselfe hath attained unto.

Theres no surer way to make the tryall both of the goodnes and defects, then by the gage of Patience. The Doctrine that is confirmed by the Teachers Patience is, and ought to bee, of great Creditt for truth, and the measure of Learning and skill in every man and in every kind, ought to bee accompted proportionably to the Measure of Patience by which hee attained, and with which he exercizeth it. If he had much Patience in learning hee is undoubtedly perfect in the knowledge that hee professeth. If hee have used much patience about the worke that he produceth, that is likewise undoubtedly compleat. Hee that is patient worketh great wisedome, but hee that is impatient worketh Folly, sayth Solomon. Whether hee speaks, or worke, or doe, its all amisse. Make the examination where you please, and you shall see that as Impatiency leads alwaies to Folly, so Folly for the most part proceeds from Impatiency. And this is one of those things that I was taught by those words, Hee that is impatient exalteth Folly.

Why if it bee but one (sayd the GUARDIAN) it is not all, and therefore you may not here make an end, for both your promise and our expectation is that you should teach all that yourselfe is taught in this matter.

I shall gladly doe it (sayd shee), because I conceive it to bee neither lesse true nor lesse profitable then the former. The second thing was, therefore, that all the high prized Follies in the world have beene cheifly sett up and are maintained in honour and Esteeme by and for Impatiency, that it may have the freer bent, and passe without Controll.

What (sayd the GUARDIAN smilingly) will you perswade us that all your womanly Niceties of rubbing floores till you may see your Faces shine in them, of whiting Linning till it passe the driven snow, of conserving, preserving, and all those other busy Curiosities for which you soe magnify yourselves, have their Creditt cheifly for the better Inducement and support of Impatiency?

I, verily (sayd shee), and all those other more boisterous and more pernicious vanities you Men ar carried with, of building, of hunting, of keeping Company, and the like, proceed from the same ground, and tends to the same end, is that which I would perswade and am confident to make proofe of. But why, I pray, do you instance our womanly affaires with such contempt?

Because (sayd the GUARDIAN) they bee utterly unworthy the Dignity of Mans Nature to take any pleasure or delight in them; and much more to glory of them. Judge in yourselves what a debasement it must needs be of those noble

Faculties of the will and reason that were made for Contemplations and pursuite of heavenly Affaires to powre out themselves in the Love and prosecution of such abject Matters.

Why, some thing wee must needs doe (sayd the AFFECTIONATE). Mans Soul cannot bee without Imployment; and since you have taken away great matters from us, you ought not to vilify these so much wherein the mind in regard of its owne working is nobly busied, however the subject bee but meane. Theres exercize of Invention, of Composition, of Order, and of all the other excellent operations of the Soule, and the Beauty, and Pleasure, and other good effects that arise from these Imployments. And herein lies our delight, not in the things themselves, as you seeme to conceive.

That cannot possibly bee (sayd the GUARDIAN). For then by how much it is more excellent to have the minds of your Families well composed then the roomes of your house curiously dressed, your Children well fed then your Table dantily furnished; by so much would your Care been greater in these matters then in the other.

You would have us then (sayd the AFFECTIONATE) spend all our time and care upon our Servants and Children, instructing their understandings and framing their manners, still watching over them to exact an orderlines and perfection in vertue and knowledge, as wee bring our houses to the height of beauty and conveniency. And so wee must become absolute School-Mistresses in steed of good Husewives.

I would have you both (sayd the GUARDIAN) carefull Guides of your house and diligent Teachers of your Children; the Neglect and disesteeme of which Office and Imployment seemes to me one of the soveraigne Follies of this world, there being no duty which Parents so much ow their Children, nor anything wherein themselves can bee more nobly exercized then in teaching their children and instructing them in Vertue and Learning. But are wee not wandred from the point?

Not at all (sayd the AFFECTIONATE), if you will but tell us whence the withdrawing of Parents from this duty proceeds.

Is it perhaps through Ignorance of the worth thereof, or through want of Love to their Children?

All wise Parents (sayd the GUARDIAN) give Instruction the prize of all other Benefitts which their children receive by their meanes.

And why, then, since it is the best Portion, are they not desirous to bestow it by their owne hands and mouths, rather then by others mercenary paps and Care (sayd the AFFECTIONATE)? Doe they want Love to performe it?

No, no (sayd the GUARDIAN). Now I perceive the Cause; they want Patience. Thats the common and the onely answere which they will stand by. And now I understand whereat you aime, and must needs yeeld unto it as an evident truth. Its Impatiency onely that hath suffred this painefull Education of our Children as too meane a matter for Persons of better rank and spirit. And it can bee nothing else but Impatiency that hath sett up on high those other vaine imployments which come in Place thereof. What you have brought mee to see in one particular is true in all the rest. The Impatiency of enduring that Paines and Care which belongs to goverment makes our Gentry and Nobility cast up their owne and their Countries busines, and betake themselves to hunting, hawking, and the like Riots. And these they magnify as noble Imployment, not because themselves are so perswaded (for their owne Consciences tell them they bee but unworthy vanityes), but because by the appearance of bodily Labour they have a faire colour for the Idlenes of their Minds, and in the Independancy that these kind of Actions have to any others, a freedome for their inconstant Affections and humours to revell as they please. And now to make a proofe whether I rightly and fully understand this matter, give me leave, dear AFFECTIONATE, to make the conclusion according to mine owne Apprehension, wherein, if I any waies faile, make you the amends by Addition and Correction of what shall bee needfull. This, then, mee thinkes, seeme to bee plaine: That every one that through Impatiency deserts his owne proper worke, first endeavours by slighting it to find excuse for what hee leaves undone, and next by amplifying the worth of that which hee set himselfe about, to have a pretence for his Continuance therein. Thus farre· you goe very rightly (sayd the AFFECTIONATE).

The Conclusion then follows of it selfe (sayd the GUARDIAN) that hee must needs become a Depresser of wisedome and an Exalter of Folly. For every Mans happines lieth in the performance of his owne proper Charge which is imposed upon him. Hee abandons wisedomes Colours therefore, who ever hee bee, that forsakes his owne stations, though it bee for the better. But such choise Impatiency seldome makes, hunting onely after that which is pleasant and delightfull to disordered sences and affections, whereof Folly is the Guide and Mistresse, and all that shee directs unto, like her selfe. The impatient Man, therefore, whilest hee leaves the good for the pleasant, runs necessarily unto the Campe of Folly, and in the end, whilst he will justify his error, turnes her Champion. And now, adding the last Commendations of Wisedome to those other foure of Strength, Excellencie, Beneficialnes, and Justice, which the CHEEREFULL taught us out of Holy Scripture to belong to Patience, wee may, mee thinks, well conclude where our CHEIFE began, with St. James : That if Patience have her perfect working it will worke us perfect and intire, wanting Nothing.

The Perfection of Patience hath beene lively demonstrated by that which hath beene already spoken, but the perfect Manner of her working seemes not to mee as yet sufficiently declared (sayd the MODERATOUR). Wherefore I should desire some further Light in this matter, which I suppose will bee given by the Declaration of those severall kinds and degrees of Patience which have beene so often mentioned to day, but no where plainely expressed in this discourse.

You have mentioned a necessary point (sayd the GUARDIAN), and which was often in my mind to have asked, but reserving it still to a convenient place, I had in the end by mine owne forgetfulnes, perhaps, lost it, which that it befall mee not with another doubt which I have, I pray give mee Leave now, whilest it is in remembrance, to crave the solution of from the CHEEREFULL, and that is, Why shee makes it a proper Doctrine of the Scripture that wee should hold it meete and just patiently to undergoe sufferings when they come unto us?

The Case (sayd the CHEEREFULL) is very plaine if you observe the arguments which I brought, that all that befalls us comes from GODS hand and by our owne Desert, which, being founded upon our Beleif of GODS absolute and immediate providence, and Mans sinfull Nature, can have no infallible Demonstration but from the Doctrine of the Scripture, which teacheth us that not so much as a haire of our Heads falls to the ground without GODS Notice, and that however innocent our actuall Lives may perhaps seeme each to our selves, yet the originall sinne with which wee came polluted into the world makes us liable to farre sorer punishment then any Man had ever inflicted upon him.

You have fully satisfied mee (sayd the GUARDIAN). All other Doctrines but Scripture fall short in these two points of GODS providence and Mans Guilt, and therefore leave the exception which the world makes oftimes against Patience but unsufficiently answered. And now, I pray, according to the MODERATOURS proposition, for the finishment of this matter let us have the severall kinds and degrees of Patience.

As there are three principall Objects, so there seemes to bee three more severall kinds of Patience (sayd the PATIENT). The first is that which constantly endures Labour and paines in well-doing, not without wearinesse—for that Flesh and Bloud cannot doe—but without giving over till the work in hand bee accomplished. And this Patience hath Idlenes for its Opposite, and Ease and Pleasure for the Bayt wherewith the Devill seekes to withdraw us from the exercize of it, and is the most common and universall Temptation wherewith hee fights against mankind.

The second kind of Patience is that which beares losse and

Injuries from Man, not without resistance—for that oftimes it may lawfully use, but ever without ill-will against the party from whom the wrong comes. This kind of Patience hath wrath for its Contrary, and revenge is the maine Engine wherewith the Devill batters it.

The third kind of Patience is that which undergoes greife and sorrow which GOD pleaseth to inflict, without murmuring or repining against him. Complaine it may, but it is of its owne weakenes and guilt, not of GODS unkindnesse. It ever justifies GOD and strives to be thankfull, not onely quiet. These are the three kinds of Patience, and as many are the degrees. The lowest is that which undergoes Sufferings without seeking redresse either sooner or otherwise then GOD appoints. The second is that which willingly enters upon sufferings that it may become more perfect, and the third degree is that which rejoyceth in Afflictions, to which measure the Apostles attained. To the second many of GODS Saints, and in especiall the Martyrs, have excelled. To the third all Christians are of Necessity bound.

Here was the end of this discourse, the close and connexion whereof with the following Stories, by reason of the scarcity of time was omitted. The stories themselves follow in order and manner as they were told.

The PATIENT first beginning as followeth :—

A noble Woman of Alexandria, finding that the greatnesse of her Prosperity offered small occasion for the practize of her Humility and Patience, that shee might not be wanting in these, being abundant in all other vertues, besought the great Athanasius to appoint her one of the Widdows belonging to the Hospitall, that by her voluntary Ministering to her inferior, shee might have opportunity to exercize Humility and Charity. Athanasius consigned a grave and sober Matrone truely fearing GOD, with whom this noble Lady having a while conversed, addressed her selfe by way of complaint to Athanasius, that hee had, by an ill-intended choise of the widow, frustrated her desires. Why, quoth Athanasius, I esteemed her to bee a widdow such as the Apostle requireth, full of vertue and goodnes. So, verily, she is, replied the Lady; that is that makes mee now beseech the change, for her thankfull acceptation doth more than repay all the Benefitts which shee receiveth from mee, that I cannot hope for any recompence from GOD at all that am neere more then doubly repayed for my Charity, and otherwise her respect to mee is such that I receive comfort and honour instead of exercizing Patience and Humility. Athanasius, understanding her, willed that one of the most froward and perverse of all the widdows should be sent home unto her, which being accordingly done, after some while Athanasius, meeting the noble woman, asked her how she rested contented with the last. Even as I desire, sayd shee; for the more vexation I receive for the good I doe, the more profitable doe I find it to bee for mee.

I have heard (sayd the GUARDIAN) in former recomptings of this Story and Authority produced for it, that the perversenes of the froward Widdow was so excessive as she forbore not now and then to lay hands upon her Benefactor, adding Blows to evill words, which, because it is not onely a proofe of the excellency of her Patience may bee an Inducement on the like occasions to perfect the same grace in us, I have thought necessary to remember, and withall to propound to your consideration, the which I confesse much affects me. That is the great difference of opinion betweene those ancient times and our proud Age, as in all other things, so especially in this matter. Who could not now adaies think they should runne much hazard of loosing the Kingdome of Heaven by living with such a Person and being put upon such things as this truely noble Lady made choise of that shee might more certainely and more fully come to the Attainement of everlasting Happines?

How necessary Patience was in old time thought to bee for the perfecting of Vertue and Glory (sayd the CHEIFE) that yong man shewed who, being willed by his Master to give some good Lesson to certaine devout Persons that came for

Instructions to him, rose up, and flinging his Garment on the ground began to trample upon it, still treading down those parts that seemed to beare up themselves, saying that a Man could not come to perfection except hee were well tryed by Injuries and so kept under by Sufferings that no swelling of exaltation should arise, at least continue, in his heart.

Your Story (sayd the GUARDIAN) is like a Jewell, of a little Bulk but of great worth ; but, comming in but by the way, will not satisfy for that which wee expect from you.

It is not my meaning (sayd the CHEIFE), though you would give mee Leave to keepe back the story which I have provided, which is of a noble Personage of the selfe same Citty of Alexandria, and setts forth Charity and Patience no lesse perfect in the Intention and in the end then that which you have heard of. There was, indeed, a little Interruption of the perfect working of these graces, but that being rightly applied may serve as much to our Benefitt as anything else.

Eulogius was a noble Man of Alexandria, endued with much wisedome by Nature, adorned with many vertues by good Breeding, with riches from his predecessors. Notwithstanding all this, finding nothing but Vanity and vexation in the things of this world, hee resolved abandoning the care of all earthly things, to sett himselfe wholly to the service of GOD ; and so, dispersing the greatest part of his substance to the poore, hee gave himselfe altogether to Devotion. But perceiving by reason of a large use of Delicacies hee was not able to endure their great Mortifications in his owne body, nor excessive Labour which hee saw divers Saints of GOD take for the Benefitting of others, hee grew much more perplexed least his Life, that was not of so great Example to others, should not in the end prove of that acceptation to GOD.

Being thus greived, one Day he saw a Leaper lying in the streets, whose Tongue was onely left whole of all his members of his Body to beg releife with. Eulogius, having considered the wretchednes of the Man and the Noisomenes of the disease, thought that there was now offered unto him an occasion for the exercize of the highest Mortification on himselfe and Charity towards his Neighbour, and stepping to the Leaper demanded if he would goe home with him and receive the most carefull entertainement and attendance that he could afford him. The poore Leaper, acknowledging the offer to bee from GOD and Eulogius an Angell of CHRIST, with all thanks accepted the condition, whereupon Eulogius, fetching an Asse, conducted him immediately to his house, serving him both in the applying of remedies and all other Offices about his Nourishment and Person with his owne hand for the space of fifteene yeares with so great Love and tendernes as no Mother could doe more to her onely Child. In the end the Leaper, by the suggestion of the Devill, began to wax so froward and peevish as nothing could content him but that he would needs be gon, though hee knows not whither. The first quarrell was for flesh, pretending that he could not any longer endure that spare and sober diet which he was kept unto. Herein Eulogius with all meeknes did readily satisfy him, but could not still his whining; but the more with gentle and humble words he sought to pacify him the more outragious the Leaper grew, telling Eulogius that his flatteries (for so hee called his faire speeches) were odious and his kindnes made him sick. Ah, say not so, said Eulogius, deare Brother, but tell mee wherein I have done amisse and I will make amends. No amends, sayd the Leaper, shall serve. Ile no more of thy tendance, no more of thy Curtesy; carry thou mee to the place where thou first found mee. GOD forbid, sayd Eulogius, that I should preferre thy desire so prejudiciall to thyselfe and mee, but rather let mee know what may content thee and I shall procure to bring it to thee for thy good, rather then carry thee hence to distruction. I cannot, sayd the Leaper, endure any longer either thy Person or the want of other Company.

That, GOD willing, (sayd Eulogius), I will speedily remedy by supply of divers holy Persons who will, I know, for GODS sake afford thee their dayly visitation. But heere the

Leaper exclaiming feircer then before, I cannot away to looke on thy face, sayd hee, and wilt thou bring others like thy selfe doubly to torment mee? Oh, what oppression, oh, what Tyranny is this that thou exercizest on me! Restore mee to the place and Condition of Life from which thou drewest mee. Eulogious, fearing his distemper so strong as hee was in doubt it might grow unto desperate resolutions, determined, by the advise of divers good persons, to carry him to St. Anthony, which, after a long and tedious journey having performed, St. Antonie after his manner came into a great Roome, where Eulogius with the Leaper and divers others were waiting for him. St. Antony, after that in generall he had instructed and admonished them, began to descend to the dispatch of every Mans particular occasions, answering, advising, and comforting them according to their severall demands and necessities, in which, having spent not onely the day but a great part of the Night, at last he called for Eulogius. It was then dark and Eulogius, knowing that neither his Person nor his Busines were knowne to St. Anthonie, thought hee had called for some one of his Disciples of the same Name, and so held his peace; but St. Antony called againe with a louder voice, saying, I speak to you, Eulogius of Alexandria, and so, drawing neere to him, demanded, What would thou with mee? Eulogius answered, Hee that hath told thee my Name hath also acquainted thee, I am sure, with my Busines. True, sayd St. Antony; but doe thou heere publickly declare it; whereupon Eulogius made a plaine and breife Narration of the matter betweene him and the Leaper, in the end adding that hee was much tempted to cast him out of his house, but before hee did it he besought his Counsell and Direction. To whom St. Antonie, in a severe manner replied, And wilt thou cast him out indeed? But GOD that made him will not cast him away. Thou wilt abandon him, but GOD will stirre up a better then thou to take care of him. Eulogius, much terrified, held his peace, and after a good pause St. Antony, turning himselfe to the Leaper with a sterne Countenance and angry voice—Thou vile Leaper, more horrible in the deformity of thy soule then of thy Body, unworthy of the Earth whereon thou liest, and how darest thou then repine and grudge against such a Blessing sent thee from heaven; knowest thou not that it is CHRIST against whom thou murmurest? For CHRIST it is that ministreth unto thee in him that for CHRISTS sake hath made himselfe a servant unto thee. Having thus spoken hee did for a good space apply himselfe to the rest of the Company, and then turning againe hee sayd to Eulogius and the Leaper, Goe home my sons and live together in peace and continue that exercize of Love and humility with which you did at first begin. Looke to yourselves that you loose not those things which you have wrought, but that you may receive a full reward, and know that this Temptation is happened unto you by the Malice of the Devill who, knowing the time of your Combate to bee at an end, would faine robbe you of the Crowne which is layd up for them which persevere unto the end in righteousnesse. But bee not you weary of well doing, and GOD, who is faithfull, shall preserve you to the end. Having thus spoken he dismissed them and they returned Home. First Eulogius died, and within fourteene daies the Leaper, following him to the fruition of that Glory which both of them runne the hazard of forfetting through want of Patience.

Your Story (sayd the GUARDIAN) ministereth abundance of excellent Observations, whereof these, mee thinks, are most necessary for us: That in all distresses of our Minds wee should seeke and follow good Mens Counsaile. Eulogius had not perhaps done so well if he had relied upon his owne Judgement as he did in taking St. Antonies Advise, which was more worth then his paines and cost, though that was not little, which hee tooke to obtaine it.

Secondly, that the Devill Labours eagerly to part holy Freindship, especially towards the end.

And thirdly, that Ingratitude is no sufficient cause to restraine Charity.

I have told you those things which I meane to carry away, and now, I pray, let the next proceede.

The double mentioning of Alexandria (sayd the MODERATOUR) seemes to call for my Story, which is of an Example or rather an Argument, which was there used to perswade Patience for naturall Defects.

Didimus of Alexandria, though blind from his youth, yet attained unto that Excellency of Knowledge as that Age had none that surpassed him. It so chanced that the great St. Antony, being drawn to Alexandria for the Confutation of certaine new sprung Heresies, became acquainted with Didimus, and finding both the sharpnes of witt and deepenes of understanding conjoyned in him with an unmatched grace in the interpretation and application of the Scriptures, he grew not onely to a Love but an admiration of the Man; but having observed a continuall sadnes in his Countenance, hee demanded one Day what might bee the reason of it, to which Didimus freely, though not without blushing, confessed that it was his Blindnes. To which St. Antony replied, I cannot enough marveile how that the Losse of that which is common to Emmits and gnats and flies, should trouble a wise man. How much ought the participation of those graces which adorne onely holy men, and even the Apostles themselves, make thee alwaies full of joy and gladnes?

This blessed Antony taught him and us to beare patiently those wants and Afflictions which, by the mercy of GOD, are recompenced with greater good, and when Impatiency assailes us to greive for those things which wee are deprived of, to turne our hearts to rejoycing and thanksgiving for those better things wee have.

It is true, sayd the GUARDIAN. Hee that well weigheth the greater things that hee enjoyeth by GODS Mercy can never bee cast downe for the want of some better things which he is deprived of by the wisedome of GOD. For certainely, if we could discerne aright, wee should perceive that even those things which are taken from us turne to our Advantage. So it was, I am sure, in this present Example of Didimus. The very Name of him breeds Admiration amongst the learned, whilest it is certaine hee was very absolute, not onely in all other manner of Learning, but even in the Mathematicks themselves, which wee think, without visible Demonstration, impossible to make any Entrance unto. Hee lost nothing by his Blindnes whilest hee lived, and by it, since his death, hee hath gained a more famous and honourable remembrance then ever any man did by his Eyesight.

If wee follow the clue that you have begun to unwind, worthy GUARDIAN (sayd the AFFECTIONATE), searching the good that may bee extracted out of every Evill that happens unto us, wee shall perhaps find that there is rather cause of rejoycing then bewailing in the most part of the suffering which befalls us. I shall tell you an Example of an excellent [Man] in his way which not onely suits to the discourse wee have in hand, but to the time, at least, to the Abuse of it, and may serve to disswade from Play and Gaming as well as to teach Patience and wisedome.

Cazimere, the Prince of Sendomiria, was a Man of rare endowments of Nature, which by learning and vertuous practize hee had so much perfected as there was fewer to be found his Equals in true worth then in Dignity. It so happened, that on a Day playing at Tables with a subject of his, named John Conor, and having won much mony of him, the Gentleman, desirous to regaine at once what hee had lost by many parcells, invited the Prince either to double his gaines by victory, or by Losse of the gaine to quitt what hee had formerly wonne; which the Prince, agreeing unto, and proving as fortunate as hee had formerly done, the Gentleman, enraged with greife and Choler, threw the Tables at the Princes head in such a manner as hurt him not a little, to the helpe whereof, whilest the standers by ranne all amazed, Conor had the Liberty to escape for that Night, it being late and darke. But next morning, being taken and brought before the Prince, all the Courtiers animated the Prince by a severe revenge to make the Offender an Example of all that should dare not onely to offer such Injuries, but even the least contempt to them to whom they owe Allegance. The wise and noble Cazimere, having paused a while, The punishment (sayd hee) that his owne shame and sorrow hath inflicted on him is more then sufficient for my wrongs and others example, and, that cleared, I am rather indebted to him for the double good Lesson which hee hath taught mee, That neither are these kind of exercizes sutable to that Imployment of mind and time which I owe to GOD and you, neither is it comely for Superiors to equall themselves by the pursuits of vaine delights and Covetousnes with Inferiors; which rules, though Conor perhaps intended not to teach mee, yet since by his flinging the Tables at my head I have learned of him, I hold it fitt not onely to acquitt him of all punishment and feare, but to restore him to my favour againe, with this condition and priviledge, that whensoever I faile in the Observance of either of these things, hee, or any of you, may boldly doe as much to mee. Thus having sayd, hee dismissed Conor and the Company, leaving in all their Minds an admiration both of his wisedome and Patience, and to us an example not onely to gather these collections which hee did, but to prize reproofes and correction of our errors at a high rate, from what affection soever they proceed in other, and not to looke whether they bee despitefully done or sayd, but whether they may not be most beneficially applied by us to the perfecting of our vertues and the attaynement of our Happines. And then, why should wee not rather love them for the good they doe us then bee angry for the evill manner they doe it in, which is onely prejudicious to themselves?

Truely (sayd the GUARDIAN) Cazimeres wisedome was very excellent in the raising of those Conclusions which you have mentioned. But that which of all other takes mee, is the Justification that hee seemes to give to Conor by the free confession of his owne Errors. Some others, perhaps, would have sayd in private, they would henceforth learne to be wiser; but very few there bee, especially amongst great ones, that would have made publick acknowledgement to have done amisse as hee did. Well, in this open condemning his error he justifieth himselfe more then he could have done either by concealement or defence, and hee made a ready way for Patience.

Hee that lookes upon his own Guilt (sayd the MODERATOUR) as all good and wise men ought to doe, can hardly take offence at others wrongs to him, however great they bee, to which purpose the SUBMISSE hath an excellent though a short story.

Whereupon the SUBMISSE told the Story which followeth.—

St. Gregorie the Great being much persecuted, both by reproachfull words and sore Injuries from Mauritius the Emperor and his Sonnes, wrott unto them in this manner: Forasmuch as I doe dayly by my sins greivously offend GOD, you shall perhaps the better please him by how much you doe the more afflict mee, that so negligently and unworthily serve him. If, as St. Gregorie did, in all our calamities and greifs wee dayly weigh what wee deserve at GODS hand, wee shall never dare to murmure through Impatiency. How heavy soever his hand ly on us, yet wee shall alwaies find it much lighter in the punishment then wee deserve.

A Man can hardly think of GOD (sayd the GUARDIAN) but hee shall find an overruling Argument to induce him to Patience. If wee think of his power, it is meet wee should bee subject to what hee appoints; if of his Justice, wee have deserved what wee suffer; if of his Mercy, wee have the assurance of reward, if we quietly endure what wee justly suffer; if of his wisedome, wee ought to judge, however it appears to us, that in truth it is best for us.

The OBEDIENT hath a good story, in my Judgement (sayd the CHEIFE), to prove and shew that this Beleife of GODS wisedome ordering all things to the Best, ought to overule us not onely in greatest, but even in the least Matters and occasions.

An old holy Man falling ill, could not in many daies take any sustenance, by which meanes growing very weake, his faithfull Disciple that attended him earnestly besought him to give Leave for the making of a certaine dainty kind of meat to make triall, if happily hee could eat thereof. The old Man agreeing thereto, the Disciple went instantly about it, and having made ready the meat, thinking to season it with Hony, hee mistakes the glasses, being very like, he poured in a good deale of stinking Oile, which done, he brought it to the sick man, praying him to eat; but he upon the first tast was not able to gett downe a bitt more, yet, loth to trouble his disciple, he held his peace without any manner of complaint, though it had much offended his Stomake. His Disciple, seeing him forbeare to take any more, besought him to eat, telling him hee must force himselfe; and see, Father (sayeth hee), I will eat some with you, and hee put a morsell into his Mouth; which hee had no sooner done but, overcome with the evill tast and smell, hee cryed out, Oh, mee! Father, what have I done? This is meat rather to poyson then to comfort you. Alas, why did you not tell mee, that I might not have urged you so much at least? To which the good old Man smilingly made Answere, My son, let it not greive thee, neither for thine owne error nor for my disappointment; if it had beene GODS will I should have eaten now of this meat hee would have so ordered that thou shouldst not have mistaken the Oile for the Hony, which, having done, thou and I both ought to esteeme it to bee GODS will, and to assure our selves its come to passe for the best as it is.

All the other Stories (sayd the GUARDIAN) have beene of admiration, this last for every daies use. And because wee shall have occasion often to call for it, it shall, if you please, bee named The Story of the Oile, which, though it was neither sweet nor pleasant in the Meat, yet may prove in the Application a Medicine of soveraigne Benefitt for the asswagement of many a sore greife that often happens amongst others upon very light matters. But cannot you, deare CHEEREFULL, all this while meet with a fitting Cue to bring in your story?

The Reference that my Story hath to the most of these things which have beene hitherto spoken of (sayd the CHEEREFULL) will, I doubt not, perswade you it hath not beene unfittly kept to the last.

Agaton having by long continuance in all manner of godly conversation gained the reputation of a Saint, certaine strangers, desirous to prove the sincerity of his so farre renowned Holiness, told him, that as the great report of his Vertues had induced them to come from farre to visit him, so the strange Accusations of many, and those no meane persons, did much distract and perplex their minds; for they tell us, sayd the strangers, that out of a haughty Mind thou takest upon thee to teach many new and unusuall Doctrines, and that thou seemest little to regard the Authority and Reasons that are contrary to thee, as though thy selfe wert onely wise and good.

They affirme likewise, that thou dost presumptuously censure divers Actions and Practizes approved by those that are much thy betters; yet thou art a bold and a continuall reproover of others faults, thereby to perswade Men that thou art an Enemy to vice. In a word, they lay to thy charge that all thy appearing Holines is but Hypocrisy, and that thou seemest to despise worldly pleasures and to contemne wealth, because thou canst not compasse them, or rather by a more commodious way hast found the satisfaction of Ambition and other evill Affections under the pretence of religion then other Men doe.

Agaton, having without any shew of distast heard them, sighing deeply, made answere that all was true that hee was accused of. But doe you, deare Brethren, shedding many teares, pray GOD for the pardon of my sinnes, the creating of a new and right Spirit within mee, that in heart I may bee such as I appeare outwardly to men.

The Strangers, much edified in the evidence of his Humility

and Patience, proceeded further, saying, Some likewise tell us that thou art an Heretick, and dost hold naughty and idolatrous Opinions. But then Agaton cryed out aloud, God forbid. Herein they doe mee wrong; however wretched Man that I am, confessing myselfe guilty of divers other Crimes, yet surely, by the mercies of God I am cleare from the Taints of superstition and Heresy. The good men, sorry to see him offended, besought him to passe by that which was onely spoken to make proofe of his vertue, and out of aboundance of charity to tell them why hee so readily confessed those former Crimes, of which they well saw he was not guilty, and seemed so much troubled at the Imputation of Heresy. Hee, constrained by their Importunity, replied, My sons, there is indeed so much of all those evill Affections in my heart of which you at first laid to my charge, and though by the goodness of God they doe not rule or sway either to do or undoe anything, but all that I doe is upon better grounds and to better ends, yet because they doe forceably intermingle themselves with my best Actions, it is not fitt for me to deny, especially when the Confession of my weaknes and Imperfection may more advance Gods Glory and edify my Brethren then I should doe by the defence of mine own Innocency, which is not mine owne, but the Guift and grace of God. And herein I follow our Lord and Saviour, who did no sinne, neither was guilt found in him, and yet notwithstanding patiently endured the Contradiction of sinners, not answering againe when hee was reviled, leaving us an example that wee should follow his steps. But as for Heresy and false Beleife in Religion, that makes an absolute partition betweene the Soule of Man and God. I may not, therefore, indure the Imputation of that which cast mee altogether from the Communion of Christ, that desirously undergoe all other Manner of reproaches and injuries, that I may bee made the more like unto him, both in the Conformity of a patient and humble Mind.

There is no truer proofe of a good heart then the ready Confession of its owne Badnes. Hee that justifies himselfe for the Inward knows not himselfe; the more wee grow to perfection the more doe wee discover our Corruptions. Hee is in a safe and a good way thats onely bad in his owne eies; but he that justifies himselfe by the good Intention and disposition of his heart when his outward Actions condemne him, is yet in the snares of the Devill.

This (sayd the GUARDIAN), GOD bee thanked, is happily brought about, and the want of our Musick have beene occasion of greater pleasure then I could have thought. Now it remaines that, calling upon GOD, wee faithfully endeavour to act what we have learned, and put in execution what wee have promised, both touching our owne selves and our living together, whilest wee doe live, cheerfully going on by humility and Patience unto the perfection of Love. Thats the end of all vertues, and the beginning of Happines. You began but foure Sisters, and are growen to seven in this exercize, and have brought it to a farre better passe then I could have imagined, and yet my heart assures mee that if you goe on adding the vertues of your second Combination, Submissiveness, Obedience, and Moderation, to the foure first, you shall bring both this and all the other great Attempts under your hands to that height of perfection which your selves desire, which GOD grant.

Love and living together, made perfect by Patience and Humility, and our very Number and Neerenes, which you speake of, bring to my remembrance a Story, as if it had beene made to this purpose, and for us.

Let us heare it (sayd the GUARDIAN).

A certaine holy Man named Anub, flying with his Brother Penon and five other Companions, in the persecution of the Sarazines, entered into a joint League to live and dy together in a certaine commodious place that they had found. The rest desiring Anub, as the eldest, that hee would instruct them how they might live peaceably together in the service of GOD; whereupon, that matter being of such consequence, Anub desired seven daies respite to perform what they desired, And in the meane space, sayth hee, let us, for the better preparing of ourselves to rule our Tongues, forbeare all manner of speach, but onely to GOD by Prayer; to which they all agreeing, Anub, going every morning to a certaine ruinous Temple of the Idolls, wherein there stood an Image of one of the heathen Gods, did openly, in all their sights, first every morning revile, and after spitt upon it, and in the end, with sticks and stones beat the Idoll, and every night kneeling downe, bowing his body to the Idoll, hee openly asked it forgivenes, confessing to have done it wrong. The solemne promise of keeping silence made Anubs Companions forbeare the appointed time, though it were as fire in their hearts. But that being expired they came altogether upon him, and his Brother Penon in all their Names demanded how it came to passe that hee, being a Christian, did reverence an Idoll, and being a Man of understanding, did every morning that which hee professed to repent at night; to which Anub answered, Herein lieth the satisfaction of your desires. Neither for my selfe or the Image have I done what you have seene, but for your Instructions. Tell me, I pray, when I smote the Idoll, did it shew either Anger or griefe? No, verily, sayd Penon. And when I bowed my selfe and craved pardon, did it swell with Conceit of Glory, or seemed it glad? Neither, sayd Penon. Why, then, quoth Anub; see wee are here, seven of us, and if it be your desires, as you professe, that wee should live in perfect concord, let this dumb Idoll bee our patterne. Let us not be puffed up when wee receive praise and esteeme, nor let us bee troubled at one another when wee conceive cause of offence; but let us carry an equall Temper in both, being still the same to our selves, and each to others, attributing the Love and honour which is given us to others abundant goodnes, and the Injuries and unkindnesses that are putt upon us to our own deservings. If you bee of this mind wee shall continue unto the end encreasing in true Amity; if otherwise, it will bee better to part at the beginning.

The Application of this Story was at that time made with

silence, and not with words, which could no waies have sett forth the Impression that it made upon the Companie, which immediately dissolved.

And here this Book finisheth, whereof the Errors and Defects are onely our owne. All the good is GODS, from whom it came ; to him bee Glorie for ever, Amen.

BOOK II

X

St. LUKE'S DAY, 1632

Resumption of the Meetings of the Little Academy—Election of the Chief to be Mother—The would-be Bishop—Cosimo de' Medici and Pucci Amatis.

THE treble Admonition which the Name and Profession of St. Luke, and the Collect and Hymne appointed for his Festival seeme to give you and mee, my dearest Sisters, hath made such an impression in my mind, and such a Commotion in my Affections as, had it not been enjoyned before, I should have made it my request that you would have given this meeting for the ease of my overburdened heart, which shame and sorrow and feare have a good while, and this day more especially, perplexed, whilest I consider the inestimable damage which wee have incurred through the fond relinquishment of many excellent workes wee had in hand, and the Remissenes with which we proceed in all the rest, which verily bodens yet further Losse and greater danger, except wee seek for timely redresse. Wee cannot keep that which wee enjoy either for vertue or Prosperitie, except we endeavour to encrease it. If wee stand still or goe slowly forward wee shalbe turned back with losse, not only of the prize which wee aime at, but even of that whereunto wee have already attained.

As the Fault which you have confessed, so the Passions which you have expressed, worthy CHEIFE (sayd the PATIENT),

MRS COLLET AND CHILD.
From the picture in the possession of Lady Lyell.

are common to us all. Wee are partakers of the greif and feare, as well as of the guilt and peril; and upon the same ground, which it seemes so affects you, have been encouraging one another to take occasion upon this day, wherein the Church celebrates the remembrance of a Physitian and makes publick supplication for the cure of all Infirmities of the soul, to sett in hand with the redresse of ours so many and so perilous distempers.

And some thing wee have conceived, which by GODS assistance wee are perswaded shall prove every way beneficial this way, if so be you draw not back through narrownes of heart, who by your forwardnes hitherto, as well as by Eminency in all other respects, have deserved and made good the Name of our CHEIFE.

If the Issue of this Busines lie upon my seconding (sayd the CHEIFE), you shall not, by GODS grace, find mee a Niggard, both for the Love of the things themselves, and of you. I should be ready (if it could be) to bee minted myself to make mony, if it be mony that is requisite for the promotion of these designes and desires of yours.

Wee are glad (sayd the CHEEREFULL) to have this liberal Promise, that you will not stick at any cost.

Nor any paines neither, nor sufferings, nor prejudice, whatsoever it may be in mine own particular, so it may be for your and the rest of this Familie their advancement in Pietie and Happines (sayd the CHEIFE). Thus I find my mind now, by GODS grace affected, and I hope by the same grace the effects shall be alwaies answerable on my part.

Though it be much which you have promised, dearest CHEIFE, yet it is no more then wee expected from you, according to the many proofs which wee have ever received from you of unparaleld Love (sayd the AFFECTIONATE). But now, leaving the prosecution of this matter to its own place and our return of thanks till the end, let us understand, I pray, what that Admonition is to us which lies included in the Name of this blessed Saint, and what should further be appliable to us out of this Festival, then that by the mention of a Physitian and remembrance of diseases wee should be invited to the Consideration of our own Infirmities, and directed to the meanes and cure.

Why, the meanes itself (sayd the CHEIFE) is in great part taught us in the Name of this blessed Physitian. What belongs to us by way of preparation wee shall find sett down therein, and if wee follow the prescript by putting in execution, I doubt not but the Cure shall follow speedily and happily by the power and mercy of the great Physitian of our souls, who never fails to perfect what hee begins in matter of Cure, except it be through the wayward default of the Patient.

I hope his mercy (sayd the MODERATOUR) shall keep us from such default; and that wee may the sooner goe in hand with what belongs to us, I pray you break the pitcher and let us see the light which wee are not yet aware of. Let us by the knowledge of the signification understand the mystery that lieth hid in this Name so much to our behoof.

The Name of Luke (sayd the CHEIFE), as the Learned in the Hebrew say, implies a lifting up, a rising againe, and a rising together.

And sounds in mine eares (sayd the GUARDIAN) as it doth in yours, a Proclamation, or rather warning-peice from heaven, that wee should joyntly with Love and Courage return to the prosecution of those excellent things from which wee are fallen. Let us lift up our eies to the Consideration, our hearts to the desire, and our hands to the receiving, and GOD shall fill us with the enjoyment of whatever wee pretend unto. Let us rise againe in our hopes, in our resolutions, in our endeavours, and GOD shall crown us with the performance of all our attempts. And let us doe it together by bonds of mutual Promise, of mutual encouragement, and of mutual Assistance, and I hope the wished event shall follow with speed and ease.

This fruitfull seed hath, I am sure (sayd the MODERATOUR),

made a proportionable Conception in every other of our minds, as well as it hath in yours, worthy GUARDIAN. But because there is no hope that any of them should come forth of that perfect and masculine feature as yours is, I shall advise the reserving of them to better opportunities, and now, in prosecution of these happy beginnings, propount that which I suppose, according to the right methods of Physick, ought first to be enquired into. That is, the searching out wherein lies the Malignitie of this disease under which we languish, and whence it doth proceed. And because I am perswaded that the painfull sence of this Infirmitie, which the CHEIFE hath made such profession of, may have made her more seriously and thoroughly dive into the Nature thereof, I shall, if you think fitt, impose this task on her.

Both in that it is likely she hath most studied what she hath been most affected with, and in that it is certaine she is in every other respect best able, it belongs to her alone (sayd the PATIENT).

Besides (sayd the CHEEREFULL), by how much I doubt wee shall have lesse of her help at last I hold it wisedome not to spare her at the first.

And her good discharge of this matter (sayd the AFFECTIONATE) shall, I am perswaded, serve both for an Introduction to her and a Confirmation to us of what is intended.

What is intended I know not (sayd the CHEIFE), but touching what is demanded, that I may not be of hindrance to that which above all things I desire the promotion of, I shall breifly tell you my opinion upon observation of that which I find in myself, without any note of Censure how it may be with others. I find, therefore, that the prime diversion from good things is bred in mee through a certaine tediousnes of mind and slothfulnes of Body, which instantly ariseth assoone as I come to the quick and life of good businesses. The beautie, the noveltie, and the honour of excellent things give such edge and encouragement to hope and desires as beares down all upon the first shock : but when it comes to the maine battail, the paines, the patience, the difficulties, the hazards, that like so many dreadfull files of pikes and shott stand in guard of vertue, and deny the prize of worthy Actions except they be forced by Combate and Conquest, doe so affright, as hope turns into dispaire, and desires into offence, and the only care is, how to quitt the feild with Creditt and safety by some handsome Colour of abandoning the Enterprize.

The next disturbance ariseth from the overmastery of self-will, that can by no meanes like but what is of its own devise, nor suffer the abridgement of any liberty either in appetites or affections, but must have its humour in the way of proceeding, or the way of proceeding according to its humour, and the intire choise in everything both for restraint and freedome.

The third Impediment comes from the want of witt and understanding, that is not able to proportion the desires and indeavours answerable to the measures of Abilities, time, circumstance, and other collateral duties. And so by an unorderly prosecution of times not only overthrows that particular which it cheifly intends, but breeds great disturbance and disappointment in other necessarie duties.

The disease, questionlesse (sayd the GUARDIAN), is right and fully discovered; Idlenes, Inobedience, and Indiscretion are those three bitter fountaines, whence that distemper and Infection flows, whereby our heads are so dazled in the contrivement, our hearts so unriveted in the prosecution, and our hands so maimed in the performance of those many good and vertuous exercizes which wee have on foot.

And the Cure is as evident (sayd the CHEIFE) by the Admission of Industrie, Humilitie, and Wisedome.

True (sayd the MODERATOUR). But how these should bee introduced into our minds is a matter of no small art and difficultie.

It is a point of skill and power (sayd the CHEIFE) only belonging to the Father of lights, from whom cometh down every good and perfect gift, such as these are; who gives liberally without grudging to them that ask heartily without fainting. Here then wee must begin.

Wee must begin, continue, and end here (sayd the PATIENT), by humble, instant, and continual Invocation, begging of GOD what is absolutely his grace, without any abilitie or deserts of ours. But yet must wee not neglect to sett our shoulders to the wheel, and to prick forward the Teemer if wee desire indeed to gett out of the slough wherein wee are fallen.

Indeed (sayd the CHEEREFULL), though health be the sole guift of GOD, yet must wee not neglect the Physitian, nor think to obtaine it (except upon extraordinary occasion) without use of the ordinarie meanes. Wee must therefore cast about to find out those remedies and medicines, by the application whereof GOD for the most part useth to convey these graces into mens souls.

Your proceedings, verily (sayd the CHEIFE), are right and orderly, but because it farre passeth that which my considerations went upon, I shall sitt a gladsome Auditour of what GOD hath put in your minds, without hope of being any ways a usefull Actour in your designes.

An Actour in the designe wee must needs have you (sayd the AFFECTIONATE), and the CHEIFE; but for being any part Authour in the Contrivement wee are content to spare you further then yourself shall think good.

That is all which I ment (sayd the CHEIFE); no waies the refusal of any performance which you shall impose on mee as beneficial and of furtherance to the busines.

With this assurance (sayd the GUARDIAN) wee shall goe on with more Confidence; and now without further losse of time, let us, I pray, come to the Resolution of this matter, which, consisting of three parts, I would distribute amongst you three, that the burden may be the lighter which is born severally, and the remedy may work more effectually with every one whilst it is of their own prescript.

Unlesse you explaine yourself, wee shall not know how to make answere (sayd the PATIENT), especially touching that matter of burden which you intimate.

No? (sayd the GUARDIAN). Doth it ly so easy that you feel it not, or doe you think because the CHEIFE hath taken all upon her you remaine discharged of that treble guilt of Idlenes, Indiscretion, and Disobedience, which she hath made such penitent Confession of?

Nay, verily (sayd the CHEEREFULL); but the sence and shame of our greater faultines hath rather stopped our mouthes, that wee have not the heart nor face to complaine before others. Well then (sayd the GUARDIAN), to make it more portable, I would counsail you to divide the matter between you, everyone taking the part which more especially belongs to them, singling out their own error, and afterwards setting down the remedy. The streigning of curtesie will make this division run out to greater length then time allows (sayd the MODERATOUR), if you put it on them. Besides, I feare Partialitie will cause it to be done unequally in the end; wherefore, I pray you to doe it for them.

If it may be without offence, sayd the GUARDIAN.

Doubt you not (sayd the AFFECTIONATE) but it shalbe with Increase of Love to you by GODS grace, and I hope not without benefitt to us.

Why, then (sayd the GUARDIAN), I would assigne Idlenes for your share; want of wisedome, or rather of Consideration, to the PATIENT.

Let it be plaine Indiscretion, replied shee.

As you please (sayd the GUARDIAN). And for selfwill, which only remaines behind, that the CHEEREFULL may take of herself.

Its very true (sayd shee). Nobody could put it upon me, if I had not a mind to it my self. Others oftimes make us idle, and nothing more common then to be made fools by better witts; but selfwill is alwaies and altogether of a mans own choise. Well, I take it now as you meane it, and by GODS merciful assistance hope ere long to cast it off so as nobody shall know mee any more by this badge from amongst the rest ; and for the better and surer accomplishment thereof shall humbly beseech you and all others not to forbeare the taking of that Authoritie which GOD hath given them over mee, but to use and improve it to the uttermost, not leaving mee to the bent and sway of mine own desires and Choises, but enforcing mee to the obedience of that which is truly good and profittable ; not seeking for peace sake to comply with my stubborn affections and opinions, but faithfully striving to subject them to the dictates of reason and Conscience.

Whether more nobly spoken or more wisely, I cannot tell (sayd the CHEIFE), but surely so as I should esteeme it more honour and more excellencie to be your partner in the accomplishment of these Resolutions then the cheif in taking the strongest hold in Flanders.

Authoritie that overaws is the soveraign medicine for selfwill (sayd the AFFECTIONATE), but for the correction of Negligence and sloth nothing will serve but Necessitie, if not of undergoing some penaltie, yet at least of giving an account. Idlenes is a base disposition, that never works but of compulsion. To think to rouse the drowzy monster from her lazy couch by any faire meanes, no, nor any foul neither, except it be a whip or a scourge, you must cast him thats sick of this scurvy upon the Pikes either of bodily suffering or shame ; and when he begins to feel his hands and his feet, you must be sure to keep him still in motion and action by a strict and severe exacting of the task imposed on him. I shall therefore for myself adde to the CHEEREFULLS request, that I may not be suffered to the guidance of mine own will, so neither to the auditing of mine own accompts ; but that they which truly love mee would look seriously and constantly to mee, that I may have no opportunity for neglect or ill performance of any of those good things that are either necessarily enjoyned or voluntarily undertaken by me.

It is very true (sayd the Patient) what the Affectionate hath told you. The best minds are like Clocks, that to goe right need dayly winding up. There be some very long, but no perpetual motions to be found. Many grounds there be of longer continuance in some kind of good things, but in the end theres alwaies an abandoning of them, but where the Necessitie of giving accompt holds forcibly. And where this Necessitie lyeth hard there may be evidently observed a greater progresse to be made by dull capacities then by the most excellent witts that can be found, if left at randome to their own libertie.

You have well confirmed this point (sayd the Moderatour). Now, I pray, lets have as good a discharge of your own part.

But then I shall not truly act mine own part (sayd the Patient).

How so (sayd the Guardian)?

If representing Indiscretion (sayd shee), I should give a wise Determination.

Well (sayd the Guardian), however you seeme to resent it most, yet in my opinion it is the lightest fault of the three.

I think so verily (sayd the Patient), and the easyest to be remedied, inasmuch as good directions are more readily obtained and more easy to be followed then such Authoritie found as can enforce obedience upon self-will, and such diligence as will exact accompt of Idlenes.

You have acquitted yourself and eased us (sayd the Moderatour) in the hint which you have given to reduce all to a short conclusion: That the likelyest meanes for redresse of all disorders amongst us is the Establishment of an Authoritie that may prudently direct and diligently exact the performance of all our good undertakings.

Undoubtedly (sayd the Guardian) there is no likelier course. And therefore I wish it may, without further demurre, be put in execution, taking the advantage which this approaching season affords, setting up a temporarie Authoritie, not for the Exercize of misrule but for the maintenance of good order, and choosing amongst our selves a Lord for this ensuing Christmas, that it may be kept not to the satisfaction of carnal lusts, but as it was at first instituted, to spiritual edification in grace and gladnes.

I know not (sayd the CHEEREFULL) why wee should not have the same libertie for good which others have for evill.

Nor doe I see any thing to the contrary (sayd the PATIENT) why wee may not attempt to bring in good things in a disguize of mirth and Jollitie, since in their own shapes they would hardly, if at all, gett admittance.

So it may serve to our own purpose, it little matters what others censure (sayd the AFFECTIONATE). Wee are too farre already engaged to have the worlds good word, and therefore I think it great Folly for feare or satisfaction of men to turn back to that which may lead us on the better to GOD. Wherefore I beseech you, without giving way to further traverse of this busines, to goe immediately to the choise, not of a Lord, but of a Lady; for so you have resolved, and so the constitution of our Family requires, it being the woman sex that exceeds both in Number and faultines amongst us.

That we may not seeme to usurpe Authorite (sayd the MODERATOUR), I pray let the Approbation of our Dearest Mother be made first known to the Companie.

She hath not only out of love to us and desire of our satisfaction (sayd the GUARDIAN), but out of her own judgement, given both consent and approbation to this matter, and that so much the rather, as hereby she shall have an Essay of their Abilities and vertues whom she hath appointed to succeed her in the government of this Family; which yet I hope, through GODS mercy for our joy and furtherance in faith, she shalbe long continued the Mother and Mistresse of.

Since the present Authoritie wee are now establishing is derived from her (sayd the PATIENT), mee thinks the new Title should not any way exceed the old, nor the translate be more large or lofty then the Original. I should counsell, therefore, that waving this ambitious stile of Lady, wee should content ourselves for our CHEIFE with one of those twaine of Mother or Mistresse which our GUARDIAN concluded with.

Verily (sayd the CHEEREFULL), it would be so much the more disproportionable to make any alteration, by how much by a particular disposition of heaven, as I conceive, not only the same Name by Baptisme, but the same surname hath by adoption befallen our CHEIFE. I would not, therefore, have any difference of stile made in the Identitie of Office, where GOD hath made an Identitie of Name in the distinction of Persons, for this reason cheifly, as it seemes to mee: That in the exercize of the same office there might be no difference in the latter from the former, but that in affections and actions she that succeeds might be altogether the same in this Familie, and this Familie in love and respect to her that succeeds, as they were to her that went before.

In this regard (sayd the AFFECTIONATE), as also that to the virgin Estate whereof our CHEIFE hath made profession, there is nothing more necessarie then Humilitie, both for Ornament and Guard, I suppose not only this swelling stile of Lady, but even that of Mistresse, may be better left then used, and with more grace to the Office and satisfaction of all parties, we shall name her MOTHER, which vertually includes the Authoritie of a Mistresse, and fully implies that which wee desire and shall expect from our Dearest CHEIFE, both now and hereafter, when GOD shall give her the full crop of Government whereof this present Action is the first fruits.

But will not the setting of Mother to the Mayd make a discord in musick (sayd the GUARDIAN)?

In old time (sayd the MODERATOUR) (and I doe not think the musitians of this Age are better Artists) there was nothing esteemed to make sweeter harmonie. Theres a Generation and conception of the mind as well as of the body, and sons and Daughters are to be begotten in CHRIST JESUS as well as in the Flesh. To them, therefore, that choose barrenes of body for more fruitfulnes of the mind, the Names of Father and Mother are no lesse truly, but farre more eminently due then to those who, by corporal pro-creation, uphold mankind. My voice, therefore, goes with you both for the same person and Name which you have propounded.

Why, heres an actual Choise mayd (sayd the GUARDIAN) before wee are aware. The Election hath outrun the proposal.

Theres no more, then, to be done but to pronounce the Choise (sayd the MODERATOUR).

I have not of a long time done anything more willingly (sayd the GUARDIAN). By an unanimous consent of the Electors our CHEIFE is elected to the place.

A faire place, but so full of danger, as in wisedome it cannot be accepted, and in Love it cannot be enforced (sayd the CHEIFE), in proof whereof Ile tell you a Storie, which you should long agoe have heard if opportunitie had served. But Ile say it was kept for an happy houre if it serve to prevent this Error and unkindnes which is now in hand. I am in good hope it will doe no lesse, if it make but half the Impression in you which it hath done in me.—

A yong man of great excellencie for Learning and Integritie of Life, being thrust upon a Bishopprick by his Freinds, desired respite before he accepted it to consult with an Unkle of his that had lived long in the desert and was full of the HOLY GHOST. The old man willed him to gett upon a great round globe that was sett up very high from the Earth, and thereon to bestirre himself, vaulting and tumbling; which he had scarce begun to doe, when, with a great perplexitie, he cried out, I shall fall. Come down then (sayd the old man), and act here upon the ground what thou canst not doe upon the globe. The other did so till he was overcome with sweat and wearines. Now rise (sayd the old man) and doe in this matter of the Bishopprick what thou thinkest best. The yong man, instructed by this Example of the great perril that attends great places, renounced the Bishopprick and gave himself to serve GOD with Humilitie and quietnes. The ambitious spirits of this world (sayth the Reporter of this storie, and that is sayd to be St. Hierome) might perhaps put off the matter with a scoff, as though melancholy and Age had made the goodman dote, but that it was confirmed by miracle. For it is certain (sayth he) that the yong man, shortly after his death, appeared to the old man, first giving him thanks, and then telling him, I had now been amongst the damned in the Hell if I had been of the Number of Bishops on Earth.

But your acceptance and Exercise of the intended Charges which GOD hath called you unto, shall, I doubt not, by his grace (sayd the PATIENT) prove to advancement of your glorie in Heaven, whilest it shall prove to the advancement of others good in this world.

It may be (sayd the GUARDIAN) the yong man was not so well qualified as you make him.

The Expression of his worth, indeed, is an addition of mine (sayd the CHEIFE), but no falsification of the truth. The whole frame of the story doth necessarily imply as much.

And when I shall have occasion I shall make no scruple (sayd the GUARDIAN) to recompt it as you have done. But since you stand so much upon the force of this Example, are you content to stand to the resolution that is made by the selfsame Authour that hath furnished you with this story?

Your demurre in so easy a question make us think (sayd the MODERATOUR) that you know some better answere then we are aware of.

When time serves, I doubt not but wee shall likewise find it (sayd the GUARDIAN).

But if neither Equitie nor Compassion move you, let your own interest prevail (sayd the CHEIFE), and be not less judicious then the Fox, that cast away the marble head that he found in the Statuaries shop, saying, However faire and lively thou seemest, yet, wanting brains, thou art a head of no worth at all.

That want of wisedome should cause miscarriage we have no doubt at all, except through your own willing default (sayd the CHEEREFULL). The supply of what is requisite is so neere and plentifully at hand. Heare my storie, and there shalbe no place left for exception.

The great Cosimo de Medicis, of whom we have heard so much, sent one to perswade Charles Pucci (it matters not whether I hitt the right Name) to stand for the place of Gonfullonier, the supreme magistrate of the Florentine Commonwealth, promising his Assistance to the uttermost, both for Puccis obtaining and exercising the same. The times being troublesome, the motion was rejected by Pucci, and many reasons alledged on his part. At last all are taken away save that of Insufficiencie in wisdome, which Pucci, a modest man, stood firmly to. Why, this of all the rest (sayd the other) needs least of all to be insisted upon. Would you accept the place if you had as much witt and understanding as Cosimo hath? If but as much as in his little finger I would make no scruple, sayd Pucci. Why, then, replied the other, when you are in the place, govern yourself altogether according to Cosimos directions, and then you shall not only have all his but your own boote, and the busines cannot but be well arranged.

There needs no application (sayd the GUARDIAN).

I understand your meaning fully (sayd the CHIEFE), and withall that, though there may be this way a supply of wisdome, yet even thereby will follow a diminution of Authoritie, which never is respectable indeed but when it is joyned with sufficiency in the same person. And this defect of Authoritie, which you sett down for such a maine point, I am sure passeth salving. The Issue will be the same as was between the frogs and the block. At the first tumbling down thereof into the water the frogs were much affected with feare and reverence. But when they saw by the lying still that it was but a block, they gete upon it, dancing and sporting themselves.

You doubt (sayd the AFFECTIONATE) we shall not give that obedience and respect which we ought?

Equalitie of Condition, Evidencie of weaknes, and Excesse of former Errors forbid, as well the exacting on one part as the giving of honour and obedience on the other, sayd the CHEIFE.

Heare my storie (sayd the AFFECTIONATE) and doubt not of the like Event.

When Amatis had by his vertue gotten the Crown of Egypt, finding that the meannesse of his original Condition made the people lesse respectful to him then they were accustomed to be towards former Kings, hee caused certaine golden vessels which had been used in the court to such homely uses as are not to be named, to be molten down, and of them made an Image, which he caused to be sett up in the most eminent place of the Citty. The beautie of the Idol drawing great concourse of worshippers, Amatis one day caused proclamation to be made, That since the basenes of the services which the gold had been formerly imployed about did not prejudice the Idol in their opinion, but they did as religiously adore it as any of the other Gods, they ought not, upon the remembrance of any forepast matters belonging to his private Condition, to derogate from that obedience and Honour which was due from them to his royal Estate.

I am overmatched, I see, both in power and policie (sayd the CHEIFE); but look to it well that you repent not when it is too late, as the unwary horse did after he had took the bridle in his mouth and let the saddle be put on his back.

Why, this adds Edge to our desires and Confirmation to our hopes (sayd the CHEEREFULL). These threats rather quicken then terrify our resolutions. Such a leader wee wish for that meanes not to goe but to run, that thinks not of creeping on the ground but of mounting up to heaven, that dare leave the shore and put out into the deep and charge boldly upon the very trenches of vice and folly. Wee have made no league with sin, albeit too often through error and weaknes we are overtaken and entangled by it. And though wee cannot with so much ease as you may, yet with no lesse desire, by GODS grace shall wee follow after that which is excellent in every kind. Your virgin Estate serves better then Wedlock to the attainment of Perfection, but doth not more necessarily require it. Wee would not, with the world to boote, take husbands, to have lesse Interest in GOD by that means. Its the hope of better serving GOD and the firmer unitiment unto him that inclines our Judgements to the married condition. Wee have made up the accompt, and find it cleare that theres no gaine of worldly comforts to be gott by marriage, except it be to them who look no higher then the Earth nor further then this Life. As for those who aspire unto heaven and intend the pleasing of GOD, its plaine the burden and the difficulties are encreased. Let us argue the matter without partialitie, and you must needs allow us not willingly to allow you to goe one foot before us. Ile put the Instance in some particulars. If Temperance be necessary to the Virgin it is doubly necessary to the married woman, who hath the charge of two bodies, her own and her childs, and therefore any error committed by her in this kind is double to that of the virgins. If the virgin overthrow her health, she beares the punishment herself. But what recompence can the Mother give, or what amends can she make, that through her disorder hath either marred the constitution or bred some incurable Infirmitie, so that the child through her default becomes lesse sound for the body or lesse perfect for the mind, that part, I meane, which followeth the temper of the body? As for Industrie . . .

Nay, deare CHEEREFULL (sayd the AFFECTIONATE), engrosse not all, I pray. Let mee have my share as well in the profession as in the confirmation of these matters. Its the first step to vertue to meane well, and the next to say well. I pray deprive mee not therefore of this benefitt, that by the obligation of my mouth, as well as by the purpose of my heart, I may be the more firmly engaged to the performance of what I now think and acknowledge to be right. Let me see, you are upon Industry. Thats my Cue, you know, more properly then any other to come upon. For Industry, therefore, worthy CHEIFE, take what part you please for yourself, and you shall see a double share belongs to us that are by you and our other friends designed for wives. If you must rise at midnight to keep your mind in frame, your soul in health, wee that have soules too and the care of a house besides, may not think of lying much longer as I suppose. I am sure it is the married womans Candle that is sett up for the watch in the Proverb. If you may not be idle, no not the turning on one hand, for doubt of falling into the enemies snares, how much doth continual Imployment belong to the married woman in the midst of so many dangers and hazards? What think you, that Envy, Pride, vanitee, wrath, malice, and all other fleshly lusts and desires stand in awe of an husband, or can at pleasure be shutt out of dores by a woman assoone as she becomes Mistress of the house? There is but one and the same way of Prevention, that is, by giving both mind and body their hands full of work, that they shall have no leasure for the entertainment of such bad guests. Painfulnes, then, and paines taking are in this respect the married womans guarde as well as the maydens; but when, over and above the care of the Estate and guidance of the house, burdens which a single life are free of are added to the wife, it must needs be yeelded that she shall not be able to goe through without a double portion of Industry at the least to that which is requisite for a virgin. As for the encrease of wisedome and exercize of Humilitie, which you are so much in love with, I pray give us leave to be partners with you and bring into stock no lesse for matter of desire and endeavour after them then you do. If GODS word must lie alwaies between your breast, to guide, to guarde, to glad the mind and heart, how shall not wee be allowed much more covetously to make provision in this kind, that are to venture upon a much more perrilous and troublesome way then that which ye have chosen? What ever you task us therefore in this kind shall be double kindnes as well in our acceptation as in your intention. As for Humilitie, it is the pale and rampier of maydens vertue, but it is the principal of all the wifely graces and the proof of all the rest. You can pretend to nothing, I am sure, in this matter for yourself but will be short of that which belongs to us if ever wee become wives.

You meane to exceed (sayd the CHEIFE), and I pray GOD

you may. To doe my best myself and to be passed by you is double gaine to mee. I should have rose from this seat the gladsomest woman alive for these last discourses of yours, if I had not been too unpardonably prejudiced by your former. You love mee not so well as I doe you, that no more regard my welfare then to thrust mee upon such a precipice. Let mee tell you another storie, if perhaps that may move you, Lamon. . . .

Spare your story (sayd the GUARDIAN), both of Lamon and of Ammon and of Goar: how one cutt off his eares to make him incapable, and the two other by sicknes and death gott dispensations from GOD for the Bishoppricks which men enforced on them. Well, suppose they did well, because they were holy men, and GOD directed them unto it for the terror of presumptuous Intruders, and not for the disheartning of them which are lawfully called and sufficiently enabled to the discharge of Offices and Dignities. And do you resolve, I pray, to submitt yourself to the Determination of the Authour whence you have derived these stories? His Conclusion in the same place shall be mine. The inference of all these examples (sayth he) is, that no man should seek for dignities, that he may not loose his Humilitie; that when they are imposed he should unwillingly accept them, that he neither run upon arrogance nor depart from obedience. Let him refuse as long as he well may, but let him not be obstinate, to the offence of good persons or the prejudice of good businesses, for it is no lesse pride to resist the just commandments of superiors then unjustly to seek for superioritie. He that takes honour to himself usurps upon GOD. He that refuseth, when GOD puts it upon him, rebells against GOD. You see by your own Doctors (for to this purpose I am sure it is what you shall find there sett down) that the perril is as great in denial as you imagine it to be in accepting. In the one is a certaine fault, in the other an uncertaine dammage. Doe, therefore, that which belongs to you, making answere not by words, but by obedience and submission.

Let not your feare trouble you; that it is which secures us; that keeping yourself in this disposition you will exercize your charge humbly, and then, without doubt, happily to yourself and us. Which GOD grant, making this daies work prove to his Glorie '

XI

ALL SAINTS' DAY, 1632

Gifts presented to the Chief—Simeon, Bishop of Selencia and Usthazanes—Tarbota, sister to Simeon—Lais—Martinian—Nonnus.

CHEIFE. The weightines of the Busines, which still appeares the more, the more I consider of it, makes mee now as unable to say anything upon my entrance into this place as I was of late upon your choyse of mee unto it. Confusion of thoughts then stopped my mouth, but now the Orderlines of Consideration hath confounded my understanding whilest going from point to point. I find nothing but disproportions in every part of this Composition. Theres too much Æqualitie between your personal worth and mine, too much difference between my Abilities and the thing you have put upon mee. I cannot reach the Alt, nor you fall to the Base. This cannot but breed a jarre. Nor can the discord of time be salved in your imposing this government on mee so much before the time. Stay till Necessitie enforce (and GOD grant that may be many yeares) and till Experience have seasoned mee for this place, if it must needs be mine. This Anticipation marres the consort. Many sufferings and much danger on all sides appeare in the pursuite of this Action, and little benefitt that I can see. Will not this hazard a giving over before wee come to an end?

PATIENT. Wee see not those terrors which affright you, and you belike see not those hopes which encourage us. Partial Consideration of yourself, worthy MOTHER, hath undoubtedly bred your mistake, especially in this latter point: whilest you terme the benefitt little wee apprehend greater then wee can possibly expresse. You shall see it in the end, and with Joy, I doubt not, give GOD thanks for making you his instrument of much better and more abundant good then you can believe.

CHEIFE. My unworthiness, which you know not of, makes mee feare the Issue of what you promise.

GUARD. Your feare is a fault. In things of your own choyse you shall doe well to looke upon yourself, and to measure out your hopes, and make your Confidence according to the scantling of your Abilities. But when GOD calls, though it be to never so great matters, wee must looke to his power, and remember that it is perfected in weaknes. The opportunitie that is now fallen, when wee least expected, and after that manner which wee could not have imagined, to make those settlements in body, mind, and Estate which belong to us in wisedome, and whereunto indeed Necessitie presseth us, makes us to beleive that the matter comes from GOD. Wee have, therefore, layd hold on the occasion, and layd on you the burden which, by joint desire of all, and by especial Injunction of them who have Authoritie, you are to take up. You have a good warrant, you see, to perswade you its GODS ordinance, and therefore you ought to have a good hope both touching the performance and the successe. I cannot think but wee must bee at some cost as well of paines as perril; but nothing like to the gaine which will follow for true profitt and pleasure. The excellencie of the thing wee aime at makes mee looke for opposition to speake plainly on all sides; but the mercy of GOD, to speake as freely, makes mee confident of the Victorie. *Through* GOD *shall wee do great Acts, and in his Name shall wee tread down our Enemies.* Goe on, therefore, with good cheare, and leave us to make answere, if any ask the question why wee have made your honour and Authoritie to outrun your Age and the common expectation of the world. Wee have reason in store to satisfy all indifferent minds, though it be not fitt to alledge it in your own presence, least wee should hazard the losse of that humilitie wherein your own safetie and the good discharge of this Office cheifly lies. Keep that intire and undefiled from presumption before, and boasting after things well done, and doubt not but GODS Grace shall make supply of all other sufficiency that is requisite for you; whether it be of wisedome or of Authoritie there shall be no lack.

If you put the allowances which the CHEEREFULL and the AFFECTIONATE have provided, you shall find the ballance even and wee shall find the peice good to the full value of that kind of soveraigne that it ought. Wherefore, laying aside all feares and care touching these matters, goe on, I pray, to the work of this day, first accepting those presents which are now offered you in testimony of Love and Honour, and towards the furtherance and perfection of the busines itself, and then making entrance into the performance of your charge by establishing the course that is to bee held in our storying. For that at least wee desire may by this meeting be settled, as being, if not the prime for worth or benefitt to ourselves, yet undoubtedly the most delightfull and most desired of all our other designes by the generaltie of our Family. I wish, therefore, that as wee intend their good in all things, so we may give you satisfaction in this.

CHEIFE. What your designes be, I know not; but for stories, which you so long after, my Resolution is, if you continue mee in the place, to make them serve for Christmas Cheare. You may casheere mee, if you please, but if you hold mee in, you must give mee leave to govern, as belongs to my profession. It must bee a very sober table that a virgin sitts at the head of, and simple cakes that are of her providing.

CHEER. Or els she shall make a foul solecisme. Chastitie no waies agrees either with fulnes or dainties; and though she keep within the verge of Temperance her self, yet if she occasion others breaking out, the soveraigne court of starrechamber will find her guilty of riot.

CHEIFE. Give mee leave to kisse those lips that have pleaded my cause so wisely.

CHEER. Theres no doubt, then, but my Law will gett passage when it comes to the question.

GUARD. Keep your Law till time serve. And now lett us goe to the tender of your presents, which will make way, as I suppose, to your desires in this and all other respects.

CHEIFE. True; for when you have put out mine eies you may leade mee where you list.

GUARD. You think wee meane to blind you with our Guifts?

CHEIFE. I am sure I shall loose not only my Authoritie but my Libertie, if I take them. Hee that thrusts a bone into a dogs mouth stops it from barking; and though you intend it not now, perhaps, yet you shall alwaies find it so: That he that takes a guift cannot by no meanes give reproof. No, nor good counsel neither. If you corrupt mee in the beginning I shall deceive you in the end. Let mee be free, if you meane to have me for an equal—how much more a superior? If you subject me with beholdingnes, how shall I be over you with confidence?

GUARD. Your feares light altogether wide of our purpose. Its the promotion of the busines which wee aime at, not the prejudice of your Authoritie. Wrong us not, therefore, doubly in your suspicions and in your refusal of that which wee offer in acknowledgement of Superioritie, in pledge of Love.

CHEIFE. If it be so indeed, Phocions Answere to Alexanders Messengers, when they pressed him to receive what their Master had sent, will direct mee and satisfy you. Alexander hath done kingly (sayd hee) in sending; Phocion must doe wisely in not accepting. Each ought to be allowed the Exercize of his own vertue. Carry back the gifts with the prayse of his bounty, and leave mee with the peace of my freedome and the prize of my Integritie. You say he bestows this upon mee rather then others for that honestie which he conceives in mee above my fellow cittizens. Let him not hazard to corrupt that which he professeth to Love. Let mee proportionably apply it, and it will, I hope, end the Contraversie. I accept your curtesy, I acknowledge your Love; but, I beseech, keep your gifts, that I may keep my Freedome and Fidelitie to you, I, and to others too; for I cannot forgett, I am sure, how I am bound by expresse promise heretofore, as well as by the Necessitie and decorum of the place which you have now put upon mee, not to take any gifts.

AFFECT. Not without Allowance, you meane, and therefore wee have provided that there may be no violating of your faith. See you there not only a dispensation, but an Injunction!

CHEIFE. You might have brought it out at first, and saved all these words.

CHEER. Wee had, then, lost much by the bargaine. Theres never a word but deserves remembrance, and more too. And though what you have pleaded semes not now to your purpose, I hope it shall to ours, making us more wary in receiving, if not altogether so absolute in refusing of gifts as you are. Lets heare, if you please, what your paper sayth.

CHEIFE. *Its fitt you should receive the gifts; but withall exact of every one Instructions how they are to be used and ordered.* Its lesse fitte now then before. Theres a double Incongruitie, in my Judgement, in taking of guifts to my profession of Virginity, as well as to my office.

PATIENT. Youl refuse the warrant then?

CHEIFE. Oh, no, however I understand not the latter part and like not the first; yet, in endeavouring to performe both, Ile prove myself the Daughter of Obedience.

CHEER. And ever may you be so. Its a greater title, and that which I more envy than that of MOTHER, which wee have put upon you.

AFFECT. Undoubtedly this last honour is but the Daughter of that first Exercise.

CHEIFE. Obedience hath been alwaies, I must confesse, both full of safety and advantage unto mee; and, therefore, I now feare the lesse, although I cannot but feare, considering mine owne weaknes and the force of gifts for perverting of Judgement and corrupting of Affections.

PATIENT. The very outside of my Present will dissolve all those Jealousies, which therefore comes as opportunely in the first place in regard of you as it doth deservedly in respect of itself, there being nothing under heaven that can challenge the precedencie of it, either for excellencie or for Beneficialnes. The purest gold of the earth is but drosse, the ravishing pleasures of the flesh are but dung, the most transcendent honours of the world are but Infamy in regard of these riches, those delights, that glory which this Book encloseth, offers, and leads unto.

CHEIFE. What, a Bible?

PATIENT. The everlasting word of GOD, the fountaine of wisdome, the Treasure of Vertue, the Wellspring of Happines.

CHEIFE. It is of a thousand times more worth, more honour, and more comfort then the tongues of Angels, much lesse yours and mine, are able to expresse, dearest PATIENT. Let us with silence, therefore, rather admire then with words goe about to sett forth that which is unutterable, the inestimable value of this holy Book, which I take from your hands with Reverence, with joy, with thanks to the infinite Goodnes of GOD that hath bestowed it on us. I salute it with a kisse in token of Love, and put it on my head in signe of Honour, and lay it up in my bosome as an incomparable treasure. I have applied the letter without; doe thou, O my GOD, apply the spirit of this thy Book within, that the light, life, power, and joy thereof may be imprinted on all the faculties and members both of the outward and the inward man. That by Beleif, Confession, and continual meditation

I H S

of those wonderfull things therein contained my soul, my Body, by Spirit, my whole man may be sanctified throughout with grace in this Life, and sealed up to the assurance of Glory in Life eternal. Say Amen, sweet JESUS, to the supplication of thy Handmayd. Amen, Amen.

GUARD. The Lord JESUS say Amen by enabling you to the accomplishment, which he only can doe, as Lord and Master. Wee as partners and fellow labourers with you say Amen by way of Petition, that you may have your hearts desire, and wee the hearts to desire and the happines to attaine what you have desired. And now prepare yourself for the entertainment of your next present, which, by your honoured Mother, our worthy MODERATOUR, is intended you.

CHEIFE. Both these Titles assure mee of a worthy gift, and fitting for mee for the present occasion.

MODERAT. I may not commend the gift, because it is so much mine, and I cannot tell whether I may properly terme it a gift or no, because it is already so much yours. But sutable it is every way, being altogether a motherly present. It is by a mothers right that I bestow it, and it is a Mothers Right that I bestow, that you may truly be invested in the realtie of Motherhood in particular, as well as in name and generalty thereof. I give you these now for children, whom I brought forth, Brethren and sisters to you at the first, that their benefitt may be doubled by your supply of what my Abilities reach not unto. I am content to part with you not my title only, but my Interest in them. They shalbe henceforth yours as they are mine. Are mine, I say; for I lessen not my proprietie, but rather double it in thus multiplying the Motherhood to them. They are become twise, nay, thrise, mine by this meanes. They are now my gift, and my grandchildren too, more then they were before. The enlargement of this Relation hath knitt the band the faster and the streighter. My affections are encreased towards them, in that they are become yours, the first of my Loves in this kind. My care is augmented for them, in that your comfort, the greatest of my Comforts, is now engaged in and upon them. I intimate not this tendernes, this solicitousnes, to stirre up yours. I know you will be to them in heart no lesse then I desire; in Actions much more then any can expect. But I make this declaration of the Intention of my Love to you, and of the unseparablenes of my Comfort from you, the rather to perswade these my children how you, as by all manner of well-doing, so in particular by the abundance of respect, Love, and faithfull service all their Lives long towards you, to endeavour the returne of those benefitts which they receive from you. So answering their obligation they shall accomplish duty to mee, and in the encrease of your Comforts double the ground of my blessing upon them. As on the contrary in causing you greif they should double their offence against mee, not only in regard that I shall alwaies be afflicted in your sorrow and wounded in your sufferings, but because I shall esteeme my self the cause, in having been the occasion, by this present action, in giving you prejudicial gifts. But I hope the best, and that my giving to you now shall prove as happy as my giving of you did to your Grandmother. The happy returne of that adventure with so much comfort into my Bosome makes mee confident, through GODS mercies, that this shall likewise be successfull.

GUARD. Its a good President, and well alledged for both parts. You have encouragement therein, and she direction. She hath a patterne of good performance, and you a proof of good speed in this Example. And, besides, the remembrance of her own Condition become so flourishing by Adoption ought the rather to perswade her with joy and hope to the exercize of the like vertue in her selfes benefitt to others. And so doing she shall indeed shew pietie at home and requite her Parents in specie, as Merchants speak, when the payment is made in the self-same Coine. For this matter serves not only to the purchase of a double blessing from you and her Fathers house, but to a full repayment of that which she owes to us and our Family, where into she hath been transplanted. For

I dare undertake on these termes to procure from the rest, whom it imports, as I now offer from my self, a formal acquittance and release of all claimes and demands whatever, that wee may have against her for the nourishment and portion that she hath divided with us, if she shall faithfully discharge what you and wee require. For however you made a more particular and full consignation of three of your own for her Children, yet the extent of her motherhood is no waies to be confined in those bounds, but must enlarge it self to the generalty of this whole Family, and in particular to my three, whom I likewise now sett over to her Motherhood, though not for cost, yet for care, though not for provision of maintenance, nor portions of Marriage and Inheritance, yet for furtherance of Education in their youth, for direction and government in their riper yeares, for faithfull Assistance and Counsel all their Lives long, for the performance of these, and these are the best parts of Motherhood. I now entreat her by what is deare unto her, and I enjoyne them, in requital, to answerable obedience and duty by the uttermost of that Authoritie which I have over them.

PATIENT. For the suiting of things the better, give me leave, by the presentment of a seventh, to make the gift more complete and proportionable. For seven, as it hath been generally above all others held the Number of perfection, so by the Pythagoreans, the great Masters in this Science, it was, as I have heard, more peculiarly attributed to Virginitie. It is, therefore, in both regards most fitt to this present. This your motherly travail tending not to life of body, but to perfection of mind, and the birth of these children being a fruit, not of your wombe, but of your Virginitie.

CHEERF. Wee have an equal part with you, deare PATIENT, in both the Mothers of this little one. And therefore, I pray, let us have likewise a part with you in the transaction, which I hope shall be comfortable to them both. The guift being yours, the Livery and ceizen shalbe mine. And that it may be every way answerable, I consigne her to you, not by the Name of her Familie whence she springs, but of her Vertue which she is to pursue. That, I am sure, will more recommend her to your Love then her Bloud, and she shall be more yours by being indeed the HUMBLE then your Neice.

AFFECTIONATE. If she degenerate not from the stock, theres hope sheel make good this and all other the best hopes that wee can have. What Modestie hath forbid in the rest, Justice requires to be performed in this last gift, that it should not passe without a recommendation of the givers worth, which truly is such as would adde prize to that which were of no prize in it self; how much more, then, when it is of the most soveraigne value that may be.

CHEIFE. The Excellency of the value beyond possibilitie or Esteeme of this sevenfold present, and the Admirablenes of the manner which you have used in bestowing it, hath carryed mee out of my self through wonderment. You must, therefore, give mee a longer time to recollect my self, before I can give any further answere then that, as I may not refuse, so neither know I how to accept such Love, such honour, and such bounty as you have expressed towards mee, beyond not only all desert, but all Capabilitie on my part of being answerable thereunto, if so be I know myself.

CHEEREF. You say well if it were youre owne, or your present strength that is to carry out the busines; but since, however great the want is in your self, there is abundance in GOD of what you most want, and excesse of bounty in him readily to bestow as much as you need, if it bee sought as it should bee, I have no doubt at all of your going through in everything to the joynt promotion of your own and our Happines. And in confirmation of these good hopes, and to the furtherance of their accomplishments, I make tender to you of this speaking present, which loudly and plainly tells how you may attain those abilities which are requisite for your Dignitie, and how you may preserve your humilitie, which is necessary to your person and condition, that so you may not loose your self in benefitting others, nor run the hazard of damnation in being exalted through the happines of welldoing.

CHEIFE. But that I see no engravement, and your words sound otherwise, I should have interpreted your meaning to be the old Inscription of Bells, *Fear God and · Honour the King.* But this, however it be good, is no waies proper to this Busines. Oh, now I have found it :—*The Bell touls to prayers, and rings out for the dead.* You would have mee alwaies to remember the last, and to be continually exercized in the first. And so I confesse neither Error before, not pride afterward, can hardly breed any Inconveniency to well-doing.

AFFECTIO. The continual Exercize of Prayer, which you are invited unto; the constant meditation of holy Scriptures, which you have promised, and the carefull Education of so many children as have been now given you, are three things that, the day being too short, you will alwaies be enforced to borrow of the Night, and oftimes, I suppose, to imploy it altogether in waking thoughts for the better performance of these businesses. In this regard, therefore, doe I here make tender, worthy Mother, of a needfull Instrument to this purpose.

CHEIFE. It is Vigilancy, I perceive, that you exhort mee unto. And that I may the more willingly sett about it, not only by compulsion of Necessitie, but by enamorment of Affections, I must desire you to light and sett up this Candle, which you have given mee, by giving mee a remonstrance of the beauty and beneficialnes of watching and watchfulnes, a vertue which, however, through the darknes of the Night, wherewith shee goes alwaies veiled, is commonly taken by the dreaming world for a Bugbeare, yet is in truth the joynt Testimony of all that have been admitted to the discovery of her face, approved to be farre away the fairest and most lovely of all other corporal exercises and perfections whatsoever. Take againe, therefore, your present, sweet AFFCTIONATE, till you have thus fitted it, and then with double thanks will I receive, and by GODS Assistance hope to put in execution, your good Counsel. And you, beloved CHEEREFULL, must shew mee the use of your Bell, both touching that which belongs to the Church and that which belongs to the Grave, ringing out a double peale by the relation of that which you find most observable in the death and in the Devotions of the great Personages of this Age. And you, dearest PATIENT, though I keep your gift, for I cannot be content to part with it, no not for a moment, yet I must desire you to unclasp it for my easier use by reading mee a lecture how I ought to read and meditate therein. The like favour I most humbly beseech of you, most honoured Mother, that you would to the gift of your Children adde the Rule of Education, that I may the better, by GODS help, performe the Mothership which you have imposed on mee. And this I think that task which the second clause of my warrant enjoyned mee to impose on you.

GUARD. It can hardly be better, and therefore I suppose the meaning is as you have made it. And now, since wee are to looke for no more touching this first point, let us passe on to the second; I meane the setting down what order you will have observed in this matter of Storying.

MODERAT. Let us make a tryal first, if you think good, before wee come to any settled determination. Matters of this nature usually come forth much otherwise in the performance then in the designe. Besides, it will not be amisse to see how the tongues and memories of the Actours serve before you give them their parts. Disuse is of great prejudice not only to the easines, but to the Abilitie of doing all things. Let this day, therefore, if you please, be for proof, and every one left to their own Liberty, so they keep themselves within the bounds of the Day, their Stories tending to make us of the number of those blessed Saints whose joynt and common Feast wee now celebrate.

CHEIFE. What you have propounded cannot be bettered. I desire, therefore, it may be accordingly performed, and that you, dearest PATIENT, would make the entrance.

PATIENT. To flee from Evill is the beginning of goodnes, and the first step to become a saint is made by leaving to bee a sinner. He that would be of their Communion must be of their Qualitie—holy as they are holy. He that committs sin cutts himself off from their Fellowship, and not only looses their Love, but makes them turn his enemies. They are all against him with Indignation that continues not with them in holines. If this were rightly weighed, it would prove a great restraint of sin and work the same effect in us at it did in Usthazanes, whom the angry frown and upbraidings of one poore Saint as he was lead fettered to the prison, brought to that sence of his misery, as to redeeme his sin he was content to lay down his life, which, how it happened, I shall tell you.

Sapores, the great Persian King, being incensed against the Christians of his Dominions by the calumniating accusations of the Jews and Magitians, by whose counsels his state and Actions were cheifly guided and ordered, began first to lay heavy taxes and mulcts on them, to their utter impoverishment, tauntingly affirming that, accordingly to their Law, they ought to submitt to whatever was imposed on them, and willingly to embrace spiritual poverty. And because he aimed not so much at his own gaine as their perdition, he gave the execution of this busines to barbarous minded persons, who added a thousand other kinds of torments to their cruel exactions, that so by the excesse of intolerable sufferings and oppressions on all hands, they might drive them to the denial of that holy profession which was become so costly and damageable unto them. But when, by the mercy of GOD strengthening his elect people, this course served not to the end that he entended, but rather to the contrary, they growing more zealous and stout in the preservation of their faith upon the losse of their goods, and their Affections, like a mighty fire checked with a little dash of water, breaking out more inflamed towards heaven by the sence of their present miseries; he proceeds to the application of more forceable Engines, thinking to quench that with bloud which he could not stifle with oppression, and wills that the Preists and Churchmen should be put to the sword, their Temples demolished, and their treasures and muniments confiscated. Amongst the first that were apprehended was Simeon, Bishop of Seleucia, eminent amongst the Christians for his dignitie and admirable holines of Life even in the eies of the unbeleivers. Having, therefore, no open crime to charge him with according to Law, they object suspicions of privy conspiracy against the State. They accuse him of holding correspondence with the Romane Emperors, and plotting with them the overthrow of the Persian Kingdome and Religion. Upon these pretences they bring him, loaden with chaines, unto the presence of Sapores, who furiously commands they should proceed in examination of him with tortures. The valiant Simeon, behaving him manfully and carelessely, without any shew of feare for the punishment that was threatened, or any signe of Reverence to the King as was expected, Sapores, with much passion, demands of him how it came to passe that he worshipped him not now, as he had formerly wont to doe. The difference of the cause, oh King, sayd hee, makes this difference in my proceedings. At other times I came not to that Intent for which I am now brought before thee, that is, to commit Treason against GOD, and therefore I then gave thee that honour which was due to thee as a king, but now I refraine from it, that I may the better preserve that honour which is due to the cause. For GODS cause I bowed down to thee as his Vicegerent on earth, but now that thou requirest I should bow down to Creatures, as to GOD, thou shalt have no Reverence at all from mee, least it should be interpreted to be any way done in Obedience to thy unjust command, or in derogation of that just worship which is due to GOD alone. Well, let that passe, sayd the king. If thou wilt not worship mee because I am a man, worship that glorious sun which shines into thine eies, the fountaine of light, and the well spring of all those benefitts and comforts which men enjoy in this world. I worship, answered Simeon, the Sun of Righteousnes, CHRIST JESUS, from whom this Sun, which thou so magnifiest, receives both light and glory, and from whose invisible vertue and power all those blessed Influences which thou attributest to this visible sun doe proceed.

Worship this sun, sayd the King, from which wee see and feel all our welfare to come, and I will adde honour and wealth to thy old age, otherwise I will cutt it short with painfull opprobious death. In vaine, replied Simeon, dost thou terrify mee with that which is my cheif desire, to suffer torments and death for CHRISTS sake.

Yet at least, sayd the King, if thou beest sencelesse of thine own good, have compassion of thy Fellows miseries, whose lives run hazard through thy obstinacy. For I vow the desolation of thy whole sect if thou persist in thy rebellion.

Thou shalt doe, oh King, what GOD shall give thee leave, sayd Simeon. To his good pleasure I committ the care of his own Church. As for mee, theres nothing can be so intolerable to endure as the performance of what thou enjoynest would bee. Sapores, perceiving that Simeon was invincible, and that both threats and promises returned back with disadvantage to himself, whilest they were so slighted by the other, willed him to bee carried to prison, that so both of them might have further respite to deliberate on this busines, being himself uncertaine how to proceed with Simeon, partly hoping that Simeon might by time and other meanes be wonne from his present Constancy.

Hereupon the Officers drag Simeon away with much despight, till comming to the Court-gates they mett with that which, causing much honour to Simeon, bred much amazement in them. Usthazanes, an old Eunuch of great Authoritie with the King, as having been his Tutor, sitting at the Entrance of the Pallace (as the manner of the Persian Courtiers was), upon Simeons comming to goe out, rose up, and with semblance of much Love and honour, saluted him as he passed by.

But Simeon answered his Curtesy and faire greetings with contempt and exclamations, turning away his face as if hee disdained to look on him, and bitterly upbraiding him for his Apostasie. For this good old Eunuch having been a zealous Christian was, in the beginning of the persecution, by the faire allurements and frightfull menaces of the King his Master, drawn away to the dissembled profession of Idolatry, and to the counterfeit denial of Christian faith which, like sparkes hid in a flint stone upon strong knocking, burst out by meanes of this sharp reproof of Simeon into the light and fire of an open and zealous confession. At first it speakes in silence by teares and sighs, but at last it proclaimes itself aloud by words and deeds. Hee goes home, and tearing off his rich apparel, as one of the cheifest accessories of his Error, hee cloathes himself with mourning, and returning to his former station begins with loud outcries to bewaile his Guilt and misery.

Wretched Usthazanes, sayd hee, with what heart canst thou endure the terror of the Judgement that canst not endure the Intimation of the Inditement? What will the Angry frowns of the Master breed in thee when the displeased turning away of the servant so amates thee?

Simeon disdaines mee and I cannot beare it. Oh, how shall I beare it when CHRIST condemnes mee? Simeons reproach confounds mee and makes my case farre worse then his thats hald in iron chaines to prison. Oh, what will the confusion of my soul bee when I shall see and heare the upbraidings of millions of Saints to the full of what it deserves, and find my self after hald away in chaines of darknes to everlasting torments?

Whilst Usthazanes is thus in the midst of his Lamentations there came some for him in the Kings Name who, having heard the matter, and much perplexed thereat, willed that hee should be instantly brought into his presence. Where, being arrived, the King prevents him, and with semblance of much kindnes demands the cause of his unusual habit and the ground of that sorrowfull Aspect which he saw in his face, and of those mournfull Complaints which hee had heard of by others.

Is there anything, Father, sayd Sapores, that is wanting to thee in my Pallace, or is there any person in my Kingdome so hardy to have done thee Injury? And if thou neither wantest any thing that thou desirest, nor sufferest any thing that thou oughtest, whence comes it that thou art thus afflicted, and with thy mourning and greif contaminatest the eternal joy and pleasure of my house?

Its no misfortune, O King, answered Usthazanes, that hath newly befallen mee, but my misdoing a good while since that thus torments mee, and causeth mee to disquiet thee and thy Pallace with my sorrow and complaints. Its the abundance of honour and favour that I received in thy Court that makes mee so full of horror and shame, and the too much satisfaction that I have given and taken in thy Pallace and to thee that have brought mee to this miserable condition in which I now am. Oh, would to GOD the uttermost of wants and injuries, which not thy Kingdome but the whole world could afford, had befallen mee rather then this which I have brought upon my self by counterfeit adoring of the sun against my Faith and duty both to the Divine Majestie and thee, for to both I am a Traitor in wickedly denying the allegiances which I owe to GOD, and in dissemblingly abusing the trust and confidence that thou hast in mee. I have fainedly broke GODS Commandments and fainedly performed thine. I am false in what I have done, and false in what I have not done, every way a perfidious and wretched Caitife. But if I have been a deceiver hitherto, Ile be so no longer. Ile return to that allegiance I owe to GOD. Ile renew the fidelitie wherein I am bound to thee. Ile cancel my hypocrisy by open Confession, and amend my secret Treasons by performance of publick service and faith to both. Heare, therefore, oh King, and mark it well. For I call GOD to record, that made heaven and earth, to avenge it on my head if I fail in what I now avow. If I had a thousand lives, I would rather give them a thousand times over to death and torments then once more bow down my knee to this visible Sun, which thou requirest, or deny any more that eternal son of GOD, CHRIST JESUS, whom thou blasphemest, to be my only Lord and Saviour.

Sapores being astonished at this strange passage, and imputing all to the Inchantments of the Christians, that had thus perverted, as he thought, the understanding of his beloved servant, after he had discharged the fury of his Indignation against them by many outragious exclamations and menaces, turning himself to Usthazanes endeavoured now with entreaties and promises, and then with arguments and perswasions, and last of all with bitter menaces and terrors to regaine him back to his utter perdition. But Usthazanes tells him resolutely that he would never more be such a fool as to worship the creature in stead of the creator, nor loose his soul for the preservation of his Life, nor make forfeiture of everlasting happines for the transitorie feeble pleasure of this world. Whereupon Sapores in great rage with him wills him immediately to be had away and his head chopt off for his obstinacie, as he called it; for his happy confession of the truth, as it was in truth. As the Officers lead him to Execution, Usthazanes remembring himself, as it were, of some important matter, praies the Officers to stay a while till he might send the King a message, and receive an answere, wherein, they willing to gratify him, he calls an assured Freind of his, a fellow Eunuch, and of special favour with the King, and desires him immediately to repaire to the King, And in my Name, sayd Usthazanes, humbly beg in repayment of all the faithfull service which I have done to his Majestie and to his Father before him, and in testimony of that favour and love which he hath made profession heretofore to beare mee, that he would now command that it might by open proclamation bee made known unto the world that I am not sentenced to death for treason or any other misdemeanour against the Law, but only for being a Christian and refusing to deny GOD at the Kings Injunction. Sapores hearing the request, willingly condescended thereunto, supposing that the bruit thereof would strike more terror and amazement into the minds of all men, and that a great Number of the Christians, seeing the rigour with which he proceeded against Usthazanes that had brought him up, and was so high in his favour, would by this meanes give over their profession, the maintenance whereof they might hereby perceive was in the Kings resolution unpardonable. This was the Kings hope in the grant of this Petition. But Usthazanes his aime was cleane contrary in the making of it. He considered that his former weaknes might perhaps have been an occasion of others falling or staggering, and therefore was desirous that the notice of his repentance and constancy might be as public as his Apostasy, that he might so recover by the example of his death whom he had mislead or endangered by the error of his life.

Usthazanes therefore, upon the obtaining of his suit marched on in great triumph. Every publication of the Cryer that was thus made sounded in his eares as if it had been a voice from heaven, assuring the remission of his forepast guilt and inviting him to the participation of infinitely better Comforts and honour then those which he abandoned at the present. In this Confidence Usthazanes gave up his life with so much joy as the overflowings thereof filled good Simeon full of comfort when he heard thereof. He neither felt bonds nor any other sufferings for the abundance of consolation which he received in the consideration of GODS mercy and Usthazanes his happiness.

The next day Simeon himself, being brought before the King and found immovable in his faith, was condemned with a hundred others to be beheaded, whom Simeon, like a good Captaine, animated with exhortations and arguments to the embracing of those lighter sufferings for the attainment of everlasting happines. To deny CHRIST, sayd hee, is death indeed, and to dy for him is the entrance into life and happines. If wee now save our lives we shall loose our souls for ever, and the deferring of death (for scape it wee cannot long) shall after a little while return to the utter destruction both of our souls and bodies which, if they fall now by the stroke of the sword for CHRISTS sake, shall by the vertue of his power be againe raysed up to the fruition of eternal happines, whereunto our souls shall immediately ascend. Thus did Simeon reason; but on the other side, the Magitians made long offers not only of life but of much honour and advancement to them if they would renounce CHRIST and adore the sun. But there was not any one that did not with great Courage run to the embracement of death rather then to the acceptation of their profers; only one old man excepted, Ananias by name, who by his pale visage and trembling joynts giving evidence of feare, Pusices, a great officer and cheif of all the Kings Artificers, stepping boldly to him, willed him to be of good Courage and not to faint now at the last. Shutt thine eies a while, oh Father, sayd Pusices, and take good heart, and in an instant thou shalt behold the light of GOD himself. Upon these words Pusices is apprehended and lead before the King, where, freely confessing his beleif in CHRIST and reprehending the Kings cruelty against the Saints, the King enragedly commands that his tongue should be pulled out by a slitt made in his neck, and so he died. And shortly after, his Daughter, a noble Virgin, was for the covetousnes of her estate maliciously accused and cruelly murthered.

The beginning thus made at Court, the persecution spred through the whole Kingdome. Amongst many admirable passages that stand recorded in the ecclesiastical histories, I cannot omitt the remembrance of one being a consequence of the present narration, and in sundry respects a fitting president for our selves. Blessed Simeon left behind him a Sister named Tarbota, a virgin of excellent beauty both of mind and body, being as vertuous as faire, although in this last she was extreme, as my Authour sayth. The memory of her brother makes her liable to the malice of his Enemies. They imagine that Simeon affronts them in his freinds and that they had taken but half their revenge of him whilest this other half of him remaines alive. Tarbota had withdrawn herself with two maids only into a retired place, serving God Night and day in prayers and supplications. This resemblance of her Brothers faith and vertue makes her become doubly odious to the Jews. To suit the punishment therefore according to their own evill affections and to make her equal in sufferings to whom she was so neere in blood and like disposition of mind, they perswaded the Queen, who languished of a sore and unknown Infirmitie, that Tarbota had bewitched her in requital of her brothers death, and that the obstinacy of the disease receiving no mitigation from the help of Physick was begun and continued by Tarbotas sorcery and Inchantment. The prejudicial opinion of Christianitie in general and the consciousnes of unjustice and cruelty used in the particular of Simeon make both King and Queen to give ready eare and easy assent to this wicked Information; and the desire of help and Intolerablenes of anguish thrusting on the Queens crudelitie, the manner of the cure which was propounded by the Jews was immediately resolved to be put in execution, although it seemes too horrible to recompt in womans eares. They tell this unhappy Queen that her life consists in Tarbotas death, the recovery of her health in the inflicting of torments, and the regaining of her Comforts in the exercize of unheard of Cruelties. Hereupon the blessed virgin is apprehended, and, after a most unjust processe framed against her upon fained suspicions of malitious accusers, is by false Judges condemned to be sawn asunder in the midst, and two parts of her Body to be hanged upon two Stakes a good distance one from another, which being done, the sick Queen after divers fond ceremonies is perswaded to walk up and down between them, her wicked Counsellors putting her in hope by meanes of this dismembred body to recover the lost vigour of her own.

It is reported, sayth mine Authour, that the incomparable beauty of Tarbota had so inveigled the heart of one of the cheif Magitians that he sent her word in prison that if she would consent unto his Love he would procure her both her own and her servants release from shame and punishment. The blessed Virgin sent him answere that the hearing of his message was more painfull and greivous to her then the undergoing of any torments or opprobries that could be invented, adding, if she had a thousand lives shee would rather loose them one after another then consent to the least defilement of her Chastitie. The desire of this close so proper for us hath made an enlargement of the Historie from what was at first intended, which was only the particular of Usthazanes, the application whereof is most evident and easie.

AFFECT. True. For if a Kings Favour and the highest honours of this country could not answere the losse of one Saints Love and esteeme, how timerous oughtest thou, oh my soul, to be of pulling the whole Court of Heaven their Enmitie upon thee?

He that thus setts the Saints by him shall hardly be overtaken with sin, at least not long kept under it. But if this repaire prove too weak at any time through strength of temptation, let him goe a little higher and he shall find a bulwark that sin can never scale nor conquer. Let him sett GOD before him, and he may boldly say with David he shall never fall. My story shall be a proof of the Inviciblenes of this Consideration, if it be rightly and fully improved, to confound all the fiery darts of Satan.

Lais was born in Alexandria of an honourable stock, with rare endowments both of mind and body, being witty and beautifull above all the women of her Age. The too much, or rather too ill ordered Love and wealth of her parents was the ground of her overthrow. For hapening upon a wanton and wilfull Education through her mothers fondnes and great estate, vaine desires and wicked appetites took such head in her that, breaking through all restraints of shame and conscience assoone as she came to liberty and opportunitie, in riper yeares she gave herself over to lasciviousnes to work uncleanes with greedines.

This wretched life of hers, and the death and destruction of so many other souls comming to the eares of Paphuntius, a man of great renown for holines amongst the inhabitants of the desert, after he had in much affliction and anguish of mind, with many teares besought GOD for the remedie of so many mischeifs and so much sin as rose by this occasion, being, as it is presumed and as the sequel shows, inspired by GOD (for otherwise it had been perhaps too bold a resolution), he changed his sackcloth into costly garments, and having washt his body, trimd his haire, and every way tired himself after the manner of wanton Lovers, he goes to Alexandria, and entering into Lais her house, without more adoe, to avoyd idle words, puts the price of Iniquitie into her hand. She conceived his meaning though he sayd nothing, and thereupon led him aside into a stately roome.

Paphuntius lookes about him wistly, and Lais, to secure him for what she thought he was afrayd, shutts the dore, presently telling him that they were safe. But not secret enough, replied hee. Then follow mee, sayd shee, and carryed him into an inner roome. Here nobody can see or heare us, you may be sure, sayd Lais. Not sure enough, sayd Paphuntius; is there yet no more private Chamber? Yes, my Cabbinet is more remote, and altogether fitt for your shamefast heart. With that she unlocks the dore, and smilingly tells him, Now you may be bold, for but GOD in heaven, none can see nor know what is done here. The holy man that looked for this Cue amazedly made answere, Doe you then think there is a GOD that sees all? I know it, sayd she, that nothing can be concealed from his eyes. And doe you, sayd he, withall beleive that there is a heaven and a hell? I beleive both, sayd she, and withall that sin leads to the one and the service of GOD to the other. And with that she sighed deeply. Thou doest well, sayd Paphuntius, to sigh, for woe is thy case above all others, that shalt give an accompt not only for thine own, but of all those other soules which through thy meanes run headlong to damnation; and answerable to the abundance of thine Iniquitie shalbe the excesse of thy torments. Consider, oh Lais, what it is thou doest, and whom it is thou dost offend: No lesse then the Infinité Majestie and goodnes of GOD, that hath given thee thy being, that hath given thee that beauty, witt, and grace, whereby thou pleasest others, and wherein thou pridest thy self. And yet is all this little or nothing in regard of that which he hath done for thee in making thee a Christian, in offering thee a Crown of happines, in affording thee all possible meanes to attaine it. Tell mee, for which of all these benefitts is it that thou heapest Injurie upon Injurie and settest thy self, as it were, to outvy his mercies with offences? Why art thou so ungratefull to GOD alone? If to him that gives thee gold (how much so ever it bee, the value is easy to be estimated) thou givest thy body, though with the penaltie of eternal damnation, how much more just and necessary is it to make returne of some good fruits to GOD, that hath given thee all that which is worthy love in thee? And not only so, but hath given himself beside, hath shed his bloud, hath layd down his Life for thee, and all this with the promise of eternal blessednes. Tell mee, is it sufferable that a woman loved by her spouse, equal to his own life, should bestow the jewels which he gives her upon Adulterers? Tell mee, I say, and let mee know wherein the difference lies on thy part, that turnest this Excellency of understanding, of speach, of beauty, which CHRIST hath bestowed on thee, to the service and satisfaction of the Devill. Remembrest thou not how he betrothed thee unto himself, and how thou plightest thy Faith unto him in thy Baptisme? Thinkest thou that he will alwaies beare what he hath hitherto borne? Let that which is past suffice, and take advantage of this time and this meanes that he now offers to redeeme thee out of the snares of Hell. How many Millions, thinkest thou, ly buried there that have not committed the thousand part of those sins which thou art guilty of? Shall his goodnes towards thee in so long-suffering be the ground of thy going on in sinning against him? Wilt thou therefore adventure to offend him, because he hath so long spared thee? Loose not this occasion, that thou loose not thy self. Deferre not thy conversion least thou diminish the helpe. There is nothing of moment but Salvation which, if a man overslip, he can never regaine nor make amends hereafter if he work it not out rightly whilest he is in this world. For GOD that doth pardon worlds of sins upon repentance in this world, pardons none at all when men are gone out of it. So that he that dies in sin is certaine to be damned. And therefore, because wee have no certainty of Life, we ought to make no putting off to repentance and conversion. Whilest Paphuntius used these and other like arguments, the Spirit of GOD working powerfully by them, Lais, that stood attentive, fell at last a trembling, and after a floud of teares that burst out of her eies, casting her self at the feet of the holy man, besought him to tell her what she was to doe. Whereupon, giving her some Instructions for the present, and commending her to the Grace of GOD, he willed her to come unto him in the desert at the end of three daies. Paphuntius departed, and Lais, to testify her own and to provoke others repentance, making a pile in the market place of all her goods and riches, with her own hands sett fire to them. The rest of the story is very admirable; you shall perhaps heare it at another time. Now let it suffice to know that she lived most penitently and died most happily; and that which you have heard was the ground of her conversion.

CHEEREF. If neither dread of GODS Majestie nor Love of the saints Fellowship prevail, yet is there a third way of preventing sin by putting ourselves upon a trial how wee could beare the punishment that is certainly due unto it; to which purpose I shall tell you a story of no lesse admirableness then those you have already heard.

There was a holy man named Martinian, who, having served GOD from his youth up, was by GODS grace for the benefitt of others endued with the guifte of miracles, so that he cured many Infirmities by his prayers only. The extraordinarienes of this gift and the eminency of his holines above all others of his time, having bred a great admiration and so a continual discourse in the famous Citty of Cesarea, from which his solitary habitation was distant but a few miles, being seated upon a desert mountaine ; it came to passe, that as one day divers of the cittizens were publickly reasoning and recompting sundry great matters which GOD had wrought by him, making the prayse of his holines the close of every sentence, a woman of the world that heard it as she passed by, being put forward by the Devill, stept boldly in amongst them, saying, What a wonderment, Masters, doe you make of this mans holines. Its an easy matter to be good where theres no opportunitie of being evill. He is rather to be deemed wise for having shutt out the temptation then vertuous for having conquered sin it self. To keep Innoceney and Intregritie in the throng of the world is the proof of a Saint, but to keep it amongst beasts in the wildernes needs no such grace, nor deserves any such prayse as you give to this man. It is evident that straw is as safe as stone from burning whilest it comes not neere the fire ; but let him come to mee or let me goe to him, and if I enflame not his heart and provoke him to folly, I am content not you alone, but the Angels themselves shall doe him reverence. The rest of this passage is not worth compting. The issue was, These foolish words were approved, and the wicked offer accepted, and an agreement presently made between this bad woman and worse Company, that she should make the trial, and if the successe were answerable to her promise she should have a reward in mony besides the praize of a good witt.

Whereupon she went home, and having apparelled herself like a wayfaring person, a meane coat girt about her, a staffe in her hand, and a bundle under her Arme, she made directly for this holy mans cell, whereat she arrived about an houre in the Night. Before she came neer she sent forth her cries : Man of GOD, for that LORD JESUS sake whom thou servest, and for love of whom thou hast left the world, I beseech thee give me shelter for this Night, that am tyred with a journey, drowned with water, and if thou succour not, in hazard to be dead through cold and hunger, and certaine to be devoured of wild beasts before morning. I have lost my way, and though I knew it I have not strength to goe. Despise mee not, however I be a sinner, yet cease not to be the creature of GOD. With this she began to weep and wail aloud. Martinian, that was at his prayers, rose up, and opening his window and seeing the woman, and perceiving that it rayned indeed, as she had sayd, very terribly, in great perplexitie of mind began, as he whose heart was continual in heaven, to reason with GOD. Ah, LORD, what shall I now doe? If I leave this woman abroad shall I not break the Law of Charitie and be guilty of her bloud if she perish? and if I let her in shall I not bring the fire into my bosome? Help mee, LORD, for I am in a great streight, and danger presseth hard upon me on every side. Let not mine enemies triumph over mee, neither let them say So would wee have it. Having thus prayed, he opened his dore, and after he had kindled the fire, giving her some dates, the only food which he lived with, he bid her rest her self till morning, and then in GODS Name goe on her journey. This done, he withdrew himself into an inner roome, and shutting the dore began to sing and pray his Psalmes as he used, and so long he was safe and quiet. But when rising from his prayers he layd him down to his rest, the messenger of Satan began to buffett him, and though he strove much, yet not being able to drive out evill thoughts he past a wearisome and watchfull Night, and in the morning rose much afflicted, doubting that the holy spirit of GOD had forsaken him, since his brest was now become such a sink of uncleannes. He had scarce sett his foot over the threshold when he was ready to pull back againe, such amazement and feare came on him to see a goodly woman in rich habiliments instead of a desolate creature that he had left in the Roome overnight. Recollecting his spirits, he demanded who she was, and how she came there, and what diabolical habit and dresse she had got. I am the woman, sayd she, whom thou yeasternight receivedst with so much charitie, and these ornaments are the bundle which I brought with mee. I pretended error for my comming, and pleaded Necessitie and danger for entrance, but it was Love that indeed forced mee out of mine owne house, and desire to enjoy thee, of whose true worth I have heard so much, that hath made mee take such paines and run such peril. The best of Cesarea would think it happines to be possessors of that which I now make tender of to thee. Bee not wanting to mee, nor to thyself in that which thou mayest with so much advantage accomplish, making exchange of misery for happines. For tell mee, I pray, what it is thou aimest at. More then heaven I am sure it cannot be, and thats as open to the married as to virgins; as accessible to him that eats as to him that fasts; as nigh him that sleeps as to him that waketh. Doth not Paul himself say that Marriage is honourable? And which of all the Patriarchs canst thou find with not one wife at least? how many of them two or more? Doest thou hope to passe them in glorie? If not, what needs thou take another path then they went? When she had thus spoken, or rather the Devill in her, perceiving by his change of countenance that the infection began to spread, she came neerer, and with smiling cheare laying hold on his hand, What is it thou doubtst of, my Martinian? sayd shee. Alas, sayd the conquered Saint, deeply sighing, If I take thee for my wife, whither shall I carry thee, or how shall I maintaine thee? Take no thought, replied the lying spirit through her false tongue; I have wealth in abundance; only now give mee satisfaction and all shalbe thine. These last words past like a canon shott through Martinians heart, laying all the holines of his soule flatt on the ground, and he without more adoe was going to the surrender of his body, when remembering himselfe a little, Stay, sayd he, a while; let me first goe out and see whether all be safe, for oftimes about this houre there come people unto mee, some for one, and some for other occasions; and although the sin cannot be hidd from GOD, yet it is best for avoyding of scandal to prevent the knowledge of men. Having so sayd he mounts up the hill to make the better discovery. And whilest he lookes about with horror in himself, GOD lookes down upon him with mercy, and sends a strong and powerfull Inspiration into his heart that he should consider well what it was he did, and what it was he lost, whom it was he pleased, and whom it was he should offend. His eies were no sooner open, which concupiscence had before blinded, but feeling his error and seing his danger, he runs into his cell, and flinging a bundle of Leaves and other light matter upon the fire, assoone as the flame began to kindle he steps into it, crying out aloud, What thinkest thou now, Martinian? Is it good being here or no? If thou canst not endure this blaste of heat, how wilt thou endure the everlasting furnace of hell? Goe to now and take thy pleasure with that woman yonder; thats the ready and sure way to the lake of brimstone and fire. Thus crying and thus burning he stood, till the fire having gott the mastery of his strength, and supplanted his feet, he fell down upon the ground. And then with a floud of tears and sighs, lifting up his hands, he fell a begging of mercy and forgivenes of the sin which he had committed in intending. Having so done a good while, at last he began to say the Psalme that begins, Truly God is loving unto Israel, even to such as be of a cleane heart. The woman, that stood by and saw all, being moved by the self same spirit of GOD, that her repentance might begin whence her sin took rise, tearing of her goodly rayment, flung it into the fire, and having clothed herself with what she first came in, casting herself down at Martinians feet, besought him to pardon what she had done, and to pray for her, For I am, sayd she, the wretchedest of all sinners; but henceforth I will serve GOD, and none but him, nor will I ever return to mine own house. Therefore tell me what I shall doe. The Devil thought to entrap thee, and behold, by the mercy of CHRIST he hath lost his bait too. Hee thought to make warre on thee by my meanes, and through the power of CHRIST and thy means I hope to make warre on him without peace or truce. The Deceiver is deceived, and the crafty is taken in his own wiles. Oh, the wisedome and the mercy of our God! What shall I give unto him for all the benefitts that he hath done unto mee? Tell me, thou man of GOD, what I shall doe for the cancelling of my sins, for the securing of my salvation? Whilest she thus spake the teares stopped her mouth; and Martinian, seeing by the truth of her sorrow the unfainednes of her conversion, having given double thanks to GOD for his own and her deliverance, after divers holy Admonitions and Instructions, dispatched her away, giving a token of recommendation to certaine holy women in Hierusalem, by whom she was lovingly received and instructed. There she lived twelve yeares with great strictnes, and at last died with much happines. As for Martinian, it was full seven months space before he was whole of those cruel wounds which he had received by this meanes.

CHEIFE. Your Stories have been of sinners Conversion wrought by meanes of Saints. Mine shalbe of Saints perfection encreased by meanes of sinners. Nonnus, being chosen from the Monastery of Tabenensiora to the sea of Eliopolis, was, upon weighty occasions of the church, sent for with eight other suffragan Bishops by the Patriarch of Antioche. Being come and lodged neer St. Julians Church, as they were one day sitting all together in the porch thereof, their attendants and much other people being with them, the Bishops besought Nonnus, who was best able, to bestow on the Company some words of Exhortation; which he gladly did, to the great Edification of the hearers. In the midst of this holy Exercise there comes by on horseback (after the manner of great personages) a famous Curtesan, waited upon by a Number of slaves, both men and women. Her garments were embroidered with gold, sett thick with precious stones even to her very shoes. Her haire, Neck, and brests were bare, save for the covering of a rich chaine and other jewels. And ever as she rod her eies went rouling up and down, now glancing upon one and then upon another. The smell of her perfumes, as she came neer, having diverted the intentions of these religious Persons, they began to look about, but had no sooner spied the cause, but, abhorring the spectacle, the most of them turned away their faces; the Bishops, over and above, fell a sighing for compassion of such sin and danger. But the holy Nonnus, cleane otherwise, fixing his eies upon her, left not to follow her with Attention till she was cleane past out of ken. Afterwards turning him to the Bishops: Tell mee, Fathers, sayd he, hath not the sight and bravery of this woman made a great Impression and commotion in your minds? When none made answere he layd his face upon his knees and fell a weeping bitterly, which, having done a while, he lift up himself againe and demanded anew, Say, I pray, hath nobody here been delighted with the view of so much beauty and so many ornaments? But everybody keeping silence, as at first, Nonnus sayd, Well, I, for my part, have had exceeding pleasure in the beholding thereof, for I am confidently perswaded that at the day of Judgement GOD will bring forth this woman as a pattern to try us by, and take our accompts touching the discharge of those offices which he imposed on us. How many houres, think you, hath she wasted in trimming and adorning herself, that there might be nothing wanting to the satisfaction of her own vanitie and of her Lovers wanton expectation? And yet are they but wretched men, that are of no worth to-day and nothing at all to-morrow. But wee, which have our Love and our spouse in heaven, in regard of whose beauty the sun and the moon are dimme; that pretend unto glory and unto pleasures that passe all possibility of apprehension for the excellency, and shall never have an end in the enjoyment, trifle out our daies without any care at all of washing away those staines which wee know and confesse doe make our souls utterly uncapable of such honour and happines. Having thus spoken he started up, and taking mee, sayth the Relatour, by the hand, he goes towards his Chamber, where he was no sooner entered, but kneeling down and knocking his brest, he thus cryed out: Pardon, oh pardon, my Lord and my Saviour CHRIST JESUS. Pardon this wretched sinner, whom a vaine woman hath outstripped in care and diligence, in as much as she doth every day more for the adorning of her body with vanitie then I have all the daies of my life done for the adorning of my soul with vertue. With what face shall I ask, with what words shall I hope to obtaine, the forgivenes of this guilt? There is nothing can be hid from thy eies; thou seest us both, and canst well tell who wee are. Thou beholdest well what each of us doth, and knowest for whose sake wee doe it. I am a Preist that come every day to thy table, and am all the day long conversant in and about holy mysteries; and yet how negligent am I in paines, how niggardly in care to make myself acceptable and pleasing unto thee! She is a woman and a sinner, and yet makes no spare of cost, nor even makes an end of study to make herself pleasing and lovely unto men. So that, woe is mee! but for thy mercy I should have no manner of hope, as I can find no manner of excuse. This he sayd at present, and gave not over to weep and mourn in the same kind all the day after. Sunday came, and the Bishops being assembled with the congregation, after the reading of the Gospel the Patriarch gave Nonnus, who satt next him, the Bible, desiring him, out of that living fountaine, to water the people with the doctrine of salvation. The holy man, answering by Obedience, went up into the pulpit, and there, not with premeditated words of Eloquence, but by manifestation of the truth and in the power of the spirit, wrought so effectually upon his Auditours, making remonstrance of the horrors of sin and the terror of the punishment due thereunto, that their hearts melted within them through dread and shame. Amongst the rest this sinfull woman was one, who, whether out of Curiositie to see Nonnus, perhaps, of whose strange Action she might have heard, or otherwise—whatever the cause, was surely by GODS ordinance—was that morning come to the sermon, a thing she had never before done, being not only a harlot, but an Infidel. But by how much her understanding was lesse, by so much did her sence and apprehension of what she heard exceed others. If others were moved, she was wounded. Every word that passed through her Eares peirced quite through her soul. Her eies ran down like fountaines, and not her face only, but her very garments were spoiled with teares. The sermon ended, and she come home, she immediately dispatched a couple of her servants to Nonnus with a letter in these words.

To the holy Disciple of CHRIST, the sinfull Disciple of the Devill. I have heard tell of thy GOD that he came down from heaven to save men on earth, and that in proof hereof, though he make the Cherubims tremble at his lookes, yet he made himself a companion of Publicans and sinners; that he disdained not to reason with a Samaritan woman, a great sinner, at the well of Samaria; and how that he thereby converted her. All this I have heard of thy Master. And now, if thou be his disciple, it is not just that thou shouldst despise a sinfull woman such as I am, denying to speak with mee, considering that I therefore desire to talk with thee that I may be directed by thee unto CHRIST JESUS.

The holy Bishop, having read the Letter, made answere againe by writing.

CHRIST JESUS knows well who thou art, and takes good notice (for it cannot be hid from him) what thy meaning and desire is. I pray thee, goe not about to ensnare mee, for I am a sinfull man, but yet the servant of Almighty GOD. But if it be JESUS CHRIST indeed whom thou longest after, and faith in him that thou pretendest unto, and for this cause thou desirest to speak with mee, thou mayest come and doe it in the presence of the Bishops with whom I lodge. For but before them I will not yeeld that thou shouldst say anything at all to mee. The poore sinner, having read this letter, without further adoe went to St. Julians Church, and finding Nonnus, who had warning thereof, in the company of the Bishops, casting herself at his feet and holding them streight, sayd unto him, I beseech thee now shew thyself like unto thy master, and drive me not away, however I deserve, but make mee a Christian. I confesse I am an ocean and abisse of Iniquitie, and therefore I pray thee to baptize mee.

Nonnus causing her to be taking up, made answere, The

holy canons forbid to give Baptisme to a harlot, except she give security not to return to her forepast wickednes. She hearing this fell down againe, and washing Nonnus his feet with teares and wiping them with her haires, spake thus: Father, thou shalt give accompt to GOD for this soul before his dreadfull Tribunall, and all my sins shall be sett over unto thee, if thou delay to baptize me and wash my soul from those infinite staines with which it is polluted. I pray GOD thou mayst have no part with him amongst his Saints, but that thou mayst be cast in his Judgement, as though thou hadst denyed him and offered sacrifice unto Devills, if so be thou doe not this day make mee the spouse of CHRIST, and present mee before him without spott of sin. The Bishops and other Preists that stood by hearing these words and seeing such Zeal and Humilitie, cryed out, They had never in their lives heard, much lesse seen, such a passage as this was; and streightwaies commanded mee, sayth the Relatour, to goe and advertize the Patriarch and to desire him to send some holy woman of good understanding to instruct and comfort this poore soul. The Patriarch, hearing the matter, was full of joy, saying it was his expectation before that GOD would doe such great things as these by the meanes of such holy men as the Bishops were; and immediately sent with us a godly matron, who was the cheif amongst the women dedicated unto GOD, and named Romana. When wee came, sayth the Authour, wee found the poore soul at Nonnus his feet, and though hee strove to make her rise, yet would she not till he told her it was to baptize her. Thereupon she stood up, and he bid her call to mind all her sins, and repent heartily for them. My sins, replied she, are more in Number then the sand, and in heavines they weigh down the sea itself; yet have I confidence in GOD, that through his bounty and goodnes he will forgive mee them all. How art thou called? sayd Nonnus. My Parents, sayd she, at my birth gave mee the name of Pelagia, but the Cittizens of Antioch call mee Margaret, for the many ornaments of Pearles and other Jewels that I have used to sett forth mine own vanitie and to provoke others sensualitie. Thy right name, then, is Pelagia, sayd Nonnus, and so it shalbe still; and hereupon baptized her, and afterwards committed her to Romana, willing her to instruct her in the perfect knowledge of the Christian Faith; which done, the Bishop went home, and turning himself to mee (sayth the Relatour): This day, brother (sayd hee), is to be kept by us with great joy and good cheere. The very Angels make mirth, and it is fitt that wee should doe likewise. See, therefore, that wee have oile for our meat, and let us drink a little wine also; for wee have made a good purchase for our Master in the regaining of this sinful woman.

You are desirous to heare the end? The Admirablenes is that which now hinders. Quiet your expectations for a while, and they shall be doubly satisfyed, when you shall have the rest both of this and those other stories which now remain unfinished.

XII

ST. ANDREW'S DAY, 1632

The Story of Lais concluded—Ephraim—The Father's Inheritance —Sir Thomas More's Story of the Juryman—Nonnus, Pelagia, and the Devil—James Devize and the Devil—Mrs. Catharine Stubs and the Devil—Inigo, King of the Draves —Amadens, Duke of Savoy—The Story of the forty Martyrs concluded—The Emperor Valens and the Christian Mother of Edessa—Oswin, King of Northumberland, and Bishop Aidan.

GUARDIAN. Though the Admirablenes, that was intimated in the rest of those two Stories which were left unperfect upon your last meeting, gave just ground of excuse for not proceeding in the recompting of them at that time, yet hath it so much encreased our desires since, as wee cannot willingly give consent to the beginning of any new matter till this old be finished. What became of Lais, and what became of Pelagia ? runs so in our minds, as gives no admittance to new thoughts till these be satisfied. You did much amisse for your own quiet, as well as ours, in going off with such a close, if you ment to deferre your going through with the Relation. You have made us restlesse through Expectation, and wee are purposed to give you no rest through Importunitie till wee have from you the full accompt of those wonderfull passages which are by your own Confession yet behind in these two stories.

MOTHER. The force of your reasons as well as of your desires beare down my former resolutions, and I see no colour, as I have no power, to wave what you propound. But I hope you will offer the same Justice as you exact, and wee shall have the full supply of what was in any kind wanting to the complement of the last daies work, as well as to these particular stories. If you distraine for our Arrears, you cannot of Equitie think of going free yourself without paying anything at all.

MODERATOUR. We cannot deny but you have right, and that were a double wrong, to presse you to make full weight, if we intended not to bring in our own parts of this Assessement. You look for stories, and you shall have them, and anything els that you desire, so you performe now what wee long for. Assoone as you have made the first of your stories perfect you shall have both ours. Wherefore, I pray, let the AFFECTIONATE proceed where she left.

AFFECT. After holy Paphuntius was departed, poore Lais, recollecting her scattered thoughts, and by those lines which he had drawn guiding them unto GOD and fixing them in him as in a center, to cut off all occasion of Diversion that any commerce or Interest in the world might breed, and, if it might be, through the example of her Conversion to bring againe to the right way some of them whom through former wantonnes she had misled, having gathered together all her goods and Jewels, which amounted to many thousands of pounds, she caused them to be brought forth into the most frequented place of the Citty, and there in open view of all setting fire with her owne hands, consumed them all to ashes, crying out aloud as shee did it, Come hither now, all you that have been partakers with mee in sin, and see how the jewels which you gave mee burn. The flame of this fire having quenched the flames of concupiscence in her own and the beholders hearts (for to this end was all this great wast made, that by the terror of such an execution upon the sencelesse accessories to lust, her sensual Lovers might be brought to the same apprehension which she was, of those everlasting torments which would in the end overtake them if they did not now with her make prevention), Lais, according to appointment, makes hast to Paphuntius in the desert, and is by him immediately led to a company of religious women, who for the Love and better service of GOD had abandoned the delights of the world, and for the surer maintenance and more abundant exercize of their heavenly desires had made a league to live and dy together. To these holy women doth Paphuntius consigne Lais, himself for a while attending with all diligence of Instruction and Devotion in his prayers that furtherance and confirmation of her faith and repentance; which assoone as he perceived to have taken good root in Lais her heart, he determines to return to that quiet and contemplation which he had for her sake so long intermitted. And esteeming it unfitt to leave her at libertie, or to the free enjoyment of those holy womens fellowship under whose governance he left her, he resolves to shutt her up betweene foure walls. Whereunto Lais, through humilitie esteeming herself unworthy of any bodies society, and desire to attend wholly without Impediment or distraction to the making sure of her salvation, easily condescends. And so it is accomplished. Upon her closing up she asks Paphuntius, with great meeknes, how she should pray and call upon GOD. Paphuntius, willing both to try and exercize her humility to the uttermost, gave an Answere that makes mee tremble in relating; and yet it troubled her not at all, so deep was her faith layd in the contempt of her self and the Admiration of GODS infinite Majestie. Thou art unworth (sayd he) with thy polluted lips to mention the holy Name of GOD, or to lift up thy hands so defiled with sin towards heaven; but kneeling and turning to the East, say over and over againe, Thou that hast created mee, have mercy upon mee. With these bitter Comforts for her soul, and the allowance of bread and water only for her sustenance, did holy Paphuntius leave this penitent. But where mans love and kindnes ends, GODS pitty and mercy begins; in comparison whereof Mans greatest Mercies are but cruelties. Hee adds the vertue of his word to this bread, and so it serves for nourishment, and he supplies strength by the consolation of his holy spirit. And Lais goes on with her repentance for three yeares space; at the end whereof Paphuntius, meeting with the great St. Antonie, tells him the case, and asketh his advice what he might think, and what he should doe touching Lais; whether it were likely that GOD had pardoned her, or would have her yet released. St. Antonie, that fetched all his Counsells from GOD, willed his Disciples that were with him to watch a whole night and to pray earnestly that GOD would direct them in this matter. Whilest all, out of obedience and Charitie, sett themselves fervently to the performance, the suit is obtained and the secret revealed to the Elect of St. Antonies Disciples. Hee sees heaven opened in a Vision and discovers with his eie a rich bed, on which lay a crown, and three Damsels appeared to him, as all things are that belong to heaven, of incomparable beauty, of inestimable worth, and of infinite Glory. Being ravished with delight, he began to say within himself, The honour and the happines of this gift can belong to no man living but my master. He had scarce thus thought when he heard a voice, All this is prepared for Lais, that was a woman of the world, and not for Antonie. Paphuntius, doubly glad for Lais, and himself now freed from care by the assurance of her salvation, makes hast to visit her, and with great rejoycing breaks down the dore which with many teares he had made up. He calls her happy, and wills her to come abroad without any feare, For thy sins (sayd he) are pardoned through the mercy of GOD. I know it, sayd Lais; for I now feel them not at all that have all this while felt them going over my head like a sore burden too heavy to beare. Tell mee (sayd Paphuntius) after what manner hast thou spent this time? When I was first shutt up, answered Lais, I made a bundle of my sins and held them steddily before mine eies unto the last, weeping and mourning over them. Verily, replied Paphuntius, it is not thy Penitency, but thy Humilitie, that

God hath had so much respect unto. Fifteen daies after this did Lais continue an Angels Life on earth, praysing and magnifying the greatnes of Gods mercy to her in the Company of those holy women. And then her soul, being parted from her body by the meanes of Death, was by the ministerie of Angels carried up into heaven, there in company of the blessed Saints and Angels to enjoy an everlasting fulnes of Glorie and Happines. .

Guard. There was more Art, I perceive, in breaking off your Storie last day, then Necessitie. The dislike of Lais her Penitency will undoubtedly make the whole to be questioned, and under the pretence of the Impossibilitie of the last part, the probabilitie of the first will be denyed by the wisedome of this Age, which will believe no further then it sees, nor approve any more then it meanes to imitate.

Mother. But however they prize it for the Quintessence of witt, yet it is undoubtedly but a Masterpeice of Folly, to make their own Affections and Abilities the Rule and measure by which the truth and vertue of forepast Actions is to be tryed. Shall not the recommendation of venerable Antiquitie gett creditt with us for more then fitts our own turns ? but all that is not proportionable to our delicacie was a fable, all that is not agreeable to our Ignorance is Superstition in the lives and practizes of the Saints. What the Authoritie of this Historie is I will not contend. Let every man beleive as he please, so hee deny mee not that for which this History, if it be a made History, seemes cheifly intended : That it becomes them to whom much is forgiven to love much—that is Christ his own Law ; and that for great sins the repentance ought to be long continued—that was Davids practize, who every night washt his bed and watered his couch with teares and professeth to have his heavines ever in his sight. Though he had pardon under the great seal by the Mouth of the self-same prophet that had put in the Inditement against him in Gods behalf, yet he lays not by the sorrow of his misdoings in his own heart, nor the solemne publication of it to others ; but proceeds in such a manner that even to this day hee seemes to doe pennance in the Church. Hee that afflicts himself only till he have obtained pardon, seemes to be sorry rather for his own losse then for his offence against GOD. He that truly hates his sin, grows still more sorry by how much he grows on to a greater measure of firmnes of reconciliation. The view of GODS goodnes as he approacheth nearer, makes him better to see the deformitie of the sin which he left behind him; and he weeps and blushes with more sence and willingnes by how much he doth it with more proof and surety of the Divine favour. Hee that casteth away repentance when he hath obtained forgivenes, shews to have put a greater prize upon it then is indeed due, as though by the vertue thereof hee had merited that which was given him by the free grace of GOD. He that knows his pardon to come altogether from mercy, can find no cause to shutt out repentance, finding it, if not so necessary as before, yet more comely. Hee thinks himself more bound to weep now for love, then he did then for feare, and setts himself to greive more heartily for his unkindnes then formerly he did for his losse and danger. Upon these grounds there was matter enough not only for Lais to continue her Repentance three yeares, but for so many as we read of in old times to make profession of it all their life long. As for the rest of this story, it is very conformable to that which wee have often seen in GODS proceedings, that where sin hath abounded, grace hath abounded much more, and agreeable to that which he hath ever promised, That where the sufferings of CHRIST abound there shall the consolations of CHRIST abound likewise. Of all the sufferings of CHRIST there was none so burdensome to him as our own sins; nor is there anything perhaps whereby wee may be made more like to him in his sufferings, then when wee take up this crosse of our own and follow him as much as is possible, with sorrow and shame for our own sins answerable to that which he underwent for our sakes, when he bare our sins and took upon him our guilty persons. The sence of this greif that made him sweat bloud in the garden, was repayd with consolations brought down from heaven by an Angel. And undoubtedly even to this day it fares so in all his members. There is ever upon the performance of this work for themselves a supply of spiritual Joy, as their repentance proves more delightfull then ever their sins were. Let none of us therefore be afrayd in this regard to begin and intend to the uttermost this duty and exercise, being assured that wee shall in the end with David have cause to say and sing : According to the multitude of the sorrows that I had in my heart, thy comforts have refreshed my soul. Lais had much afflicted herself with mourning and many sufferings, and GOD filled her mouth with joy and her tongue with laughter. She by repentance wore a crown of thorns about her heart, and GOD by revelation gave her an earnest of that immortal Crown of Glory which he ment to put upon her head. He that sows in teares of Repentance, shall even in this vale of misery reap in joy, by the hope and assurance of eternal Happines which GOD shall give unto him, and that according to that measure of fulnes which himself desireth. If he sow plentifully he shall reap plentifully ; if he sow sparingly he shall reap sparingly. Let no man be afrayd to doe this work thoroughly : for for every seed of paines and greif that he thus setts, GOD shall, even in this life, give him a whole sheaf of joy and gladnes into his bosome.

PATIENT. Undoubtedly you are in the right, and the ignorance or misunderstanding of this point is that which makes men now adaies to hasten away from their repentance. Assoone as it hath brought them a little quiet and comfort, they lay it aside, thinking it as unseemely as mourning garments to a Bridal. And hereby it fares with them as it doth with those sick persons, who, finding a little ease by the medicine, presently give it over, and betake themselves to the Aire, to Exercize, and to nourishing diet for the full recovery of their health and strength ; but the effect is cleane otherwise then they expected. They either fall into a relapse, or continue lingring in distempers. Whereas, would they have gone through with the course perscribed by the Physitian, they should have had, though not so soone, yet much more abundant enjoyment of that pleasure and delight, for the greedines whereof they put away the Physick. Answerable without question is the error and the event in the spiritual disease of the soul. The pricepitation that we use upon our conversion is that which keeps us ever after so crazy; wee think to gett strength by attempting greater matters and hope to attaine joy by carrying up of our affections to higher contemplations. And because evill humours were not thoroughly purged, nor the dead flesh quite eaten out by the corrosive of repentance, our hands fail us in the performance, and our hearts faint us upon every Temptation, and we walk a burden to ourselves by continual heavines, a scandale to our Brethren by much frailty and many failings; so discompting in a tenfold proportion the shame and sorrow which we refused to make perfect in our repentance, which certainly, if it be effectual to bring hope out of dispaire, confidence out of shame, rejoicing out of greif, and good resolutions out of sin, would be a much more operative medicine to encrease them, if it were, as it ought to be, applied to the full and to the last.

CHEEREF. That the world shall be afrayd of I wonder not, it being, like Sampsons lion, very gastly to look upon. The watchings, the Fastings, the Teares, the sighs, the sufferings, that it is clothed with, makes it appeare very dreadfull afarre off. But they that have tasted the hony and found the strength and the sweetnes that repentance swarmes with; that these, I say, should so childishly draw back through vaine affrightment of others feares, rather then their own sence to the contrary, and loose so much for want of making perfect the work, seemes strange. And as it cannot but be a strong delusion of the world, so undoubtedly it is a proof that they who are thus beaten off remaine still more of the worlds partie then themselves are aware of; and are at the best, however they conceit themselves, but children in the faith of CHRIST, which holy Faith, as it first began to be preached from this point (for not not only John the Forerunner, but our LORD himself began his Gospel with Repent), so undoubtedly it is still to this day grafted in mens heart upon this self-same stock, and grows up and fructifies for the most part answerable to the vigour and strength thereof. A sound repentance and throughly performed, sends up a large and fruitfull shoot of Faith. That it grows withered and weakly as it doth in most mens hearts now adaies, proceeds cheifly from defect in the foundation. A slight repentance cannot serve to nourish but a starveling Faith. The better cultivating therefore of this Plant of Repentance then is usual in the world, is necessarie not only for the encrease of Joy, but for the maintenance of Truth.

AFFECTIO. You have so well amongst you explained that which might seeme liable to exception in my storie, as from henceforth I shall make no scruple to tell both parts together, which till now I confesse I had; not that I conceived any thing amisse in it, but because I know the misconstruction which these times use to make of all those things which are above the pitch of their own reach.

GUARD. The Commentarie is answerable to the Storie, and the doctrine will, I am perswaded, seeme as strange to common Judgement as the example. But that is no prejudice to the truth, that it is not approved by the general vote of the world, so it bee confirmed by evident proof of scripture and constant practize of the Saints as this which hath been now delivered appears to bee; for I remember to have read that St. Augustine confesseth himself to be ravished with the delight that his teares bred by the sweetnes of them, making gage of that infinite Joy which he hoped for. If it be so sweet to weep here on Earth, what will it be to triumph in heaven with CHRIST? sayth hee. St. Hierome, writing to Eustochia, tells her that sometimes after his many teares and continued looking up to heaven he seemed to be in the midst of the heavenly Quires, singing with great Jubile, Wee will run after the pleasant savour of thy most precious Balme.

MOTHER. There is no more intended, I perceive, in this argument, and therefore I beseech you, most honoured MODERATOUR, that since you have had what you desired, you would make good that which you promised.

MODERAT. It was not forgetfulnes of my promise, but study to performe it somewhat answerable to Expectation, that hindered mee from presenting your demand by the tender of my storie concerning the famous Ephraim, which is recorded in his life.

AFFECT. Is your Storie of that Ephraim, I pray, who not to his own, but to the advancement of GODS glorie and the Edification of the standers by, on his deathbed told them : I have never in my life sworn by the Name of my GOD, nor spoken filthy nor idle word ; I have never cursed any man, nor have had contention in law with any, and yet went alwaies afflicted, often weeping and sighing for the great dread and terror which he had of the day of judgement, the remembrance whereof, as himself left written, was alwaies present in his mind? If this thought wrought so upon his Innocency, what ought it to doe upon my guiltines?

MODER. This very Ephraim of whom you speak, having upon these grounds which you mention, given himself, according to the manner of those times, to a solitarie life, comming on a time to the Citty of Edessa, whither he often repaired to benefitt himself by the conversation of good men, and to endeavour himself the Conversion of Sinners ; as he travailed full of these thoughts, drawing neer to the Citty, hee besought GOD with much Entreaty that the first person that he should encompter might be of furtherance to him in his holy purposes. With this hope he views the gates with much solicitousnes, whether GOD had heard his prayer or no. He meets a woman whom garish habit and wanton carriage proclaimed to bee a strumpett. This falling out so contrary to Expectation, he fixeth his Eie upon her with manifest shew of Greif and Indignation, which she perceiving, setts herself with answerable Constancie and contempt, to view him.

Ephraim, doubly troubled for his own disappointment and her Impudency, cries out aloud and angerly: Art thou not ashamed, oh woman, to stand gazing and looking upon a man? Cast thine eie down to the ground, and look on that, as befitts thee. To which she readily, and with great boldnes, taxing him of that self same thing which he reproved her for, made answere: It befitts me, that am a woman, to look upon man, of whom I am, and of whose ribbe I was shaped; but thou, that art a man, oughtst to cast thine eies down to the Earth, out of which thou wast taken and formed. Ephraim hearing this, rested all amazed, thanking GOD for so wholesome an Instruction; and used often with much admiration to recompt the Answere, wherein she had drawn out so compendious an Abstract of the several duties of man and wife in marriage, which then is made perfect to the height of vertue and fulnes of comfort when the wifes eie, by reducing all her desires to the subjection of her husband, remaines immovably fixed on him as her temporary end, and the man his eie being alwaies fixed on the earth by the remembrance of his frail beginning and end, exercizeth his Authoritie with humilitie, and takes his comforts with sobrietie.

Your turne, worthy GUARDIAN, is next.

GUARD. My storie hath as great affinitie with the CHEERE-FULLS as this last had with the AFFECTIONATES. Its concerning the punishment of sin and the paines of Hell, though in a more easy, yet in no lesse usefull manner represented to our Consideration then they were by the storie of Martinian.—

There was a wise man, as his Neighbours calld him, and a good Father as himself thought, that having many children, and desirous to leave them well provided, had gathered a great Estate in the world, and loaded his soul with much guilt before GOD. At last GOD opens his eies and shews him his Error, and he concludes that he was a Foole in graine to loose his own soul for any other bodies pleasure, and but an unkind Father, that had heaped up GODS Curse for his Children. Upon these thoughts he grows to a conclusion, that whatsoever come he will make his Repentance perfect by Restitution. And to make his children capable of the Necessitie of this intended course, one Night as they satt at table round about him, he thus bespake them : My sons, you know how much I love you by that which I have done for you. Theres nothing that I desire from you but love againe, and that I hope I shall not want. How say you ? Hereupon they all began joyntly to make large protestations of the greatnes of their obligation and excesse of their affections. I am glad to heare this, sayd the goodman ; but I desire withall to have some proof whether the Effects will bee answerable to the words. They besought him to tell what he would have done, and he should see that their expression fell short of what was in their hearts. That I shall require, sayd he, is only this, That you would each of you one after the other hold his little Finger for a quarter of an houre in the flame of the Candle there. His children, hearing this, began to smile, supposing that their Fathers dotage was a signe of his approaching death, whereby they should come sooner then they thought to the enjoyment of their own libertie and his wealth. The Father, seeing they made light of the matter, began with many entreaties and much earnestnes to perswade them to it. But he speaks in the Aire ; neither faire words nor threats could perswade them to such a madness, as they termed it. Why then, sayd hee, yourselves be the Judges whether it were wisedome for mee to goe down quick into hell, and to ly there for your sakes burning in unquenchable flames from head to foot, world without end. Nay, verily, by GODS grace it shall not be so. Ile restore what I have unjustly gott, and make amends where I have done wrong ; and if I leave you not the wealth of the world, I shall leave you (if yourselves turn it not away) GODS blessing, which is a farre surer portion and better Inheritance.

PATIENT. It was a wise remonstrance and happy returne, and worthy to be imitated by all Parents in the like case. That a Father should leave his children on the Parish through riot or any kind of unthriftines or Negligence, is such a crime as makes him more then an Infidel. But if doing what he ought he cannot advance much in worldly Provisions for them, it matters not at all. GOD is faithfull, and will some other way make supply for his children. Let every good Father build on this, and for himself, so he have not failed in that diligence which he was bound to in this kind, hee may without any feare at all depart the world, though he leave nothing behind him, knowing that GOD will not call him to accompt for the portions, but for the breeding which he gave his children. If he bring a good Inventorie of spiritual graces and vertues, by his care and paines conveyed to his Children, he shall have the reward of a good Father, ever to be proclaimed, as Abraham was, GODS Freind. But if otherwise (whatever the world perswade him), he will be found what he least feares perhaps, not only no good Father, but a Denyer of the Christian Faith, which teacheth that hee that first seeks not the kingdome of heaven for himself and for those who are under his charge, seeks it not at all, nor may with any reason ever hope to have a part in it, till he change his opinion in this point. But I doe wrong by this discourse, which will hereafter find a fitter place, to interupt the present busines. Pardon mee, I beseech you, worthy GUARDIAN, and proceed.

GUARDIAN. My Storie is at an end.
MOTHER. Why then, goe to the second.
GUARDIAN. Doe you look for two at once?
AFFECT. If you make not double payment now you pay us not the full, but will remaine in arreare, either for this present day or the last, which was against the covenant that wee made at first. That our honoured MODERATOUR so ment, is plaine by her Example.
GUARDIAN. Since you have reason and president for it, I cannot bee against it, although not so well provided as I wish to performe it. Let mee see; Sir Thomas Mores storie suites so well, that Ile seek no further.

At a certaine Faire (I know not whether it were Sturbridge

or no) there happened to arise a Contraversie between a North countryman and a Londoner. Being brought instantly to trial in a Pyponder Court (if I mistake not the Name) the Jury, whether by contrivement or accident, proved all, save one Southerne Man, to be the North-country-mans acquaintance and Neighbours, whereupon with little adoe they all resolved, having an Eie rather to Freindship then to Justice, to find for him, being the plaintife. Lets goe then, quoth the Foreman, since wee are all agreed. Nay, stay, I pray, Mr. Dickenson (that was his name), sayd the Southerne Jurer; mee thinks both reason and law are on the defendants part. With that they all fell upon him, as an Oule in an ivie bush. With what doe your two eies see more than our two and twenty? Not so, quoth the goodman, I presume not to be wiser in understanding, but I am carefull to doe nothing against my conscience. Why, have not wee consciences too? replyed they all joyntly. I will not judge your consciences, sayd hee, and I must desire you to satisfy mine, before I give up the verdict with you. With that some of them fell a reasoning the matter. But the Foreman, knowing that bad causes loose alwaies by debating, shuffling all up, prayd the southern man not to enter now upon arguments, nor stand minsing of conscience, but like a good fellow to goe along with them for company. You say well, replyed the honest man, if there went no more on the busines then so. But you know that wee must all at last and altogether come before GODS judgement-seat, and if wee doe, having done according to our own consciences. I hope, sayd the company, wee shall doe well enough. True, replied he, but what shall become of mee, that doe against my conscience? Mee thinks I now see how it will be. You are called up to heaven, and I am cast down to hell, and then I cry out to you, Oh, Mr. Dickenson, see what befalls mee now for your sake; because I went for company with you at the giving up of such a verdict against mine own conscience, I am now going to hell; I pray, according to promise and good freindship, goe now along with mee. Will you then bee as good as your word? No, verily, you meane it not, I am sure, at present, and much lesse would doe it then. Hold you therefore, I pray, contented, if I part company with you in this busines, that wee may not then part upon worse termes.

AFFECT. This is a storie that every day will be usefull and appliable, there being, as I suppose, no one more ordinarie argument of misleading to be found both in small and great matters then this of going along in company with others in our opinions, in our desires, and in our Actions; and for the most part how much better natured any man is, the greater is the danger. It seemes impossible to stand either with modestie or Love for a man to goe another way then his freinds or betters take. And yet if he goes against his own Conscience he takes the broad way to Hell. The best freind in the world will leave a man at the grave, and yet the very slightest acquaintance takes great offence if a man run not headlong to the Devill to keep their goodwills. Hee that will sell his freindship at this rate, let him keep it for mee. As farre as we may goe in GODS Name, let us goe together. But to part with our interest in GOD for the best Company in the world, and to renounce our own part in everlasting happines for any other bodies earthly pleasures too, is such an height of madnes and miserie as no man durst require of another, but that he is himself, and thinks him from whom he expects such kindnes, to be an Infidel.

GUARD. Your descant sounds right in mine Eares, deare AFFECTIONATE. Hee that truly beleives Hell cannot but be afrayd of going to Hell himself, and ashamed to urge any other to goe thither for his sake. He that truly beleives it, as Lais and Pelagia did, makes light all other losse and sufferings to escape that.

MOTHER. I understand your meaning. Where did I leave?

CHEEREF. Why, at that point which, both for us and this approaching Festival, is perhaps of all others the most necessarie to begin with. I mean that by the example of Nonnus his sobrietie, wee should think of regulating our forepassed excesses,

IHS 223

reducing our corporal Feastings upon spiritual occasions to that proportion and temper, both for quantitie and qualitie of Food, as may serve to the cheering up and quickening of the heart, not to the deading of the spirits; so that our devotions and not our Lusts may receive heat and vigour.

MOTHER. That which you shall now heare will confirme the necessity of this practize, That when wee give our selves to outward rejoycing, we ought to stand more warily upon our inward guard, and to be doubly heedfull no waies so to discompose our selves, but that upon the first Alarum wee may be ready with our spiritual Armes to encompter our Enemy, who alwaies goes about like a roaring Lion seeking to devoure. And if he cannot hope so much, yet will he not fail to doe his uttermost, at least disturbe and contaminate our mirth when ever wee sett our selves to the partaking thereof, such a cancred Adversarie is he to all that which brings content to man.

Holy Nonnus is scarce settled to his wine and his oile (those were the dainties that made his meal a Banquett) when all is interrupted by an unbidden and unwelcome guest. The Devill come in naked, and in a dreadful shape, and after hideous murmurings, as if he suffered some great violence, upbraides and reviles the blessed Saint, calling him decrepide and doting old man. What, sayth the enraged spirit, can it not suffice thee to have taken 30,000 Sarazens, and to have offered them up to thy GOD? Can it not suffice thee to have driven mee out of Heliopolis, mine own Jurisdiction, and to have turned the Inhabitants thereof, that were so devoted to my service, to the worshipping of thine own GOD, but thou must now at last strip mee of this Remainder of my hopes, by whose meanes such an excesse grew every day to my kingdome? Cursed be the day of thy Birth, and cursed be that floud of Teares wherewith thou hast overthrown the foundation of my dwelling, this pillar of my hopes. I can neither beare nor resist the mischief that this wretched old man doth mee. This (sayth the Authour) the Devill roared with such loud yellings, that the other Bishops and Pelagia in their general apartements understood it all. Nonnus, being neither moved nor amated with any of that which he saw or heard, the Devill instantly addresseth himself to Pelagia, and blasphemously taxeth her to have dealt with him as Judas did with CHRIST, selling him to his Enemies hands in recompence of all those Honours and favours which she had received of him. Pelagia, being taught and heartened by her spiritual mother and holy Nonnus, recommendeth herself to CHRIST and defies the Tempter, and he for that time vanisheth. But two Nights after he comes to her againe, as she was in bed with Romana. He wakes her and demands wherein he had been wanting to her that she had so unkindly abandoned him. Hee setts before her eies the riches, the pleasures, the honours, whereof by his meanes she had been possessor and partaker, and offers largely to content her in whatsoever she could wish, if so bee she would now vindicate him from that scorn and contempt would be put upon him by the Christians through her conversion to the Faith. But wise Pelagia defies him and his offers, and tells him she had given herself wholly to CHRIST JESUS, who had done so much and so many things for her as could not be recompted. Hee hath ransomed mee out of thy power, sayd she, and hath lead me into his own heavenly Chamber, the holy militant church. He shall fight for mee, and deliver mee from thy malice and thy wiles. With this the wicked spirit departed, and Pelagia, upon Romanas waking, tells her both of her danger and her victorie. Romana encourageth her to proceed with Faith and good hope, assuring her that, being so armed, the Devill should be afrayd to come neer her, much lesse to doe her any harme. The next morning, Pelagia, sending for her steward, wills him to make a perfect Inventorie of her Estate; which, being accordingly brought her in writing, she makes tender thereof to Nonnus. See here, Father, sayd shee, the wealth that I have gotten by the Factorie of the Devill. I beseech thee, let it be disposed of to better uses. As for mee, the Treasures of my LORD JESUS CHRIST are sufficient; other riches I desire not. Then calling her Familie, both men and women, she made them all free, and, with liberal gifts, gave them hearty and wholesome exhortations to be partakers and Imitators of her repentance, as they had been partners and Instruments in her unrighteousnes. As for the remainder of her Estate, holy Nonnus, sending for the cheif officer of the Church of Antioch, consigned it all into his hands with this Charge. I abjure thee (sayd hee) by GOD, to look well that no parcel of this wealth be converted to thine own use, nor that any of it be imployed about the Church in ornaments or otherwise; but that it be wholly and faithfully distributed amongst widdows, orphanes, and other poore people, that so it may at last prove beneficial in the spending that was gathered together with so much sin and damage, as thou knowest. The consideration of this undue getting so affected Pelagia, as she rather chose to live of Almes then to keep any thing of her former wealth towards her future maintenance. The eight day being come, this holy convert, putting off the white garment with which, after the custome of those times, she had been apparelled at her Baptisme, disguiseth herself, and to prevent all hinderances not acquainting any whosoever, departs secretly in the Night to put in Execution a strange attempt, and such as before hers, wee shall, it may bee, scarce find a President for. The good Romana, next day missing her, grows much perplexed. Her Love makes her sorry she had lost Pelagias Company; her Experience of mans frailtie makes her feare the devill had circumvented her. But Nonnus bids her bee of good cheere. Daughter (sayth hee), there is no cause of mourning for Pelagia, but the contrary. She is safe, and, with Mary Magdalene, hath chosen the better part, which shall not be taken from her. Shortly after this the Bishops meeting brake up, and everyone returned to their own homes, without any Inkling, though much diligence had been perhaps used to know, what was become of Pelagia. At three yeares end, sayth the Authour, I my self having an earnest desire to goe up to Hierusalem, asked leave of Nonnus to this purpose; whereunto he willingly condescended, and, upon parting, sayd unto mee, Brother James, when thou comest to Hierusalem, enquire amongst those that live solitaries for one Pelagius, and visit him on my behalf; verily, thou shalt find a great servant of GOD. I forgat not this charge, sayth the Authour, but when I came to Hierusalem began to ask for Pelagius, and was immediately directed to his little habitation, which was on mount Olivet. Comming thither and knocking, Pelagius opened his window (for other entrance there was none) and demanded what I would. I come, sayd I, from Nonnus, the Bishop of Heliopolis. A holy man indeed, sayd Pelagius, and as it were another Apostle. Beseech him to pray for mee, and doe thou likewise, Brother Deacon, remember mee in thy Prayers to GOD. I was not a little amazed to heare these particulars, both of my self and my Bishop, being no waies able to call to mind that I had ever seen this holy person, whose pale visage, hollow eies, wan lips, and rivelled cheeks seemed to mee to represent the Image of Death. Our Discourse ended, sayth the Authour, Pelagius shut the window and withdrew to prayers, and I came away much edified by this angelical spectacle. Afterwards, sayth hee, I visited many other devout persons, who all bare ample Testimonie of the exceeding grace of GOD that was in Pelagius the Eunuch, so they called him. But whence he came, or who he should bee, nobody could tell. Being thus full, not only of love but admiration to this unknown Saint, I determined, sayth the Authour, to visit him once againe, and to enjoy a little more of his heavenly conversation. But when I had knocked one or twice and saw no answere given, supposing the Intention of his Devotion to be the cause of his silence, and not meaning to bee troublesome, I went away for that time, returning the next day at a convenient houre. As I cast it but with no better speed then at first, the third day I came againe, and, after knocking and calling, perceiving upon diligent Attention no manner of motion or noise from within, I began to suspect that all was not well, and so, taking heart, thrust ope the window forcibly. This done, I, looking in, saw Pelagius lie dead upon the flore. Of this I gave instant notice, and thereupon not only all the Professors of the self-same course of life, but many other people, came running from Hierusalem, who, with joynt consent, brake down the dore, and after many teares bestrawed upon the body, they took it up to fitt it for the grave; which they had no sooner begun to doe but they perceived that it was a woman. Hereupon they all lift up their voices together with cries and teares, magnifying the Divine power and wisedome, saying, Glory be to thee, oh GOD, who hast so many hidden treasures upon Earth, not only amongst men, but amongst women also. Upon this, drawing neere, sayth the Authour, I began with better heed to advise the face, and immediately knew it to be that of Pelagia, the strangenes of the alteration being that which had formerly deceived mee. Hereupon I made known her conversion and all that you have heard related, sayth the Authour; which, doubling the affections and wonderment on all hands, brought an infinite Number of people to her Funeral, which was performed with great joy and great honour, as was meet for her that had perfected holines in the Feare of GOD here on earth, and was now made perfect by GOD in everlasting happines as touching her soul, with assurances that her body likewise should, in due time, ascend to the participation of the self-same joy and glory.

GUARD. Your Storie is mounted so high by admiration, that it passeth the reach either of censure or application.

MOTHER. And well doth one that writes it, though in breif, conclude with an allusion to the Name of Pelagia, That in her a man may well and worthily admire the Ocean of the Divine Judgement.

GUARD. Then belike you have more then your Relatours Authoritie, which you have so often mentioned.

MOTHER. Theres so manifold and so good Authoritie, as I have heard for the proof of this storie (at least, that which I cheifly insist upon, thats the first part), as mee thinks it should be a harder matter to doubt it then to beleive it. But let every one think as they please, so they give mee leave to think that Nonnus his influence upon Pelagia her great diligence in adorning her body was right and necessary for us all that pretend to have our loves in heaven, and to say to my self and you, that wee have no reason with any confidence to look up to GOD and our LORD JESUS CHRIST as the spouse of our souls, except wee bee as carefull to put on those spiritual abiliments, which may make us lovely in his eies, as earthly women are to trimme and dock their bodies to the liking of their earthly Lovers. Surely, whatever the world think, as CHRIST deserves no lesse, so neither will he accept lesse then the uttermost of our diligence and care in this behalf; which, God grant, wee may henceforth faithfully imploy, that wee which are called to be heavenly may shew our selves heavenly, as they which are earthy doe approve themselves to be earthy.

GUARD. Wee all joyne with you, both in opinion and desire, touching this matter. But why, I pray, doe you so abandon the second part of your story, disavowing the maintenance before you heare any opposition?

MOTHER. I abandon it not as any way faulty, either for point of truth or vertue; but because I see no special usefulnes in it to the present busines, I would be loth to contend, if any should call it in question, as perhaps some may, to whom the Devils apparition and discourse will seeme scarce probable.

PATIENT. Why, verily, it seems strange to mee that these like passages should so hardly gett credit in these latter times, wherein there are every day so many certaine proofs and experiments of them. Amongst all the rest which wee have heard read, that of Mary Smith, of Kings Lin, in Norfolk, suits marvelously with that which you have related touching the Devills assaulting and endeavouring to seduce Pelagia. Two several times the Devill appeares to her in prison in the shape of a black man, and the last of these two times he had a paire of hornes on his head, and that was as she was comming down the staires to conferre and pray with some Divines. His Counsell to her was, that she should confesse nothing to any of them, but continue constant in her made promise, rely upon him, and he would save her. That this could not be a fancy in Mary Smiths apprehension, the manner of her end approves beyond exception. That it should not be a made tale of any other, but truly reported by her self, the Fidelitie of the Authour that wrott it, and the Confirmation of so many witnesses as he alledgeth, forbids any ingenious mind to have any suspicion.

MODERA. Surely theres a great resemblance of the Devills proceedings in these two Stories, and so is there likewise of GODS infinite mercy. Mary Smiths end may be admired as a Sea and Abisse of the Divine Judgement as well as Pelagias. She made an open confession of her sins, shewed hearty repentance for them. She renounced the Devill and defied him, and found both shelter and comfort in her recourse to CHRIST. She made a good profession of her faith, and shewed the proof of a good hope in her willingnes to dy, when she might have lived longer. When she was offered a repreive she refused it, and made choise of instant Execution, no waies, as it seemes, out of dispaire and wearines of this present life, but out of the desire and hope of immediate entring into a better. He that shall weigh these things rightly, and give those allowances which are due on both sides, shall find that proportionably theres no lesse ground of wonderment in this story of Mary Smith then in that which hath been recompted of Pelagia.

GUARD. The apparitions and assaults of the Devill to recover those which have been his especial instruments, have been notably confirmed by this late and fresh Example. But mee thinks his longsome discourse, and, above all, his blasphemous comparisons, as it is very mistrustfull to heare, so it carries some difficultie to believe.

MOTHER. What would you have thought if I had told it out as large and full as it is sett down in the story itself? The detestation which I see affects you made mee abridge it much, but leave it out altogether I durst not, having no diffidence of the truth, and thinking it the more observable in regard of another passage very like, as mee thinks, and very lately added by the same Author, the Devill I meane, which I am sure you cannot forgett.

PATIENT. Wee cannot call to mind what it should be that you intend, and therefore desire you would declare it at large, as if it were altogether new.

MOTHER. Why, it was out of our supper readings, as the other additions have been. And the particular which I meane is that of James Devize, doubly confirmed by him upon two several examinations, and this it is. The Devill did often, and with much Importunitie, in the likenes of a brown dog, solicit this James Devize to give him his soul, thereupon promising that hee should have power to be revenged of whom he would. James Devize his answere or excuse (I know not well what to terme it) was, That his soul was not his own to give, but was his SAVIOUR JESUS CHRISTS; but as much as was in him to give he was content that he should have it. But this reservation pleased not the Devill. He presseth him againe and againe; and having still the same answere from this wretched man, to witt, that he would give him his own part, and no further, the spirit of blasphemie tells him that he was above CHRIST JESUS, and therefore must absolutely give him his soul, and then he would give him power to revenge himself against whom he disliked. The last time that the Devill appeared about this negociation was the Tuesday before Devizes apprehension; and when he could not prevaile with him to have his soule absolutely granted unto him, he departed from him, giving a most fearfull cry and yell, and withall caused a great flash of fire to shew about him, but afterwardes troubled him no more.

MODER. A strange passage, undoubtedly, and as in many other respects very observable and appliable, so surely to this purpose which you have alledged it, To sett forth the impotencie of Ambition and Affection that Belial hath, to make competition, as I may say, in everything with CHRIST JESUS. But what shall we say? that the apparition of evill spirits to wicked persons being so frequent even now adaies, the apparition of good Angels and divine visions to good men is grown so rare, as scarce one or two examples are to be found in a whole Age. The puritie of our Religion for point of Doctrine being equal, as wee are taught, if not above most of those times wherein such favours abounded, should seeme to make us capable as they were.

CHEEREF. That the light of the Gospel drives away the spirits of darknes and abates their power I have often heard given as a reason of our freedome from those many delusions with which our Forefathers were vexed by the Devill; but then mee thinks it should withall bring us into better acquaintance with those holy Spirits which, as the blessed Apostles of our LORD teach us, are continual admirers of the Gospel and constant Attendants of the true Professors thereof.

GUARD. It is not for us to enter into such high points; but to tell you what I have heard for a reason, and shall think a good one, till I know a better: It is the want of true practize of that holy truth which wee professe that debarres these times of ours from this kind of honour and consolation. If you make the Assessement by knowledge and sound doctrine, the world is rich of good men; but if by vertue and holines, you shall, I am afrayd, find it such a bankrupt as never was the like. Who can give mee a Saint amongst those many thousands of beleivers which he knows? And if he give mee one, and he himself dares take the title, yet if you lay his holines by the patterns of old, your self will suspect it is scarce right, such a difference will appear both in the substance and the lustre. And shall we then marvell that the Angels, GODS special ministers, should walk so invisible to us, when wee walk so imperfectly, so insincerely with GOD, their and our great Master? Wee must goe altogether out of the world in our Affections before wee can enter upon these Earnests of heaven; and bid adue to all confidence in meanes, all consolation in things below, all love of ourselves, before wee look for such familiarity of Love, comfort, and assistance from the Inhabitants of heaven. They are as ready now, I am perswaded, if wee would meet them half way, as the Saints did in old time, by setting their affections on things above. But to come down quite to the Earth, where wee ly groveling, were too great an Indignitie for them, and would bee too dangerous a confirmation of our Error.

AFFECT. That which you have now delivered, worthy GUARDIAN, seemes so much the more consonant to truth in my judgement as I see it answerable to that which I have heard and read touching this matter. There have not wanted, through GODS infinite mercy, in these last and evill daies of ours, some notable examples in this kind, amongst which that of Mrs. Catherine Stubs deserves, perhaps, both for the certaintie and all other respects, to be held amongst the cheifest. It seemes by her speech and behaviour that the Devill did visibly appeare unto her in some dreadfull shape. Certain it is that he did sorely combate her, and was driven away by the sword of the spirit. Every argument that she useth, and almost every word, is out of Scripture. With these Armes she contesteth with Satan, with these she defends her self from all his fiery darts, with these she beates him, yet he flies away like a beaten Cock, as her self termes it. But whatever the Devills appearance was, whether to the eie of the body or the mind only, its plaine that the vision of the holy Angels was real and evident, both to the flesh and to the spirit. Oh, would to GOD you saw but that I see, sayd she to them that were about her; for behold, I see infinite millions of most glorious Angels stand about mee, with fiery charriots ready to defend mee, as they did the good Prophet Elizeus. These holy Angels, these ministering spirits, are appointed by GOD to carry up my soul into the kingdom of heaven, where I shall behold the LORD face to face, and shall see him not with other, but with these same eies. The rest of her discourse is very remarkable, and cleares all suspicion that what she apprehended was by certain eiesight, and not by beguiled

Imagination. But neither she nor any of those others which we have heard of were thought worthy of this honour and comfort till they had utterly renounced all their Interest and dependencies on this world. You know the solemne Farewell that she gave to all earthly things before she had this earnest, and anticipated welcome to heaven. She bequeathes her child to her husband, and tells him, Hee is no longer mine, he is the LORDS and yours. I forsake him, you, and all the world, yea, and mine own self, and esteeme all things but dung that I may winne CHRIST JESUS.

PATIENT. That a Soul thus refined and purified from the drosse of corruptible Affections should invest the bodily faculties with the power of discerning spiritual objects, seemes not unproportionable to reason, as it appeares very agreable to experience, there being perhaps many other instances to be brought of them who, upon the like disposition of mind to that of Catherine Stubs, have upon their deathbeds testified to have been made partaker of the like consolation. But whether the want of this perfection of holines be the cause that so few now in their lifes time are thought worthy or capable of those kind of heavenly visions, is too deep a ford for us to adventure upon the determination. Wherefore, seeing you are, it may be, unwilling to passe so abruptly from this discourse of this holy woman, let mee, I pray, remember you of that other passage which immediately follows in the story upon that which last recompted, affording, as mee thinkes, consideration very weighty and proper both for the times and this present subject wee are upon. The child being taken away, she espied a little puppy or bitch, which in her health she loved well, lying upon her bed. She had no sooner espyed her, but shee beat her away, and calling her husband to her, sayd, Good Husband, you and I have offended GOD greivously in receiving this bitch many a time into our bed. Wee would have been loth to have received a Christian soul purchased with the precious bloud of JESUS CHRIST into our bed, and to have nourished him in our bosomes and to have fed him at our table as wee have done this filthy curre many times. The LORD give mee grace to repent it and all other vanities. And afterward could she not abide to look upon the bitch any more. I have told it you in the very words of the book, thinking it not fitt to make any alteration in a matter of such consequence.

CHEEREF. It is doubtlesse a passage of great moment to shew the issue that all vaine delights have, turning in the end to anguish and vexation of spirit.

AFFECT. And it is a lively instance of the tendernes of a good conscience that finds great guilt in it self upon little offences.

MOTHER. How dare you call it a little offence which she her self censureth to have been a great one! Her opinion is plaine to the contrary, and her argument invincible. He that cannot find in his heart to shew his Christian brother that love and kindnes which he shews to his beast, must needs grant that he loves his own sensual delight better then CHRISTS satisfaction. If that very Proverb which they have so ready in their mouths to prevent all opposition to their vanities, Love mee and love my dog, serves to evince this truth beyond all possibility of denial, they break of friendship with him that will not for their sakes love that which is odious, heare that which is intolerable, and make much of that which is naught worth. All this is to be done and more to gentlefolks dogs, and yet will have us beleive that they keep their love and their honour and their allegiance to CHRIST JESUS our LORD intire and untainted in the contempt and neglect and injuries of his lively members. Offer a great Lady that bestows every day a hundred kisses on her dog, and receives as many from him, a poore mans child to kisse, and she starts back as if an Adder were ready to leap upon her; and yet she cannot deny but that the child is farre more deare to CHRIST then her dog can be to her, nor can she make any doubt but that CHRIST, if he were present, would embrace him with the Armes of his glorie. Bring a poore naked person into a great mans roome, where a dog stands pearching at the trencher, and see what a hubbub will arise; and yet theres no question made but CHRIST comes along with the poore Man, and feels himself both the good and evill entertainment which that other receives.

St. James will by no meanes allow that the rich man, in his gay clothes and gold ring, should be preferred in our affections before the poore man in vile rayment. And what will the setting of those affections, the shewing of that kindnes, the taking, the bestowing of that cost on our dogs, which wee doe not, wee cannot afford the lively members of CHRIST JESUS, amount unto in his judgement, think you? Let them turn and mince and colour the matter to the uttermost that witt and art and eloquence can devise, and yet it will not in the end be found lesse then the having no respect at all to the faith of CHRIST, no, not to the majestie of GOD neither. Mark well, and you shall see a strange irreligiousnes accompany this humour. Their dogs must goe along to church and there play with them. Theres the greatest of their own devotion, a continual disturbance to others. Such an Insolency as I am perswaded the most sottish of the heathen durst never offer to their dunghill gods. And is our LORD JESUS CHRIST and his service only worthy of such affront, that wee cannot forbeare our own wanton delights in our dogs; no, nor forbid our dogs theirs in their friskings, barkings, lickings and kissings, whilest his worship is in solemne performance? Is it the dog, think you, or the Devill, rather, that stands pawing upon the hands that are joyntly stretched out in supplications, that lies slavering the lips that are sounding out GODS prayses, and oftimes with the brush of his taile interrupting the veiw of heaven from the eies that are lifted up unto it? You see to what a height this sin grows unto. They quickly come to sett at light the Devine Majestie it self, that so much forgett the Nobility of humane Nature as to make more of a dog then a man. It is not meet, sayth our SAVIOUR, to take the childrens bread and give unto dogs. The crums that fall from the table ought to serve their turns. Those superfluities of our tables and affections which cannot be converted to the use of man may be perhaps afforded to dogs, and thats all that CHRISTS doctrine allows. But to give them any part, much more precedencie of that which belongs to men; to feed them, to cloth them, to tend them, to provide for their ease, their cleannes, their ornament, to bestow our time, our paines, our thoughts, that they may be sweet, faire, precious dogs, worthy of our Love, fitting for delight, acceptable and uncontroulable in all companies; whilest in the meane space the poore members of CHRIST perish for want of food, rayment, and harbour is such a contradiction not only to that particular rule which CHRIST JESUS gave in this matter, but to the very foundation of his religion, as if any dare pretend to make any reconciliation in this point, wee may boldly shutt him off with St. Pauls censure, He is proud, and knows nothing.

CHEEREF. Undoubtedly he knows but a little of Christs mind that thinks CHRIST will allow the wast of any Love or Cost upon our dogs, or any other such like cattle, for our pleasures sake. CHRISTS advise is that the overflowings of our affections and estates should be derived upon the poore and needy, rather then upon our freinds and kindred; how much then will he resent the diversion of them upon vile beasts? What excuse will they render to him for their lavish cost and kindnes unto dogs, who, upon mention of the poores Necessitie, made an apologie for a little extraordinarie cost and kindnes that was bestowed upon his own body?

AFFECTION. Surely they must have some other advocate then the spirit of GOD, and goe upon some other Law then the Gospel that hope to carry out this matter at the great day of tryal. Catherine Stubs puts herself upon mercy, and seeks by repentance to cleare her guilt. They that dare stand upon Justification may have better heart than she had; I doubt they will not have so good successe to have the Angels come down to fetch them up to heaven. I am now altogether ot her mind, that it was a greivous offence; and though I am ashamed of mine error that I thought otherwise, yet am I glad that I made it known, whereby this discourse hath followed to the rectification of mine own and perhaps of some others minds too, who, it may be, as I did, looking upon the Excellencie of other vertues in her, may be perswaded to think this a lighter or lesse dangerous Exorbitancie then indeed it is. Her example can be no colour for any bodies Imitation that heares her confession and detestation of this sin at last. She could not abide to look upon the Bitch after she well bethought her of the Love she had born and the kindnes she had shewed more then she would willingly have afforded many a Christian Soul. Thats all (that nobody may mistake) which she accuseth her self of, that she would have been loth, not that she would not at all have done as much for CHRISTS members. I am perswaded that if experiment had been made, she durst not respectively have done lesse for the least of them that belong to CHRIST, then she did to the bitch. She durst not have refused to admit them, not to her table only, but to her cup; to receive them, not only to her bosome, but into her heart, and to goe out of her bed for them, if it were not fitt to take them into it. That which she laments is, that she could not have done this so cheerfully to the poore for CHRIST his sake, as shee did it for her own lust to a filthy curre, as she termed it.

CHEEREF. And verily there was great reason; for the truth of our Love to CHRIST, both for substance and measure, is to be found by the Nature and manner of our Love to his members here below. Hee that loves CHRIST with all his heart hath, with David, all his delight in the Saints on earth and upon such as excell in vertue, and thinks nothing els worthy either of Love or Honour. Ile give you a proof of this by an admirable Example which I lately read. And because I find it so well sett down, as it cannot be mended, Ile give it you in the very words of the Authour :—

Ingo, King of the Draves and Venades, after his conversion to the Christian Faith, making a stately Feast, not as Ahashuerus, to shew the bounty of his own, but the glorie of CHRISTS kingdome, sett all his Nobles, which were at that time Pagans and unconverted to the Christian Faith, in his

Hall below, and certaine poore Christians in his Presence-Chamber with himself, with kingly Cheare and Attendants; at which they wondering, he told them, This he did, not as King of the Draves, but as King of another world, wherein these were his consorts and fellow-Princes; these he saw with a spiritual eie clad in white robes and worthy his company. To them he would give civil due in the regiment of the Commonwealth; but those he must love and honour in his heart, as beloved and honoured of God.

MOTHER. No Discant can adde grace to the plaine song of this story.

GUARD. Yet give mee leave to paire it with another very proper to the subject wee are on:—Amadeus, Duke of Savoy, Grand child to him who for his vertues was chosen Pope, bore with great Patience the falling sicknes with which it pleased GOD to exercize him all his life long. One day certaine Embassadors of other Princes, upon discourse it may be of their Masters pleasures, besought him to see his dogs of chase. Tomorrow (sayd he) if you come Ile give you satisfaction. The Embassadors failed not at the appointed houre, and the Duke that was provided lead them forth into a Gallerie, out of which he shewed them, pointing with a little rod that he held in his hand, a very great number of poore people sett at meat, and served both with plenty and decencie. These, my Masters (sayth he), are the hounds which I keep, every day feeding them as you now see, and with them I hunt, not for corruptible dainties and sports, but for eternal glorie and happines.

MOTHER. Well, then, I perceive as long as there be poore and vertuous people in the world, theres no place for dogs of Pastime in the heart of a wise Christian; no, nor in his house neither, but under the table. Your Storie and your Arguments amount to as much. As for Mrs. Stubs, the sure Answere in my Judgement will bee, that what she did amisse in this kind she did out of Ignorance and want of consideration, which he that shall here have repentance, cannot pretend. If any think it strange that such darknes as this error includes should remaine in such an illuminated understanding as she alwaies seemed to have, let him remember that the best of our Perfection in this world is but like that of the Moone, whose lightsome orbe is blemished with many dark and black spots. Theres no such absolute puritie in understanding and affections whilest wee are here below, but that there will be ever found some admixture of Error in both. Assoone as it is discovered it must be detested ; thats necessarie. We cannot willingly entertaine the least sin without breach of Freindship with GOD. But for whatsoever is unwittingly done amisse, theres abundance of mercy with GOD to passe by it, and excellencie of wisedome to extract both our own and others Good out of it. Take the present instance into consideration, and you shall find it as I say. Mrs. Catherine Stubs is made humble by that remembrance of her Error, and so becomes more capable of the Divine Consolation which she was to enjoy. Wee are made wiser by her Error, and come better to know the heinousnes of it by her confession and repentance then we could have done by any others admonitions that were innocent. GOD suffers this sin in her practize a while, that it might appeare more sinfull in the end by her censure and condemnation. They that think her a Saint must beleive what she sayd by the Spirit of GOD instructing her, and not follow what she did through the evill example of the world misleading her. And so, if it please you, let us give an end to this present matter and this daies work.

GUARD. Not so, I pray. The good successe of my first motion this day touching the perfection of those two Stories which were last day left unperfect, makes mee think it cannot prove amisse to desire from our MODERATOUR the fulfilment of that admirable storie of the Fourty Martyrs for which she hath been beyond all reason a longsome Debitor to us.

AFFECT. A story of Martyrs began this Festival, and no story more proper to conclude it. Martyrdome is a condition that belongs to all Saints, if not in full Act, in faithfull

Resolution. There is no man may hope to enter the Kingdome of heaven that is not at a point to lay down his life for the purchase of it.

MODER. I shall willingly doe what you request, and so much the rather as besides that which you expect touching the Martyrs, you shall heare that of a Mother, which will make my story doubly sutable and usefull.

As the Guardians profession of the Christian Faith, and making himself partner in their sufferings brought matter of joy to the Martyrs all night long, so it bred much greif next morning amongst the heathen. They saw a double shame to their Religion in what had happened. He that came to it in hope of Life dyed, and he that went from it made it to be worse then death. Hereupon Agricola, to make a short end of that which he was afrayd might turn to further damage, enragedly commands to take the Saints out of the water, and after the breaking of their legs, wills their bodies to be burned. The breaking of their legs gave end both to paine and life. As the blows descend their souls mount up to their wished happines, and as they part they sing, Our soul is escaped as a bird out of the snare of the fowler; the snare is broken, and wee are delivered. Only one, the yongest and the strongest, Melliton by name, remaines yet alive, and him the executioners (whether out of compassion or out of designe, I know not) resolve to leave behind. All the rest of the bodies they fling up into certaine cartes, and begin to drive away to the place appointed for their burning. Amongst many Christians that stood by, Mellitons Mother was one, who, more amated at this kindnes then at all the former cruelties, stepping to her son, lifts him to the ground, laies him on her shoulder, and makes hast to overtake the cartes that went before; and as she goes thus loaden, she speaks to this purpose: Oh, my son, the son of my wombe, and the joy of my heart, how blessed shall I live hereafter if thou shalt now dy for CHRISTS sake. Courage, my Son! Courage, I say. These light afflictions, which are but for a moment, shalbe repayed with a more exceeding and eternal weight of Glorie. Take heart, oh thou light of mine eies, that I may enjoy thee in everlasting light. When thou wentest to the warre for thy Prince, I sent thee forth with teares, because danger was much and the gaine little. But now I march with triumph, because I know there is a Crown and a kingdome that attends thee. The cold water hath brought thee to the gates of Paradise, the consuming fire shall give thee full possession of it. Thy Companions, my Son, thy noble and happy Companions, are gone before; make hast to overtake them, that with them thou mayst enter into the presence of the LORD and into the fulnes of his Joy. To all these words Melliton gives no answere, but cheerfully breathing out his soul into her bosome, gives the full assurance of her best desires; which she perceiving, takes him from her shoulders into her Armes, and undantedly casteth him upon the other Martyrs. This done, she follows with the rest to the place of execution, and there staies till she sees that body which had received life and nourishment from her brought to ashes, being farre more glad to have offered him up a burnt sacrifice to GOD, then to have kept him alive never so much to her own Comfort.

PATIENT. Let me adde a Paralel, and there will be a large feild for your admiration and observation to exercize themselves in. Valentz the Emperor, having out of his zeal to the Arrian heresy deprived the orthodox Christians of Edessa both of their Bishop and their Churches, comes at last in person to see a famous and magnifique Church that was in that Citty, bearing the Name of St. Thomas. When he comes he sees the Catholicks, whom he had hoped to have seen either perverted or dissipated, exercizing their Religion in great Numbers, and with great boldnes, in an open feild under the walls of the Citty. At this spectacle he grows so enraged, as after many contumelious words heaped on the President General, he gives him a blow on the face, and wills him henceforth, with armed hand, to prevent such assemblies; and if they would needs come together, he bids him use both whips and clubs and other warlike Instruments for their chastizement. The President, whose name was Modestus, thus enforced and affrighted, gathering all the trayned band together early in the morning, goes to the performance of this charge. As he passeth over the market place, there comes a woman half-dressed, leading a child in her hand, and without any shew of care or feare, breaking through the midst of his troopes, hastens to the place where he was going. The President wills her to be brought back, and demands whither she made such disordered speed. To the Assembly of the Catholicks, sayd the woman. Alas, poore soul (sayd hee), dost thou not know the Emperors Commands? I know it, replied she, and that all these persons and provisions are intended to the slaughter of them, and therefore it is that I make such hast to this holy meeting, longing to undergoe joyntly with them whatever is to be done or suffered for our common Faith. But why dost thou carry this Infant with thee? sayd Modestus. That being partaker in an holy Death, replied she, he may be partner with us in everlasting happines. The President amazed (as well he might), goes back to Valentz, and recompting this passage, tells him he might by one Instance know the mind of all the rest of the Orthodox, and perceive that the event would be contrarie to expectation. For wee shall, sayd he, gaine nothing but the reproach of crueltie in attempting by foul meanes to overthrow such invincible Constancie. The force of these arguments, and the wonderment of the fact it self, wrought so on the mind of Valentz as he forbore to put in execution the violence which hee intended. And the holy woman that brought her son a free will offering went away, not only with his and her own life, but with the safetie of the whole Church.

GUARD. Wee had lost much if wee had gone away without these last Stories.

CHEEREF. And wee shall be guilty of more by having heard them if wee put them not in practize. To know these things and not to follow them will procure double stripes.

MOTHER. Wee shall not scape at so easy a rate. Our Commendation of good will make our Condemnation the sorer. If we imitate not what wee advise and propose to others, wee shalbe tenfold punished, and wee deserve it.

AFFECT. Wee are necessitated to be better then ordinarily Christians are, or els our case wilbe farre worse, in that wee know the way and the reward of weldoing; of both which points, as farre as I can perceive, the world is utterly ignorant. If our stories be right, the practize of the world is very wrong. And in fuller remonstrance thereof and further pennance of my unwary Errour in lessening the fault of Mrs. Catherine Stubs, which her self so much aggravated, give mee leave to the confession which I formerly made, to adde by way of satisfaction the recompting of a most noble Storie as any you have heard, containing not only a cleare proof of that wholesome doctrine which I have learned from you touching the difference which wee ought to make in our affections and esteeme between the members of CHRIST and all other creatures whatsoever, but serving notably for a pattern to all such delinquents as I have been, how they ought to make amends and reverse the ignorance of their words and deeds when ever they are convicted of opposition or maine difference from the true and lively power of Christian Faith and doctrine. And because the Story is or special weight and consequence, not only in regard of the substance of the fact but of many other circumstances, I shall tell it you as neer as possibly I can without any variation from the original relation of venerable Bede himself, the native truth being a condition that is perhaps of more satisfaction then addition of ornament, in those examples propounded for absolute Imitation or proof of Doctrine not commonly received in the world such as this present is.

Oswin, King of Northumberland, was a man tall in stature and of a comely aspect, affable in speech, and curteous in behaviour, and of open handed bounty both towards the gentry and commonalty, so that great store of noble Personages flockt out of all the parts of this Ile to his Court, the Eminency of his rare parts both of mind and body, and the Excellence of his worthy Actions drawing them on to his love and service. Amongst all his other vertues and modesty, and as I may so speak, glories of GODS spiritual benedictions that were in him, his Humilitie is recompted to have been exceeding admirable, as by one example will be abundantly manifested. He had bestowed a very good horse upon Bishop Aidon, although, good man, he used commonly to performe his journeys on foot; yet, notwithstanding, for the better passage of rivers and other such like occasions, he had accepted of the Kings guift, and one day as he made use of it by riding, a poore man encountering him begd an Almes. The good Bishop being full of pitty, a special observer of the poore, and a father of the afflicted, instantly dismounting, wills that his horse, with all the royal furniture belonging to him, should be given the poore man. The King had speedy notice thereof; whereupon, going in to dinner with Aidon, he sayd, What is this that thou hast done, my Lord Bishop, in giving to the poore man the royal Courser which thou shouldst have kept for thine own use? Were there not meaner horses, or other kind of things good enough to have bestowed on the poore man, although that thou hadst not parted with that horse, which I gave thee for thine own personal service? The Bishop cutting him short made answere: What is this that thou sayest, oh King? Is that son of a Mare which I have given away of more esteeme with thee then that son of GOD for whose sake I have given it, and that son of GOD to whom I have given it? Aidon having thus spoken satt him down in his place, and the King and his servants that had been a hunting goe to the fire. As they stand warming themselves the King takes the matter and the Bishops words into better consideration, and hereupon ungirding his sword and giving it to an officer to lay aside, he comes hastily to the Bishop, and casting himself down at his feet, desired him that he would be appeased with him; for never hereafter will I speak any more of this busines (sayd hee) nor from this day forward sett any stint touching what or how much of my mony and goods thou shouldst bestow and give amongst the sons of GOD. The Bishop hearing this starts up as one much affrighted, and taking up the King, told him that he would be wholly freinds with him, if, casting away all manner of heavines, he would now sett down to meat chearfully ; which, whilst the King in obedience strives to performe, shewing himself pleasant and merry, the Bishop on the other side grows so troubled and overgone with greif, that teares burst out of his eies. One of the Bishops Preists observing this, demanded of him in their own language, which neither the King nor any of his servants understood, what might be the reason of this sodaine passion. I know, answered Aidon, that this King cannot live long ; for such a King as this I never saw. I perceive plainly that he will be shortly snatcht out of this world, for this people are no waies worthy of such a Governour as he is. And in very truth this sad presage of this holy man was not long after accomplished. This blessed King was traiterously made away, and Aidon himself lived only twelve daies after the others death—death in the worlds accompt and in the eies of flesh and bloud, but in truth the entrance of life and everlasting Happines.

XIII

CHRISTMASTIDE, 1632

St. Lawrence—Jeames Baynham—Windelmuta's Burning— Marian's Burning—Bishop Farrer and Thomas Hanks— The Martyrs of Saluce—The Priest Macarius and the Avaricious Virgin.

MOTHER. Its a hard task, beloved CHEEREFULL, that is upon us, and double to that which was last yeare enjoyned. To outvy idle pastimes by worthy Stories was not much; the pleasure lies the same way in both those matters. Its the Delight of the mind thats sought by gaming, and, therefore, when a better satisfaction was offered in the same kind, it was no great difficultie to content them from whom we tooke the lesse. But the Belly, you know, hath no cares; and therefore I know not how you can apply your Stories to quiet its grudgeings for those delicacies which you have robbed it of. They must be very materiall Stories that can make recompence for the losse of so much good Cheere as your austere Temperance hath rentrenched.

CHEER. The Pleasure which I have hindred had, I am sure, by this time beene lost if it had been taken. The savour of Dainties is past assoone as they are gone downe into the Belly. You are now, therefore, no worse by forbearance then you should have beene by enjoying. Bring mee any of those who have filled themselves with the best of meats and drinks, and if he find any sweeter relish in his mouth by all that which

Gluttonie could devise, then you now doe upon that Pittance which Temperance hath entertained you with, and I am content to be challenged of injury in what I have done, and bound to make amends in what shall be desired.

MOTHER. Nay, verily; we would not now by any meanes make exchange for disposition either of mind or of body with them that have most filled themselves with Dainties. The Sweetnes of their good Cheere is vanished, and the fulnes that remaines is a Burden. We are now in the better case by their owne judgements, and so shalbe till supper returne, when the poverty of two dishes, and those but plaine ones neither, Mutton and Veale (for I heare of no others provisions) will not be able to minister that happines which a well covered table would doe.

CHEER. They will not afford that Honour perhaps in the worlds esteeme; but surely for matter of pleasure there need be no envy, it being most true in matter of Diet which Socrates sayd of Riches, That the surest and readiest way to be wealthy is not to encrease mony and substance, but to cutt of unnecessarie desires. So verily for a man to keepe good Cheere alwaies there needs not the providing of much or dainty good, but the paring away of wanton appetites. He that eats by the judgement of his Pallate, and not of his owne or others fancies, may alwaies, if he please, sitt downe to a Feast, it being ever in his power, by the right preparing of his stomach, to convert whatever is sett before him into Nectar and Ambrosia. Tell mee, I pray, whether you thinke there be ever a feast in the Kingdome that will rellish the Guests better then our sober Commons is like to doe our good Company to Night? And if you eat with as much pleasure as any whatsoever, why should you esteeme your Cheere lesse or worse then the best can be even for the very present? As for afterwardes, when the Table is taken away there will be no compare. You shall have as much advantage over others in your rest upon an orderly supper, as you have now for buisines upon a sober collation. So then, both for the night and day theres the pleasure of ten houres, for one that you should have had by the allowance or such excesse as we have formerly used. And how can you then any way make Temperance or me your Debitor, that have not abated anything from the delight of your mouth, and have added much to the delight and ease of every other facultie and member both of Mind and Body? If you have now no lesse pleasure in eating when you come to your meales, and much more in all other respects all the day long, why should you then thinke any other Cheere or entertainment better then that which you have?

GUARD. We approuve what you say to be true, and are content to accept what you provide as good and great Cheere; but alwaies without any prejudice to the Stories that wee are now come for. It was your promise, and therefore we may claime them by way of debt, though not of recompence. We acknowledge to have no Damage by what you have taken from our Bellies; but if you give not the Dainties which we expect for our mindes, you shall faile in that which is right for your selfe and due to us.

MOTHER. The demande is so right as cannot be put of without much wrong. Wherefore I pray, beloved CHEEREFULL, without any further delay proceed to the satisfaction of it. Let the Banquet of Stories be brought forth, and that answerable to the Festivall, rich and plentifull with dainties, that our Guests may report they have Christmas fare for the mind at least, albeit but ordinarie entertainment for their Bellies.

CHEER. You say well; and to this intent I have chosen out a Storie which includes all the ingredients of Christmas magnificence. It is of St. Laurence, his name speakes Bayes: thats the first, you know, of all the preparations which belong to this great Festivall.

MOTHER. Never was a name more fitly imposed on a man. The Laurell, its the glorious meed of Victors, and who ever more victorious than St. Laurence, that triumphed over Emperors, and by his Patience in suffering overcame the very patience of his Tormentors?

CHEER. A good fire is the next of our Christmas provisions. And here you shall see one kindled if you draw nigh it by attention, will warme the coldest heart, and inflame it with the Love of heaven, making us blush to thinke how little we are willing to suffer for him for whom St. Laurence was willing to suffer so much.

AFFECTIO. And by the light thereof, if you looke well you shall see the monstrous deformitie of the worlds practize at this time, especially in nourishing our Bodies and arming our Lusts to fight against CHRIST, at the same time when wee celebrate the remembrance of the Martyrs that layd downe their Lives for CHRISTS sake. They regarded not their Bodies to please CHRIST, and we regard not CHRIST to please our Bodies. How doe wee condemne ourselves in commending them!

CHEER. A Christmas light guilded and engraven with the pourtracture of all manner of vertues will not be wanting. St. Augustine sayth that St. Laurence his Passion was a Candle set up to enlighten the whole world. As for good Cheere and Dainties, which is ye maine, though all the Martyrs be Dainties at GODS table (and how then shall they be otherwise in our esteem?) yet in very truth St. Laurence is rost meat for our soules to feed on.

MOTHER. You say very true. There is not perhaps amongst all the Martyrs any one Example wherein we shall find more abundance of admirable and appliable matter, then in this of St. Laurence, if there were time to improve it now. You need not goe on to further resemblance—there could not a story be chosen more proper every way. Wee pray you therefore proceed to the narration it selfe.

CHEER. The country of St. Laurence is commonly sayd to be Spaine, and Osea, a city of Arragon, the place where he was borne, where his Parents Names stand recorded to have been Orentius and Patrentia, and there is an Anniversary remembrance of them, as Saints, in that Church to this day. Being thus borne of Saints, it is no question but his breeding was in all holines, and accordingly wee may presume his whole life was answerable. We may well thinke he had beene long trained up in CHRISTS schoole that came forth so compleat a champion, but leaving what wee know not, weel beginne where we find certainty; and that is, how he was chosen by Pope Sixtus to be the Cheife of the Deacons, and had the treasure of the Church committed to his custody. These treasures (that you may not thinke that holy Bishop to have beene a horder up of wealth for Covetuousnes, as his successors now be) are by St. Ambrose specified to have beene certaine monies which were kept in store, for the necessarie sustenance of the Ministers and the charitable releife of the poore Christians. At this time was a cruell Persecution at Rome, and the cheife Minister thereof was named Valerian, who, understanding that Pope Sixtus by his preaching and his counsells was a meanes, not onely of drawing many Gentiles to the Christian Faith, but of putting forward many Christians to the prize of Martyrdome, sends for him, and by all Artifice that could possibly be devised, both of faire and foule words, of Threats and Promises, assaies to supplant him in the profession of that holy faith whereof he had beene a Doctor to others. But Sixtus, remaining immoveable, and seeming to deride both his menaces and offers, Valerian in great rage wills him to be carried to Prison. In the way, as the Guard led him, Laurence overtakes him, and without respect of any thing els, for the longing that he had to goe with him into Bonds and unto Death, cries out amaine, Whether away, Father, dost thou goe without thy sonne? Whether dost thou make such speed, oh holy Preist, without thy Deacon? If it be to offer up thy selfe a sacrifice to GOD, thou doest against thine owne usage, that was never wont to offer without a minister. I have hitherto served thee in this nature; what now appeares offensive in mee that thou shouldest reject mee? Hast thou found me to degenerate, either in fidelitie or valour? Thou committedst to my ministry the dispensation of CHRISTS Blood amongst the faythfull, and wilt thou now deny mee the

communion of thine owne blood? Wilt thou refuse him a
partener in thy sufferings whom thou hast made an associate
in the consummation of the Sacraments? Haveing accepted
me for the greater charge, wilt thou put me of from the lesse?
Consider well however the greatnes of thy courage may be,
yet the goodnes of thy judgement will by this meanes be
called in question, and thou mayest happily be censured as
undiscrete whilest thou art commended for valiant. The
Scholars imperfection is the Masters disgrace. How much
renowne have many great Persons wonne through their
scholars vertues? How many famous Captaines have
triumphed for the Victories of their souldiers rather then their
owne? Remember that Abram offered up his sonne, that
Steven went to Martyrdome before Peter. Doe thou like
them, my Father. Manifest thine owne valour first in thy
sonnes, and obtaine the victorie in his Conqueste. Offer him
for the truth whom thou hast delivered from error, and taking
mee a long with thee in thy suffering, goe approved in thy
judgement and accompanied to thy Glory.

I refuse thee not, my sonne, answered Sixtus, nor doe I
leave thee behind as a Coward, but as a select Champion
ordained for a greater Triall. An easy Death best befitts my
Age and weakenes; a sorer Conflict attends thy strength
and youth, and a more noble Triumph is reserved for thee.
Weepe not, my son, thou shalt quickly follow; three daies
hence thou shalt obtaine what thou desirest. This space of
time is to be inserted for decency betweene the Preist and the
Levite. It fitts thee not to strive in thy Masters presence,
least it should be thought thou needest helpe to overcome.
Why doest thou make suit to be a partner in my sufferings?
Lo, I bequeath them wholly to thine inheritance. What
wouldest thou doe in my company? It belongs to weake
Scholars to goe along with their Masters. They that are
strong come as safely after, and much better, being single, that
so they may enjoy that full measure of Glorie which they
deserve. It would be greatly to thy disadvantage to have a

helper in this combate, that knowest how to overcome when thou art alone. Why doest thou so urge our going together? Elisha wanted not the grace when he was left by Elias to doe wonders of himselfe, and greater then his Master had done. I leave thee behind, as he did, to follow and to passe mee in my sufferings. Thou shalt endure more, and obtaine more; I consigne unto thee the whole succession of my Vertues. Onely this I give in charge: Let the treasures of the Church which thou hast in keeping be speedily divided amongst the poore.

St. Laurence, being thus comforted, not with the hope of life and worldly Happines, but with the assurance of a painfull Death for CHRIST his sake, departes with much joy, hasts to the performance of his Masters injunction. Hee spends the rest of that day and the whole night after in visiting the Christians that had retired themselves into certaine caves under ground and other secret places, for safety of their lives and the free exercise of their religion. At one of these places he restores sight to a blind man, and at another cured a woman that was greviously tormented with continuall headache. These mighty deeds that made him admirable in their eies made him more humble in his owne. He craves it, as a favour of the congregation, that he may wash their feet. They yeeld, as they tell him, because CHRIST gave the example of what St. Laurence desired.

And so at one place he performed this service to above seventy persons. After he had washed and kissed their feet he fills every mans hand proportionable to their needs, till he had quite emptied his owne of all the treasure, mony, and stock that was under his custody. If the hight of his other excellencies seeme unimitable to us, yet surely we can find no excuse why wee should not accompany him in this descent, even coupling that honour that we receive from GOD or Man with the exercizes of humility, and the beneficence that we shew to any of GODS Children with abundance of respect to their Persons. The necessity of the godly Poore are for our

Compassion onely, not for our Contempt. They doe well indeed to thinke the lesse of themselves for their Calamitie, but we ought rather to prize them the more, considering that in their lowly estate and afflictions we shall finde a greater resemblance of our Masters condition then in our owne honour and Prosperity. St. Laurence, having thus every way fitted himselfe by the putting on of that spirituall Armour that was needfull, and by the dispatch of those affaires that were of impediment, comes forth at last into the open feild. As soone as it was day he goes to seek his Master, Sixtus. And as he goes he meets him, led to execution with two other of his Fellow Deacons, Fielicissimus and Agapetus—those were the Names of this happy, lovely paire.

A holy œmulation of their approaching Blessednes makes him melt into teares, and breake forth into Cries. Take mee likewise, Holy Father, now along with thee. I have done what thou enjoynedst; the treasures are dispensed. Why should I stay behind that have no more to doe? These words aloud and often repeated by St. Laurence, caused his instant attachement by the Guard, whereof notice being given to the Emperor, he immediately causes the Prisoner to be brought unto him, having in his greedy hopes conceited a double prize, of Sixtus his Church treasures, and of Laurence his Christian faith. But Laurence disappoints his expectation for that time by silence. Though he were often demanded, yet he would not answere one word, and is therefore by the offended Prince committed to the Guard of one Hypolitus. In this Prison, amongst other delinquents, there was one Lucilius, who, through excesse of Greife had wept out his eies. St. Laurence offers him both his sight, which he had lost, and œternall happines besides, if he would beleive in CHRIST. Lucilius agrees, is immediately baptized, and instantly receives what was promised; his blindnes and his sorrow fall away both together; he seeth the things of the earth plainely, and feeles those joyes of Heaven he could never have beleived.

The observation of this and other the like Cures (for many

other are sayd to be wrought by St. Laurence in that prison) caused his Guardian to take a singular Affection unto him, and so, with much respect and kindnes, he setts upon him to perswade that he would freely disclose those treasures that the Emperor sought after, alledging not onely the security of his life, but the certainty of his promotion in riches and Honour would thereupon follow. If thou wouldest beleive in GOD Omnipotent, and in his Sonne CHRIST JESUS, I will not onely, freind Hypolitus, sayd St. Laurence, shew thee those treasures which thou demandest, but make thee a certaine partaker of œternall Life and happines. And hereupon St. Laurence tooke occasion to preach the Gospell of GOD, which, by the operation of the Holy Spirit, became so effectuall, as Hypolitus with his whole family, being 19 Persons, were converted and forthwith baptized. After this Valerian (that was one of the Tyrants Names) and Decius, the other, sending for St. Laurence, endeavoured with gentle words and large promises to draw from him the place where the treasures lay which he had openly confessed to have beene in his Custody. Gladly will I doe what is required, sayd St. Laurence, if I may be allowed fitting time for the performance thereof; three daies respite I must have for the collecting them together.

Its granted, sayd Valerian, and let Hypolitus goe with you as Assistant and Guard. Upon this agreement all three departed contented, Valerian rich in the assurance of these treasures, Hypolitus blest in the further enjoyment of his Prisoner, and St. Laurence glad in the hope of doing more good and suffering more Evill. At the three daies end St. Laurence returnes, and finds Valerian, accompanied with Decius. The receiving of the treasures was a busines that both desired to be interested in. Being willed to make good his promise, he stretches out his hand to a great Number of poore people, blind, lame, sick, and impotent, that he had brought along with him, and, as some say, upon those very Cartes that had beene given him for the conducting of the treasure. Loe here, most mighty Emperor, sayd hee, the wealth of Sixtus, the tresures of the Church, which you so earnestly enquire after. There is no tongue able to express the rage of those Passions which the mockage of St. Laurence, so they termed it, drave these Tyrants into. They commanded his Cloathes to be stripped of, and his Body to be torne with Scorpions, an iron instrument that beares that name from the likenes that it hath to the forme and to the effects of the Scorpions claws. When this seemes not to move him, the Tyrants will their ministers to put in practize on him the uttermost of all those Engines which the schoole of cruelty could afford. Hereupon they sett before him a long row of dreadfull torments, and tell him he must looke to undergoe them all if he continue his obstinacie. Unwise Men, sayd he, you are, that thinke to scare mee with these things, which I have alwaies longed for as greatest Dainties. Instruments of tortures you call them, and so they shall all prove to you, but for mee matters of delight. You will never be able to satisfie my unsatiablenes of these Delicacies. If these be delicacies, cryed out enraged Decius, tell where we may find other madmen of thy Fraternity to beare thee companie in this feast. Those whom thou askest after, replied St. Laurence, are too good, too happy for thine unworthy eies to behold. Decius perceiving that his courage was too great for lighter meanes to worke upon, wills that St. Laurence should be loaden with Chaines, and carried before him to his Pallace, where, with length of time and all exquisite tortures, he ment to be revenged to the full. Being there seated in his throne, he wills St. Laurence to doe what he was commanded, and not to rely upon his hidden treasures, which should not at all stead him against those cruell torments which should otherwise be inflicted upon him. My Confidence, replied the blessed Saint, is onely in the treasures of Heaven, the Bounty, mercy, and goodnes of GOD. By these treasures shall I be kept free in soule and in spirit, although the body perish under that thou threatenest. Hereupon Decius gave commande that he should be first beaten with rods, and afterwards hoysing him up into the Aire by an

Engine whereupon he was fastened, they burnt his sides with certaine hot plates of Iron made fiery hot to that intent. In the midst of that torment the Martyr lift up his voice, gave thankes aloud to JESUS CHRIST, that had made him worthy to suffer these things for his sake, beseeching him to shew mercy upon his Servant, that, being accused, denied him not, and being examined confessed him to be the sonne of GOD. Thou art a great Magitian, I perceive, sayd Decius, that makest light of these things; but all thy cunning shall not help thee; for I sweare by the immortall gods, that unlesse thou instantly resolve to sacrifice to the gods, I will inflict such torments on thee as never mortall man endured the like. Thy torments shall have an end, replied Laurence, in a short space, and even that little whilest they last I shall not feel them, by the power and vertue of CHRIST JESUS. Doe what thou canst, thou shalt wearie thyselfe and not mee. That will wee try, sayd the Tyrant, and thereupon commands his whole body should be scourged over with certaine Whips that had leaden bullets tied to the end of the Cords. The bruising of the flesh rayseth up the Courage of the spirit. St. Laurence seemes at ease, and the Tyrant grows wild with rage. He bids, Teare his flesh with iron Combes, pull his Joynts in sunder with the rack. This is immediately done, but all proves in vaine. St. Laurence continues cheerefull, not onely constant, not through insensiblenes of bodily paine, but by the supply of heavenly refreshment. One of the Souldiers, named Romanus, sees an Angell standing by St. Laurence in shape of a goodly young Man, wiping with a Cloth the sweat from his face and the gore from his wounds. At last Decius, tyred out of Patience, bids, Lead away the Martyr for that time to prison againe; where, assoone as he was entered, Romanus brings a vessell of water, tells aloud what he saw, professeth that he will henceforward serve no other GOD then CHRIST JESUS, and desires to be baptized, which is accordingly performed by St. Laurence. News thereof going instantly to Court, Decius wills that Romanus should be brought to him. Romanus comes without delay, and by his voluntarie Confession prevents the Emperors demande, but encreaseth his anger. Assoone as he comes in sight, he calls aloud, What is thy pleasure with me, oh Emperor? I am a Christian. My pleasure is, sayd the Emperor, that thou shalt loose thy life for thy Christianity. And so he did. The executioner takes him away instantly, and cutts off his head without the gates of the citty. Thus he that came after went before, for one houres worke in the Vineyarde at the end of the day receiving the agreement of everlasting Happines. By this time night drew on, but fury takes no rest. St. Laurence is sent for, and againe the Tyrants both together set upon him with Calumnies of Majick, proposall of sacrifices, and dreadfull menaces. Decius tells him that if he persist in his willfulnes, the whole night shalbe spent in tormenting him. Then shall it be a glorious day of Jubile and triumph unto mee, said he, and not a night of darknes and horror, as thou conceivest. Beat his mouth with stones, cryed the Tyrants, and bring forth the Bed that is prepared for his lodging this happy Night. It was a great Instrument of Iron made in fashion of a gridiron. On this they stretch forth the Saints Body, and afterwards putting fire under, they began to rost him alive. The Superintendencie of the Tyrants themselves caused great solicitousnes in the ministers. They applied the Coales œqually, that every member might have his part; and yet so moderately as by Continuance of life the torment might bee lengthened out. Whilest he lies in this manner he lookes upon Decius, and, See wretched Man, these Coales are a refreshment unto mee, and this fire nourisheth what thou seekest to destroy. And all this through the power of my LORD JESUS CHRIST, whom, when I was accused I denied not, and when I was examined I confessed, and now, being rosted in the fire, I blesse and magnify. This ardent love to our SAVIOUR kindled in St. Laurence his heart made him not to feele at all the outward flames that rosted his body, which, being now quite eaten through on one side, he calls again to Decius, whose enraged visage gave evidence that the flames had peirced further into his heart then into St. Laurences body, Give order, sayd he, I pray thee, oh Decius, to thy ministers to turne my other side to the fire, that so, being thoroughly rosted, thou maiest eat thy fill of my body, and make account to satisfie thy appetite with my flesh, and not with the treasures of the Church, which by the hand of the poore are conveyed already into Heaven.

And now the Conquest being acheived, the Combate ended, the glorious Martyr turnes himselfe to CHRIST, and giving thankes for his sufferings, is immediately received up to the enjoyment of his Crowne. The body, that was left all night upon the Gridiron, was next day honourably interred by the Christians, of whom Hypolitus, being accused to the Emperor as cheife, was in reward of his Piety, and of his constant profession of the Christian faith in Conformity of his Name to that other Hypolitus whom the Poets speake of, adjudged to be torne in peices by wild horses. This is the story of St. Laurence, which I will end with Mr. Fox his conclusion:

The GOD of might and mercy graunt us grace by the life of St. Laurence to learne in CHRIST to live, and by his death to learne for CHRIST to dy. Amen.

MOTHER. Undoubtedly we have an excellent patterne in the one, and a strong encouragement in the other. We can hardly find a more perfect rule then his Actions, and a more enforcing argument then his sufferings, both to direct us in the leading of our lives according to CHRISTs will, and to perswade us to the ready laying of theme downe for his sake, when hee calls us to it. Who can thinke any service enough, or any suffering too much for such a Lord and Master as CHRIST JESUS is, who turnes the sorest Paines to delight, and extracts pleasures for his Saints out of the most horrid torments that mans rage can inflict upon them? He that lies broyling on a Gridiron in others eies, lies in his owne Conceit upon a Bed of Pleasure. Oh, the mercy and power of our LORD JESUS CHRIST to them that love and put their trust in him! It was so with the three Children of old; they walked in the furnace as in a Garden.

And even in these last dayes wee have had by new examples the seale of these elder truths, and that we may know it was all the free grace of GOD, and not any waies the merits of his servants Innocency, in some of them, who could not, as St. Laurence, glory in their constant profession of the truth, from which through humane fraylty they started at the first, that the grace of GOD and his mighty Power might be fully manifested and more perfected in and by their weaknes.

Jeames Bainham, overwrought by feare, abjures the truth under the Name of Heresy in the daies of Henery the 8th. He recants with his mouth what himselfe beleived, and subscribes with his hand to that which others offered. He goes in procession before the Crosse at Pauls, and stands with a fagget on his shoulder before the preacher all the sermon while, and so with a small fine he is dismissed out of bodily Prison and from the greivance of Men. But his freedome proves his misery, his Liberty without GODS favour is a thousand times worse then the prison, and his life without the truth is growne odious to himselfe. He bewailes his error in private to his freinds one by one; at last he makes publig Confession of it before the whole Congregation of the faithfull in a Warehouse in Bow Churchyard in London. This done, he goes next Sunday to St. Augustines with an English testament in his hand, and the obedience of a Christian man in his bosome; there he puts himselfe forth in open view, and weeping, tells aloud that he had done no lesse then denied GOD in departing from the truth. And if I turne not againe unto it, this word of GOD, sayth he, shewing forth the testament, will damne mee both body and soule at the Day of judgement. Forgive me all, good people, and take heed that you fall not after the example of my weaknes. Death can be nothing in respect of that hell which I have felt, and for all the world I would not againe endure what I have done. This publig Act he seconds by his letter to the Bishop, and is thereupon apprehended, and after much cruell handling comes at last to the Stake ; and what doe you thinke doth it prove ? As flesh and Blood formerly doubted? No. Heare his owne words, and see the selfe same tender mercy of GOD which St. Laurence acknowledged, made good on him likewise. When the fire had devoured halfe his legs and Armes, he calls out to the lookers on, Oh, yee Papists, Behould you looke for miracles, and here now you may see a miracle: for in this fire I feele no more paine then if I were in a Bed of Downe; but it is to mee as sweet as a Bed of roses.

PATIENT. The livelines of this noble expression will hardly be parralleld; but the selfe same gratious working of GODS holy spirit, as St. Vincent sayd of old, in strengthening the Tormented more then the Devill can doe the Tormentor, and in sweetening the bitternes of most cruell paines so as they should be very tolerable to the Body, and no way able to diminish from all fulnes of joy in the spirit, might easily be confirmed by a Cloud of better examples, as well as those of former times if need were.

MOTHER. Though it need not for gaining of beleife in them that beleive already, yet it will be profitable for encrease and confirmation of beleife in them that beleive most. Nor is there any thing that can better suite both the day and ourselves. Wherefore, if you thinke good, let us not passe from this subject till we have by addition of more proofes fortified it a little better.

GUARD. You say well. Instances are the best arguments in this matter; and however we perswade ourselves, I am in doubt that beleife of this trust is not so full and sound as it ought to be in most of us. For did we really beleive it in others, we could not be so affrighted in applying it to our selves. That fire should not paine, though it burnt, nor torments afflict when they were most felt, nor Death affright at all when it most dreadfully ceazes, are such grounds as, being rightly layd, would make us as forward to be Imitators as we are ready to admire the Patience and Constancie of Martyrs.

PATIENT. Indeed that was Windelmutas foundation. When a noble Matron that loved her dearly besought her for the prolonging of her life to dissemble the profession of her faith, and to be content to keepe it in her heart, Ah, sayd shee, doe you know what you say? *With the heart we beleive to righteousnes, and with the tongue wee confesse to salvation.* And when upon her seeming to contemne death, it was told her she had not yet tasted how bitter Death was: No, sayd she, neither ever shall I: for so much hath CHRIST promised to all that keepe his word. Neither will I forsake him for sweet life or bitter death. Nor was CHRISTS mercy less then her hope. She went to her death with a merry and joyfull Countenance, desiring the executioners to looke well that the stake were fast, that it deceived her not by falling. She layd the powder to her brest, she stretcheth forth her neck to the cord, and bowed downe her head as one that would take a sleepe. What thinke you? Was Deathe terrible to her at all?

MODERAT. How contemptible was it to Marian, a woman of low ranke in the world, but of high degree in GODS kingdome, when for her resolutenes in the truth she was condemned to be buried quick. Seeing the Coffen brought hooped with Iron: Have you provided this pasty Crust to bake my flesh in? sayd she.

AFFECTIO. But fire is intolerable. You shall have instances for that too. When Richard Jones, a knights sonne, bemoaned the painfullnes of his death to Bishop Farrer a little before his burning, If you see mee once to stirre in the fire, sayd the Bishop, then give no Creditt to my doctrine. And what he sayd he well performed: for he stood without moving to the last, holding up his stumps till one Richard Gravell beat him downe with a Staffe.

Thomas Haukes his freinds had the same dread of burning as the other had. They thinke the paine of the fire to be unsufferable, and as he is going to the stake, earnestly desire that if he find it possible for a man to keep his mind quiet and patient in the consuming of his body, he could give them a signe, and that which they pitched upon was that he should lift up his hands towards heaven before he gave up the Ghost, and stretch them on high above his head. This he promised to doe, and so enters the fire, and there continues till his speach is choaked, his skinne riveled together, and his fingers quite consumed by the violence of the flame. Now every one gives him for a dead man, and their expectation is come to an end; when on a suddaine, like a man that remembreth what he had almost forgot, he reacheth up his hands all on a light fire above his head to GOD ward, and with great rejoicing, as it seemed, clapped them thrice together; upon which grew a marveilous outcry and applause from the beholders, and especially on their parts that knew the meaning. And straightway the blessed Martyr, sinking downe into the fire, gave up his spirit.

MODERAT. The little paine that the fire put the holy Martyrs to in Queene Marys dayes was not onely well knowne, but notably testified by some of the cheifest of their Persecutors themselves. A vengeance light on them, said Bishop Bouner; I thinke they take a delight in burning, and then what shall we gaine by the match?

GUARD. This speach paints him forth in the selfe same colour that Decius appeared in, broyling much more painefully in flames of rage and Dispite then St. Laurence did on his gridiron. And verily, if you will observe the passages on both sides, as well in ancient as moderne times, you can hardly be perswaded but for the most part the Martyrs themselves felt much lesse of all that which they suffered then either their Judges or Tormentors did. Make comparison of demeanour both in the comming unto and the continuance of the execution it selfe, and you shall see it evident, by the difference of tempers, that you shall perceive the Martyrs full of Confidence, of cheerefulnes, of Charity, leaping, singing, praying: they that condemne them, and they that carry them away to death, goe raging, cursing, quarelling, with bent brows, hanging lips, and staring eies. The ones talke is all of joy, nothing but Heaven, Angells, happines; the others tongues runne all upon Devills, Hell, and damnation. Yf the fulnes of the mouth be a true signe, as truth it selfe has taught us, of the abundance of the heart, wee must needs conclude that there was much more reall Comfort and Gladnes in the inward, then appearing misery in the outward estate of GODS servants : and on the contrarie, the persecutors were even for that present in much worse Condition for point of paine and greife and bitter sufferings.

MODER. A very fresh proofe of this difference of temper we lately heard in our supper readings.

GUARD. You meane touching the Martyrs in Saluce, Anno 1619 ? Its worth the recounting againe, and besides, here be many that never heard it yet, I suppose.

MODERAT. Peter Marchesy, a Notary of Acceill, in the vally of Maire, rich both in the world and to GOD ward, having by his example in saying prayers at their meetings, as well as by his wisedome in conducting their affaires, much advanced the reformed religion in those places, was committed to Prison, in June, 1619, by the Governor of Denier, and thence brought into the inquisition at Saluce.

Maurice Mungie, a souldier of good note, that had borne the office of a sergeant in the Dukes warres, whilest he sollicites the others deliverance, is himself attacked for the same Cause of religion, and both are joyntly condemned to suffer death at . . .

Upon the 21 of October they are brought forth to execution early in the morning by foure a Clock, the Monkes that had been laboureing all night to pervert them accompanying them on foot, and the Bishop in his Coach, to the Gallows. Marchesy goes formost, the executioner stopping his mouth that he might neither pray to GOD nor speake to the people, and another goes along still beating him with a Cudgell. At last he getts the liberty of a few words, but they were sweet ones : I see the heavens open and the Angells attending for mee. No, replied a Monk that stood under the Gibbet, Those are the Devills that stay for you in Hell, wicked and damned wretch that thou art.

Mungie is brought out after him, and as he comes he cries out, Bee of good Courage, Companion, wee have wonne the Victory! What, thinke you, did they feele for paine that thus triumphed for joy? We have wonne the victory, sayth he. So they had indeed, of flesh and blood, of Men and the World, I, and of their very persecutors too. They could not but goe away confounded in their owne hearts as well as in others Judgements. The same teares of the people, and many they were that applauded them as Martyrs, condemned the other as their murtherers.

GUARD. Mongie was a souldier, and he proclaimes victory. Hugh Laverock was old and impotent, and he congratulates the recovery of his owne and his blind companione, John Apries, their infirmities at the stake. Every man in the schoole of Martyrdome useth his own expression, but all play their prizes with the same contempt of paine and death. After they were chained the stake, Laverock cast away his crutch and heartens John Apries. Bee of good comfort, my Brother, sayd he, for my Lord of London is our good Physitian; he will heale us both shortly, thee of thy blindnes, mee of my Lamenes.

MOTHER. Both the delight and profitt of this subject is so great as I should hold it no small sinne to put an end thereto, but that I see the time is outrunne, and wee ourselves come to a stand. Wherefore, if you please, let us now differre what wee cannot well accomplish.

GUARD. You say-well for this matter; onely one thing which I doe not so well understand I would bee glad if I now might receive satisfaction in, and that is, touching St. Laurence his calling the poore the treasures of the Church.

MOTHER. I will tell you a story that shall cleare the point, sutes well with the day, and serves marveilously to our admonition. Martyrdome in full act is but for some few, but the care and esteeme of the poore belongs to all Christians. And if in this we doe not imitate both St. Laurence and St. Steven, theres no reason to think of being partakers of their glory.

There was a Virgin in Alexandria, a Virgin rather in name than in truth, being rich and covetous, who, under pretence of love to her kindred and providing for them, was altogether busied in worldly affaires, and could by no meanes be perswaded to exercize any Charity. Amongst the rest she had one Neice, on whose content and preferment both her study and affection were cheifly sett. Many holy men having in vaine assayed the cure of this infirmity, Macarius at last resolves to make triall what GOD would worke by his meanes. Macarius was a preist of a hundred yeares old, of great fame for holines, and of most remarkable compassion to the poore, having turned his owne house into an Hospitall of sick folke, and wholly imploying both his mind and body about the tendance of their Persons and the releife of their Necessities. To this Virgin therefore one day Macarius goes. There is a parcell of Jewells come into my hands, sayd he, Emralds and Jacincts and other precious stones of such worth, as in truth inestimable, and yet they may be all had for a small summe. A hundred pounds is the price. I am well assured there be many of them more worth alone then you shall pay for them all. You may, I doubt not, by the sale of some one reimburse the mony that you now lay out, and keepe all the rest for your owne honour and your Neices ornament. The covetous mayd hearing this (after the usage of those times, with great humility to aske favour, and with highest reverence to entertaine Preists) fell down at Macarius his feet, beseeching him that no body but she might have the Bargaine. Goe along then with mee, sayd he, and conclude it your selfe. That shall not need, Father, answered the Mayd; see, here is the mony ready told out. What you doe in this matter I will stand to, and shall besides have an everlasting obligation for the benefitt. Macarius taking the mony, without more adoe layd it all out for the releife of the poore that were under his charge. The Mayd after some daies waiting, loth to suspect any thing amisse of so holy a man, and yet not able to conceive any reason of such unexpected delaies, meets him one day as he was going from the Church, and modestly remembers the busines to him. Alas, sayd he, that I have not yet given you an accompt. I layd out the mony, and the jewells are safe. Come home and you shall see them. If you like them, then well; if not, you shall carry back your mony againe, and I will pleasure some other with the bargaine. She, hearing this, follows him cheerefully, till being entered into the Doores, he turnes about, and askes her whether she desired first to see the Emralds or the Jacincts. It matters not much which first, so I may have them both, replied shee. With that he leads her into a ground roome, and shewed her a number of poore, sick, and impotent women. These, sayd he, are the Jacincts. Come up and you shall see the emralds. And so he carries her where the men lay, some of whose infirmities were very noysome to behold. Seeing her amazement, he tells her with great seriousnes: These are Jewells in GODS esteeme, and I hope they cannot be otherwise in yours. These are a prize in your hand, with which you may make purchase in heaven, and therefore I know you will not repent you of the bargaine that is so much to your advantage. The poore Virgin, having no power to reply, departs home in great anguish of mind, which instantly breeds sicknes, and whilest she thus doubly mournes her losse and her infirmity, GOD, trebling his strooke by the death of her Neice, brings her to a right sence of her error. Shee feeles her sinne in her owne punishment and bewailes it; reads her danger in anothers Judgement, and intends to prevent it. She thankes GOD for his unspeakable mercy, Macarius for his good Counsell, ratifies the disbursement which he had made, and imploys all the rest of her wealth in the same kinde and trade, making Godlines her ornament, and growing rich in good workes, and so approving her selfe both to GOD and Man a true Virgin in the spirit as well as in the flesh.

XIV

CHRISTMASTIDE, 1632—ST. JOHN THE EVAN-LIST'S DAY

Eustratius and the Holy Virgin—Julian the Apostate and Theodorus—Marcus of Arethusa—Henry II. of France and the Tailor—Henry II. and Andelott.

MOTHER. Love is the Summe of St. Johns Doctrine, whose feast we now celebrate. And the height of Love is to lay downe our lives for whom wee love. So he proves GODS love to us, and so he requires wee should prove our Love to GOD and to his Children. You shall heare an example, and that in our owne sex. GOD make us imitators, as I know you cannot but be Admirers of it.

Eustratius being chief Governor of Alexandria, sets forth a proclamation in Dioclesians name, That whosoever denied to sacrifice to the Gods should be condemned to death. Amongst many others that made light of this matter, Theodora, a Virgin, is accused to be one. Eustratius sends for her, and she instantly appeares, with her eies cast down through shamefastnes on the ground, but with her heart, through sanctified thoughts, lift up to heaven; her body she presents before the Tribunal, but her soule remaines fixed at GODS Mercy-seat. I would know, sayd Eustratius, who thou art. Why, a Christian, sayd Theodora. I meane, sayd the Judge, of what condition, whether free or a servant? I have told thee already, replied she. I am a Christian, and CHRIST hath made mee free from sinne. And in respect of what belongs to the vainglory of the world, if happily thou intendest that, I was borne of illustrious and noble Parents. Its very true, sayd Lucius, one of the assistant Judges, shee is of the best and highest blood in this Citty. And how, then, wilt thou defile (faire Mayd) sayd Eustratius, such excellency of blood with such enormities of Crimes? Its flat rebellion against the Emperors, to deny the worshipping of their Gods, which they have enjoyned. Come, now, and casting sweet Incense in the fire on the Altar, purge away this evil odour, that taints thine honour and endangers thy life. But then I shall defile my selfe much more, sayd she, polluting my soule, and becomming an adultres to that great and glorious LORD of heaven that hath espoused mee to himselfe with his owne blood. To him I owe, and to him I must preserve the spotles Chastity of my mind, as well as of my body. Verily, sayd Eustratius, thus doing thou shalt loose both ; for unlesse thou sacrifice to the Gods thou shalt goe to the stewes. If thou forceably wrong mee, sayd Theodora, thou shalt adde to the Crowne without any minishment in the purity of my virgin Chastity. Thou mayest cut in peices my body, and outwardly distayne it ; but thou shalt not touch my soule, either with greif or shame. That GOD hath reserved to the subjection of his owne power only, and I am confident that his Mercy shall extend to the preservation of my body also ; and though thou shut me up in the stews, yet shall not the filth thereof be able to soyle mee any whit. A fond woman thou art, sayd Eustratius, to rely upon the Crucified ; shall he defend thee from violence, that could not deliver himselfe from death ? A fond Man thou art, answered Theodora, that blasphemeth him that by his death subdued the world. He suffered indeed, but of his owne accord, ministring Power and supplying strength to that selfe same force which was used against him. And I know that he can keepe mee safe against all the violence and Malice of hell it selfe, and I am confident that if I depart not from this hope and trust, he will performe it, and much more. Three dayes respite are given thee, sayd Eustratius, for the honour of thy kindred, otherwise this obstinacy deserves no favour. Bethinke thy selfe well, and come with a better mind. But she at three daies end returnes the former answere, and thereupon Eustratius wills the threatened sentence to be put in execution. Assoone as they had put her in the loathsome place she lookes up to heaven. God, sayth she, the FATHER of my LORD JESUS CHRIST, that freed Peter out of bonds, and from the waiting of the Jews, free mee from this perill, and disappoint the hopes of the enemies of thy Name! Let the might of thy goodnes be manifested in the preservation of thy handmayd! Whilst she thus prayes, a yong Man clad like a Roman Soldier, by the Authority of his habit and the feircenes of his words making all the rest give way (though they were many that like ravenous wolfes stood contending for a Prey), enters the roome and shuts the dore after him. Theodora, much affrighted both at his presence and his Actions, lookes up pitifully into heaven as one that doubts to be abandoned of him from whom she most expected help. Whereupon Didimus—that was the Souldiers name— comming nigh, with blushing cheekes and broken words to testify his owne, and to secure her modesty, tells her that she should not be afrayd of the habit which was put on for her safety, nor doubt the losse of her Virginity from him, who was ready to lay downe his life for the defence of it. Come, let us make interchange of garments, sayd he, and goe thou out for the preservation of thy Chastity, and leave me heere for the exercize of Charity and the Combate of fayth. Theodora gladly yeelds as to GODS ordinance; and so, putting on the others apparrell, muffling her face as one ashamed, passeth away unknowne. She was no sooner gone, but another enters, and a while mistaken in the womans habits, courts Didimus for Theodora; but finding no correspondency to his lustfull affections, and going about to use force, Didimus uncovers his face, and he, thinking it to have beene a reall

Metamorphosis, began to cry out, Come in, oh Men of Alexandria, and see a wonder past beliefe: The woman is transformed by the Christians GOD into a Man! GOD hath made no exchange of persons, sayd Didimus, but we have made exchange of garments onely. The souldier that went out was the Virgin whom you misse, and I am her that came in, a Romane Souldier in habite, but a Souldier of CHRIST JESUS in heart. She is safe escaped from your lusts, and I gladly remaine here a sacrifice to your rage. The newes of this being come to the President Eustratius, he wills Didimus to bee brought, and enragedly demandes who had given him Counsell to this deceit, and what was become of Theodora. It was GOD alone, sayd he, that gave me Counsell and heart for the performance of what I have done, and he that hath thus freed Theordora knows where she is; as for me, I know nothing, but that she is a Christian, and because I am so likewise, I have put my life in hazard for the securing of her Chastity. Thou shalt be doubly tormented, sayd Eustratius, both for the fraud that thou hast used, and for the faith which thou professeth; yet if thou wilt deny the last, I will forgive the first, and pardon thy offence which thou hast committed, if thou wilt recant the opinions which thou holdest. I should never have had the heart, said Didimus, to doe what I have done if I could have the heart to doe what thou requirest. Thou mayest well offer me up a burnt offering to CHRIST JESUS, but surely thou shalt never perswade mce to offer sacrifice to any of thy Gods. Eustratius, hearing this, commands his head to be cutt of, and his body to be burned. Blessed be GOD, sayd Didimus, that hath accepted my service, and doubly rewarded me in letting me dy a Martyr, and Theodora live a Virgin.

St. Ambrose (if his story be the same, for, because he gives no Names to the Persons and sets Antioche to be the place where those suffered, some have made a question whether these be not another couple from those which he writes of), adds that Theodora, hearing of this sentence, made hast to the place of execution and there discovers herselfe, and with many arguments and much earnestnes pleaded for her owne death and the others safety. Oh, faithfull servant of CHRIST JESUS, sayd she to Didimus, I chose thee a champion of my Virginity, and not a substitute for my Martyrdome. If my chast honour runne perill, I have need of thy assistance ; but if it be blood which they thirst after, I have myselfe wherewith to make payment ; I need no security for the discharge of this debt. I am sentenced to death, answered Didimus, and not thou, oh Virgin-spouse of CHRIST JESUS ; what need we loose two lives when one will serve? One will serve indeed, replied she, but that ought to be mine. If thou thus dy through my cause, thou leavest mee not so much a live woman as a guilty, and that of a double fault, thy present death and my former flight ; although, indeed, I fled not from the sufferings of Martyrdome, but from the pollutions of sinne. Thus did, sayth Ambrose, this noble payre contend which should dy. The cruell Judge puts an end to this pious strife, and by condemning them both to die, contents them both to the full. The Pythagorians, sayth St. Ambrose, exalt to heaven the freindship of Damon and Pithias, who offered one to dy for the other. But how short doth it fall in all degrees and parts of this wonderfull passage ! They were men, both of them ; one of these a woman. They were grounded freinds ; these had never before seene each other. There, one of necessity was to dy ; these both came voluntary to it. They offered themselves to one Tyrant ; these to many, and they much more cruell ; for he pardoned the guilty, and these condemned the innocent. In this case is much more excellencie of wisedome, for their humane freindship onely perswaded ; here desire of Martyrdome prevailed. They sought mere applause ; these the honour of GOD.

GUARD. This great desire of Martyrdome, and this holy contention for dying, with which your story ends, seemes to call us back to the further opening of that rich and happy veyne which we yesterday began ; I mean, touching the exceeding Connsolations wherewith GOD useth to refresh the spirits of those whose bodies he appoints to suffer for his Cause. I pray you, therefore, let this daies stories be likewise to the proofe and confirmation of this necessary, most profitable truth.

AFFECTIO. This blessed Virgin and Martyr, Theodora, brings to remembrance a noble Confessor of the same Name, in whose sufferings, and from whose Mouth, you shall receive a notable Confirmation of that which you desire.

In Julian the Apostates time, Theodorus, a yong man, being convicted to have beene one of those who sung Psalmes at the removall of the Martyr Babilas his body, was by the Emperours Commande most cruelly tormented from morning to Noone; all which he endured with that Constancy and Cheerefulnes as if he had beene a beholder of some enemies paines, and not a sufferer of it in his owne body. The President appointed for the oversight of this busines, comming to the Emperor, tells him, Its best timely to give over this matter, least they prove a derision to the Christians, in proving themselves so weake as not able to make them feele paine. Whereupon the Emperor wills that not onely Theodorus, but all the other Prisoners, should be set free. Afterwards divers aske Theodorus how it was possible he could endure such horrid Torments.

I wanted not the sence of Paine, sayd he, but there stood by mee a young Man, that ever and anon with a fine Linen wiped away the sweat, and sprinkled my body with a most cold water, whereby not onely the heat and the smart of the stripes and wounds was mitigated, but I was so refreshed and delighted as when I was taken downe from the Engine of torment it greived me more then before.

PATIENT. Marcus of Arethusa was a Companion of Theodorus in the sufferings of the selfe same persecution, and in the setting forth of the selfe same grace and mercy of our Lord JESUS CHRIST, in turning the paine that is undergone for his Name sake into ease and rejoycing. His mirth in invincible torments shews the hand of the Lord to have beene as powerfull with him, though the Ministry of Angells was not so visible, as in Theodorus his Case. This holy Bishop haveing demolished a magnifig Temple of the Idols at Arethusa under the favour of pious Constantine, is upon the Change of relligion under Apostata Julian eagerly sought for by the heathen, his owne private as well as publique enemies of the Christian Faith. At first, according to CHRISTS generall advise, he sought safety by flight; but understanding the apprehension and ill usage of his owne Person to redeeme them from bonds and vexation, they that thirsted not his bloud onely, but his shame and smart in the highest degree, forgetting as well the humanity that belonged to themselves, as the honour which was due to his Age and excellency of vertue and Dignity, first stript him naked and cruelly beat him. That done, they cast him into the common Jakes of the Citty, and anon, after drawing him out againe, put him into Schoole boys hands, who with their iron stiles, with which in those times they used to write, did pounce and prick his body all over. Being thus wounded from head to foot, the men take him againe from the Children, anoynting him with milk and hony; and so, chosing out a place where the sunne shonne extreame hot, they bring him up in a wicker basket to be devoured of wasps and flies. As he hangs in these torments they began to treate with him about the building of their temple, for which they aske at first a great summe of Mony; and upon his constant refusall, doubting that his poverty was not able to furnish so much, they fall to halfe, and in the end pitch upon a very trifle, which they urge him hard to give, being now more ambitious to get the Mastery, then formerly covetous either of revenge or Mony. But Marcus tells them they loose their labour, as well as perswading as in tormenting. For I hold it, sayth he, as great a wickednes to conferre one halfe-peny in any such case of impiety as this is, as to give the whole summe which you require. And that they might perceive his light sence and esteeme of that which bred horror in them to looke upon, he merrily tells them by way of derision, How am I advanced on high, despising you that ly groveling on the earth below!

MOTHER. There can be little question made, as I suppose, by him that well scans the words and carriages, but that the Martyr himselfe felt lesse paine of the torments then they which caused them to be inflicted on him.

PATIENT. If any should thinke otherwise, the event will make it evident. The Persecutours themselves, for their owne ease and quiet, give over the pursueing of that Cruelty which they cannot make him sensible of. They let him downe and depart, confounded in their own Consciences and disquieted in their Minds, and leave him triumphing in his Victory, and us to learne from his mouth, as my Authour concludes, the example of true Piety and faithfulnes.

CHEEREF. From his Mouth we may learne not onely an example of that true Piety and faithfulnes which belongs to the servants of CHRIST JESUS, but of that great Pitty and faithfulnes which CHRIST JESUS our Master useth to proceed with towards his servants, alwaies making way for the Temptation that it is easy to be borne by the spirit, however intolerable it seemes to the flesh. And touching that other part, the terror, confusion, and anguish of mind, that useth to attend the persecutors of GODS Saints, I shall tell you a fresh and very admirable example, wherein you shall see a Victory more wonderfully then perhaps you have yet heard of, in regard of the great distance of Conditions in the Persons; the one a mighty King in the ruffe of youth and jollity, the other a poore Man, by trade a Taylour, and otherwise of so little note in the world as his Name is perished, being omitted by the first relatours, cannot now be easily found; but what it may be is perished on earth, is certainly registered in heaven, his Name is there enrold in the lists of Saints and Martyrs. And that which I shall tell you stands recorded in the Martyrologe, and in the French History, in the words whereof I shall, as neere as may be, deliver the matter.

Henry the Second of France, after much sport at his

Queenes Coronation in the year 1548, caused a generall procession to be made in July, where he was assisted with the Queene, the Princes of the bloud, Cardinals, and all the Orders and Estates of Paris. At his returne from the Bishops Lodgeing, where he had dined, he would see certaine Christians burnt, detesting the Errors and Abuses of the Church of Rome. Amongst the which there was a Taylour, who some few dayes before had made answere of his beleife befor the King and many Courtiers, and spake boldly to the Dutches of Valentinois, the Kings Concubine, telling her that she should rest satisfied to have infected France, and not seeke to pollute so holy and sacred a thing as religion and the truth of the Sonne of GOD with her giltlienes, and that it was to be feared that GOD, for this Cause, would send some great plague upon the King and Realme. But the King being incensed, and not amended, being carried away by the allurements of her that did bewitch him, having commanded that his processe should be dispatcht, he would be a Spectator himselfe of this Taylours execution, standing in the Lord of Richports Lodging in St. Anthonys Street, right against the Scaffold, where—contrary to the expectation of the Cleargy and Courtiers, who used to tell the King that the Lutherans were nothing els but such as carried vaine smoake in their Mouthes, which, being put to the fire, would soone vanish—the Taylour shewed a wonderfull Constancy and Patience, having discovered the King, who, perhaps, discovered himselfe the more to amate him. The Taylour began to behold him so constantly, asn othing could divert him, yea, the fire being kindled, he had alwaies his eies fixed upon that object. As the King was faine to retire himselfe, yea, he was so troubled, as he confessed, he thought this Mans shaddow did still follow him, and that for many Nights this spectacle did present it selfe unto him. Whereupon he protested he would never see nor heare any such people. But, forgetting his protestation tenne yeares after, he heard things which he should have given attentive eare unto, and pretending to see a great Personage burnt, whose words did merit Credit, he lost both sight and life.

GUARD. The observation of Faustimus and Tobitas cheerefull Constancy in unsufferable Torments inflicted on them, made Calocerius—as wee lately heard read—with great reason to cry, Vere magnus Deus Christianorum ; Verily, great is the GOD of the Christians! Happy had it beene for this French King, if from the same premises he had made the like inference as they did. Hee had then beene likely to have saved not his soule onely, as Calocerius did by his Conversion, but his life, too, which Calocerius lost instantly for the Confession of CHRISTS Name, and this unhappy Prince lost afterwards in and, as I suppose wee may boldly say, for the persecution of CHRIST his Members.

MODERATOUR. It seemes by that which hath been related that the same spirit prompted him if he had given as good care as Calocerius did.

PATIENT. The affrightment that continued with him so long was more then a prompting, and, as it seemes, wrought effectually with him for the present, when it drew from him that resolution never more to see nor heare of any such people. But belike he had forgott this old promise when he made those new threats which your story speakes of.

MOTHER. He forgott it till it was too late, but his deaths wound brought it fresh to memory, by that which is constantly reported of him ; but he should have remembered it before, and surely GOD gave him a faire warning before he gave him his full payment.

CHEEREFULL. I wonder such a warning as you intimate should be omitted in my Authour. I doe not remember any passage there that can be fittly driven to this sence.

MOTHER. You shall find it registered by a Historiographer no lesse authenticall then yours, whoever he bee. Thuanus reports, how that a yeare before this Capitall and flatt intended breach of his promise, which cost him his life, he was much incensed by the wily Circumventions of the Guizians, and in particular the Cardinall of Loraine, against the Protestants ; and by striking at the Cheife to breed more terror amongst them of lower ranke, he sent one day purposely for Andelott, Generall of the foot, having given him Notice of the busines by his Brother, the Cardinall Chatillion, and his Unkle, the Constable Momarantzy. Andelott appearing whilest the King sat at dinner, accompanied with the Dolphin, who sate somewhat below, the King, with expression of much Love on his owne part, and acknowledgement of many great services received from Andelott, gave him to understand that there had been divers Complaints made against him, as one not well affected in Religion. I desire, therefore, sayd the King, particularly to know your beleife touching the Masse and the Sacrament of the Altar. Andelott, with great Confidence, made a full and plaine Answere in every point agreable to the doctrine of the Protestants. The King, seeming much troubled thereat, gently willed him to consider well what he sayd, and the danger that would ensue upon his perseverance in such opinions. Whereupon Andelott, with much more Courage and freedome replied, That nothing could have befallen him more desirously then that ample Testimony which his Majesty had given of his singular affection towards himselfe and his whole Family, and of his gracious acceptance of their loyall dutifulnes and services. But in Case of Religion, it being GODS cause, he might for no cause whatsoever use dissimulation in any wise. My goods, my estate, my honours, sayd he, are all in your Majesties hands to dispose of as you please, but my soule is onely subject unto GOD, from whom alone I received it. To him, therefore, as the highest LORD am I bound in this matter to give absolute obedience in all things. The King was so moved at this stoutnes, as not able to restrain his passion; he tooke the Dish that stood before him, and with as great unwarines as Choler, flinging it away, gave the Dolphin, that satt by, a very sore blow therewith, and immediately arising from the Table, willed Andelott to be carried away to prison, and shortly after deprived him of his Generalship of the Infantery.

GUARD. This passage everyway deserves enrollment both in bookes and memories. It is an excellent president for great personages in the like occasions as Andelott was, and serves marveilously to lead us on to the discovery of the true Cause of this Kings miserable end, and the utter desolation of his posterity. The effect of this rage lighting on his Son was a faire warning what would be the issue of his progresse in this quarrel. And if, when he ment nothing but Curiosity, as in the first case, and certainly ment Love to the Person whom hee converted, as in this second, and was in both mislead, onely perhaps through blind Zeale to the cause, notwithstanding his opposition to the truth wrought so much to his owne damage and danger; he had just reason to feare no lesse then indeed befell him, when with purposed malignity he sett himselfe to entrap GODS Saints, and sought the rooting of them out for the uncontrolled exercize or his owne evill Affections.

AFFECTION. The Ignorance of this story makes mee, and most heere, I am perswaded, uncapable of the Benefitt which you and others that know it have. I shall therefore intreat that wee may heare the particularities of the fact whereupon you reare these weighty and usefull observations.

GUARD. You say well. As there is not perhaps any one passage in these later ages to be found, wherein the frailty of mans wretched estate appeares more conspicuous then in this, so neither is there, it may be, any one whence more remarkable observations and more profitable, may be collected, as well for private men as greater Fortunes. I therefore second this motion, and desire that our beloved CHEEREFULL, or you, worthy MOTHER, or rather both together, would give us a full accompt of this matter.

XV

CHRISTMASTIDE, 1632—HOLY INNOCENTS' DAY

The Martyrdom of Romanus—A Child Tortured—Fourteen French Martyrs and their Mothers—Maximinian and the Boy Martyrs—Feast of Circumcision—Christmas Gifts for the Guests—The Priest and the Tavern—Oxford and Cambridge Scholars—A New Year's Gift.

MODERATOR. This Day would have led us of it self, had wee not beene before upon them, to the Consideration of Sufferings, Death, and Martyrdome. Theres no reason therefore to alter the subject, which doubly agrees to the Feast and to that which went before.

The Innocents were Martyrs, and served up like flowers to GODS table. And wee undoubtedly might compose many sweet Nosegaies out of their Example; but having riper fruits in store, wee will not seke about for that which would perhaps lesse satisfy.

You shall see a Martyr compleat in all manner of vertue and sufferings; and that wee may every way suit the Day, accompanied with a Child, who in Innocence and Youth œqualls them whose Feast wee celebrate, but in understanding passeth Men. You heare a Child confessing the truth with his tongue, a Man confessing it without his tongue, that every way GODS praise might be perfected, and the Enimy and Avenger stilled. And that you may give the firmer creditt to it, you shall have it in the words of an Authour against whom, for matter of ancient miracle, no Exception lies.

Wee will begin, sayth the Authour, with Romanus, the notable and admirable Souldier and true servant of CHRIST, whose history sett forth in Prudentius doth thus proceed; so lamentably by him described that it will be hard for any man almost with dry Cheeks to heare it :—

Pitiles Galerius, with his grand Captaine Asclepiades, violently invaded the Citty of Antioch, intending by force of Armes to drive all Christians to renounce utterly their pure religion. The Christians, as GOD would, were at the time congregated together, to whom Romanus hastily ranne, declaring that the wolves were at hand, which would devoure the Christian flock; but feare not, sayd he, neither let this iminent perill disturbe you, my Brethren. Brought was it to passe by the great grace of GOD working in Romanus, that old men and matrons, fathers and Mothers, young men and maydens were all of one will and mind, most ready to shed their blood in defence of their Christian Profession. Word was brought to the Captaine that the band of armed Souldiors was not able to wrest the staffe of faith out of the hand of the unarmed Congregation, and all by reason that one Romanus so mightily did encourage them, that they stick not to offer their naked throates, wishing gloriously to dy for the Name of their CHRIST. Seeke out that rebell (quoth the Captaine), and bring him to mee, that he may answere for the whole sect. Apprehended he is, and bound as a sheepe appointed to the slaughter-house, is presented to the Emperor, who with wrathfull Countenance beholding him, sayd: What? Art thou the Authour of this sedition? Art thou the Cause why so many shall loose their lives? By the Gods, I sweare thou shalt smart for it, and first in the flesh shalt thou suffer the paines whereunto thou hast encouraged the hearts of thy fellows. Romanus answered: Thy sentence, O Emperor, I joyfully embrace; I refuse not to be sacrificed for my brethren, and that by as cruell meanes as thou mayest invent; and whereas thy Souldiors were repelled trom the Christian Congregation, that so happened because it lay not in Idolaters and worshippers of Devills to enter into the holy house of GOD, and to pollute the place of true Prayer. Then Asclepiades, wholy enflamed with this stout answere, commanded him to be trussed up, and his bowells drawne out. The Executioners themselves, more pittifull in heart then the Captaine, sayd: Not so, Sir, this man is of noble Parentage; unlawfull it is to put a noble Man to so unnoble a Death. Scourge him then with whippes (quoth the Captaine), with knaps of Lead at the ends. Instead of teares, sighs, and groanes, Romanus sung Psalmes all the time of his whipping, requiring them not to favour him for Nobilities sake. Not the bloud ot my progenitors (sayd he), but Christian profession maketh mee noble. Then with great powre of spirit, he inveighed against the Captaine, laughing to scorne the false gods of the heathen, with the idolatrous worshipping of them, affirming the GOD ot the Christians to be the true GOD, that created heaven and earth, before whose judiciall seat all Nations shall appeare. But the wholesome words of the Martyr were as oyle to the fire of the Captaines fury. The more the Martyr speakes the madder was he, in so much that hee comanded the Martyrs sides to be lanched with knives, untill the bones appeare white againe. Sorry I am, o Captaine, quoth the Martyr, not for that my flesh shalbe thus cutt and mangled, but for thy Cause am I sorrowfull, who, being corrupted with damnable errors, seducest others. The second time he preached at large the Living GOD and the LORD JESUS CHRIST his well beloved Sonne, eternall life through faith in his blood, expressing therewith the abomination of Idolatry, with a vehement exhortation to worship and adore the Living GOD. At these words Asclepiades commanded the Tormentors to strike Romanus on the mouth, that his teeth being stricken out, his pronunciation at leastwise might be impaired. The Commandement is obeyed, his face is buffeted, his eyelids torne with their Nailes, his cheekes are scorched with knives, the skinne of his beard is plucked by little and little from the flesh, finally his seemely face is wholly defaced.

The meeke Martyr sayd : I thank thee, o Captaine, that thou hast opened unto mee many mouths, whereby I may preach my LORD and SAVIOUR CHRIST. Looke how many wounds I have, so many mouths I have, lauding and praysing GOD. The Captaine, astonished with this singular Constancy, commanded them to cease from the tortures. He threateneth cruell fire, he revileth the noble Martyr, he blasphemeth GOD, saying : Thy crucified CHRIST is but an yesterdaies GOD, the Gods of the Gentiles are of most antiquitie. Heere againe Romanus, taking good occasion, made a long oration of the eternity of CHRIST, of his humane Nature, of the death and satisfaction of CHRIST, for all mankind, which done, he sayd : Give mee a Child, o Captaine, but seven yeares of age, which age is free from malice and other vices, wherewith riper Age is commonly infected, and thou shalt heare what he will say. His request was granted. A pretty boy was called out of the multidude and sett before him. Tell me, my Babe (quoth the Martyr), whether thou thinke it reason that wee worship one CHRIST, and in CHRIST one Father, or els that we worship infinite Gods ? Unto whom the Babe answered, That certainely whatsoever it be that Men affirme to be GOD must needs be one, which with one is one and the same; and inasmuch as this one is CHRIST, of necessity CHRIST must be the true GOD. The Captaine thereat cleane amazed sayd : Thou young villaine and Traitor, where and of whom learned thou this lesson ? Of my Mother (quoth the child), at whose knees I learnt this lesson, that I must beleive in CHRIST. The Mother was called, and she gladly appeared. The Captaine commanded the Child to be horsed up and scourged. The pitifull Beholders of this pitiless Act could not temper themselves from teares ; the joyfull and glad Mother alone stood by with dry Cheekes ; yea, shee rebuked her sweet Babe for craving a draught of cold water ; she charged him to thirst after the Cuppe that the Infants of Bethlehem once drank of, forgetting their Mothers milk and Pappes ; she willed him to remember little Isaac, who, beholding the sword wherewith, and the Altar whereon he should be sacrificed, willingly proferd his tender neck to the dent of his Fathers sword. Whilest this Counsell was in giving, the boucherly Torturer pluckt the skinne from the Crowne of his head, haire and all. The Mother cryed, Suffer, my Child, anone thou shalt passe to him that will adorne thy naked head with a Crowne of eternall glory. The Mother counselleth, the Child is counselled; the Mother encourageth, the Babe is encouraged; he receiveth the stripes and the sores with smiling Countenance. The Captaine, perceiving the Child invincible and himselfe vanquished, committeth the silly soule, the blessed Babe, the Child uncherished to the Prison, commanding the torments of Romanus to be renewed and encreased as the cheife Authour of this evill.

Thus was Romanus brought forth againe to new stripes and punishments, to be renewed and received upon his old sores; insomuch the bare bones appeared, the flesh all torne away: wherein no Pitty was shewed, but the raging Tyrant puffing out of his blasphemous mouth like a mad Man, these words cryed out to the Tormentors, saying :—

> Where is, quoth the Captaine, where is your might?
>   What? are ye not able one body to spill?
> Scant may it, so weake is it, stand upright,
>   And yet in spite of us shall it live still?
> The Grype with talaunt, the Dog with his tooth,
>   Could soone, the dastards, this Corps rent and teare;
> He scorneth our Gods in all that he doth,
>   Cut, prick, and pounce him, no longer forbeare.

Yea, no longer could the Tyrant forbeare, but needs he must draw neerer to the sentence of death. Is it painfulle to thee (sayd he) to tarry so long alive? A flaming fire doubt thou not shalbe prepared for thee by and by, wherein thou and that boy, thy fellow of rebellion, shalbe consumed into ashes. Romanus and the Babe are led to the place of execution. As they layd hands on Romanus, he looked back saying, I appeale from this thy Tyranny, O Judge unjust, to the righteous throne of CHRIST, that upright Judge; not because I feare thy cruell torments and mercilesse handlings, but that thy judgements may be knowne to be cruell and bloody. Now when they were come to the place, the tormentor required the Child of the Mother, for she had taken it up in her Arms, and she, only kissing it, delivered the Babe. Farewell, she sayd, my sweete Child; and as the hangman applied his sword to the babes neck she sung on this manner :—

> All laud and praise with heart and voice,
>   O Lord, we yeeld to thee,
> To whom the Death of all thy Saints
>   Wee know most deare to bee.

The Innocents head being cut of, the Mother wrapped it up in her garment, and layed it to her brest. On the other side a mighty fire was made, whereinto Romanus was cast, who sayd, That he should not burne. Wherewith a great storme arose (if it be true) and quenched the fire. The Captaine gave in commandement that his tongue should be cutt out. Out was it pluckt by the hard rootes and cutt of. Neverthelesse he spake, saying, He that speaketh CHRIST shall never want a tongue. Thinke not that the voice that uttereth CHRIST hath neede of the tongue to be the minister. The Captaine at this, half out of his witt, bare in hand that the hangman deceived the sight of the people by some subtle sleight and crafty conveyance. Not so (quoth the hangman) if thou suspect my deed, open his mouth, and diligently search the rootes of his tongue. The Captaine at length, being confounded with the fortitude and courage of the Martyr, straightly commanded him to be brought back into the Prison and there to be strangled, where, his sorrowful life and paines being ended, he now enjoyeth quiet rest in the LORD, with perpetuall hope of his miserable body to be restored againe with his soule into a better life, where no Tyrant shall have any power.

PATIENT. That which in this story is most wonderfull hath, even in these latter days of ours, by the mercy of God beene by fresh examples ratified.

Anno 1546 there were at . . . in France fourteene Martyrs brought together to the stake, the fire being made over against the house of Stephen Mangen, where they had used to keepe their Assemblies. Before their execution it was told them that as many as would not be confessed should have their tongues cutt out. Seven yeelded, the other refused. Amongst the last seven Mangen, who was one, after the cutting out of his tongue pronounced audibly three several times, *The Lords Name bee praysed*, confirming that which you heard in Romanus, That he which looseth his tongue for CHRISTS sake shall have no misse of it for the setting forth of his prayse.

CHEEREFULL. The Mother of Peter Clarke, one of these fourteen Martyrs which you spake of, will be a good companion for that holy woman which tooke such joy in her little sons Martyrdome. When shee saw her sonne John Clarke come home, after cruell whippings in his body, with a marke of infamy branded in his forehead, she cryed out with a loud voice, *Blessed be Christ and welcome be his prints and markes.*

AFFECTIONATE. William Hunters Mother deserves no lesse honourable remembrance. Visiting her son in prison, she saluted him with much Joy, telling him she thought herselfe happy in bearing a child which could find in his heart to loose his life for CHRISTS Name sake. *For my little paine which I shall suffer, but a short brayd*, sayd hee, CHRIST *hath promised mee a Crowne of Joy, and may you not be glad of that, Mother?* With that his Mother kneeled downe on her knees, saying, *I pray* GOD *strengthen thee, my son, unto the end; yea, I thinke thee as well bestowed as any child that ever I bare.*

GUARD. Blessed be GOD that we find so many Parallels in this decrepit Age of the world, to those ancient Examples. But how comes it that the faith and grace of our LORD JESUS CHRIST, which shoone so gloriously of old in childrens brests, is so eclipsed now, as there is none of us can out of their present remembrance find a Match for this blessed Infant that accompanied Romanus in suffering, and is now a fellow sharer with him, not onely in the Glory of heaven, but even in his honour upon earth? It cannot be but Grace is the same Grace that it was wont, and serves to actuate childrens soules as of old; the fault lies altogether, I am afraid, in ourselves. It is not so effectually applied on the Parents behalfe, for that it should bee lesse abundant or lesse powerfully afforded by GOD now, then at first, I cannot think: sure tis the Parents fault, that doe not rightly prepare the ground for this heavenly seed. If there were as right tilth and as good husbandry used nowadayes, why should not there bee as good a crop of fayth and vertue in our Childrens minds as was in theirs of the Primitive Church? And so much the rather I doe suspect this to be the cause, as, mee thinkes, I have observed in all these stories an evident acknowledgement on the Childrens part, that they had learned of their Mother. I shall tell you a story which will confirme your opinion, and seale up the beleife of many other things which have been discoursed of:—

Maximinian, having sent for two young Children of Nicomedia, Brethren, and very nobly borne, began with such faire words and promises as Children use to be taken with. Afterwards he sent for some of that which in their presence he had offered up in sacrifice, persuading them to eat of it, and they should have no harme. They, turning away their mouthes, fell a weeping and, as they were able, stamerringly told him, they had not so learned of their Parents, but it was a cleane other way that they had beene used unto. Hereupon hee grew angry, chid them sharpely; and when that prevailed not, hee willed them to be sorely beaten with many stripes. But when the children, strengthened by GODS holy spirit, yeelded not at all, a certain Sophister that stood by and had beene a cheife instigator in the matter, seeing this, told the Emperor he doubted not to make them eat quickly so he might have the ordering of the busines. For what a shame will this be, said hee, that the Romane Emperor should be overcome by Children that cannot yet speak plaine. Having obtained his request, he compounded a certaine plaster of very keene mustard, with which, after he had shaved of the haire, he anoynts the childrens heads very thick. That done, he carries them into a Bath or stove fire hott, where the flame instantly, like a flash of lightning, seized upon their heads. The poore children, not able to stand upright for the torment, bow their faces towards the ground, and after a little while the younger falls dead on the floore, which, when his brother saw, he bidds him joy as lowd as ever hee could. He embraceth him, he kisseth him, and proclaimes him Conqueror, crying out amaine and without intermission, Brother, thou hast gott the victory, Brother, thou hast gott the victory! Thus embracing, kissing, and crying did the Child stand, till at last he fell downe dead himselfe, with his Brother in his Armes. The spectacle was very ruefull even to the persecutors themselves. As for the Christians, it seemed so admirable as for the remembrance thereof they built a Church over their bodies, which they call by the Name of the Infant Martyrs.

MOTHER. The passage of this Festivall having been hitherto so sutable in true good Cheere and Christmas Mirth, as every body, I am sure, rests well apayed in their entertainment, I would be glad for a perfect finishment of the busines, that in no kind wee might bee wanting to that which any body can require touching Christmas, that our Love might be likewise expressed to our freinds after the usuall manner of this day, by the presentment of some such guifts as might serve both for use and Benefitt to themselves, as well as for such loving remembrance of us as belongs to Christian freinds.

CHEEREFULL. These two conditions of Durance and Beneficialnes which you require in your present, cutt of that hope which otherwise I might have had, to discharge my part of this matter with ease and satisfaction out of the storehouse under my charge, now well replenished with many dainties through the kindnes of your loving Neighbours.

MOTHER. Tis very true; the perishable nature and sleight degree of good that is in these kind of provisions, yielding no other benefitt then such fading pleasure as die in the very enjoyment, debarres you from this advantage. Besides, this would bee more wrong than bounty perhaps, whilst you should pay your private Debt out of a common Stock. Let every one therefore resolve to bring in their share out of that which is truely their. owne. The warning, I confesse, is somewhat short, but according to the Spanish proverbe (Out of a full Ambrey a feast is quickly made) I am sure theres none can be unprovided to this Intent.

CHEEREFULL. Wee are richer then wee are aware of if it bee as you say.

MOTHER. Theres none more deafe, I perceive, then he that will not heare. The storehouse of Temperance under your guard, the wardrobe of Sobriety under the Patients, the workehouse of Industry under the Affectionates, are not unfurnished, I hope, to fitt the whole countrey, not onely our small number of Freinds with New Yeares Guifts.

GUARDIAN. Scarreborough warning.

MOTHER. You understand, I see well, the progresse of the busines, and aime at your owne ends in pleading for others; but neither yours nor our most honoured MODERATOURS priviledges may exempt you from this common service. I must humbly desire, what I may not enjoyne, that shee will bring her part of floures and fruits out of her Nursery of Education, and that you will out of the Treasury of Charity seeke such jewells which may fitt the severall occasions and conditions of our freinds.

And first to beginne with, our good Cousen and Guest, whose kind acceptation of our frugall entertaynment deserves the best of our acknowledgement, his reall approbation of Temperance, outgoing by example what you intend in rule, gives assurance that there is Nothing out of that store house that will not by him be esteemed as a dainty.

CHEEREF. I have a story very proper to that holy calling which he intends, and very usefull, as I suppose, in these corrupt times, if there were fitting space to make application as large as the story would well beare.

Mother. To what is it now destrayned?

Cheerefull. To the purity of the heart.

Mother. Why, thats the perfection of all other vertues, and that which I am assured our good cosen chiefly pretends unto. The conclusion could not have beene in a better point; and for all that it might be further extended unto, doubt you not but his Learning and good heart will improve it to the uttermost, and much better then you can doe.—

Cheerefull. An old holy man being by commande of superiors called from that retired life which he led, to Alexandria, as hee passed the streets, saw one in a Preists habit enter, together with some others, into a Taverne; at which, much greived, hee setts himself over against the dore, and upon the Preists coming out, singling him from the rest of the company, My reverend Brother, sayd hee, knowest thou the worth of thy profession and the excellency of thy ministry, that it is not inferior to that of the Angells? That Apostate Julian under severest punishment forbad the Preists of Bacchus and Venus to sett foot into Tavernes; how can it befitt the Ministers of Christ Jesus, the fountaine of sobriety and purity? That Purity (replied the Preist in an arrogant manner) which Christ requires is that of the heart, which, whilest it is preserved intire, neither place, nor company, nor any other outward thing can defile. He had scarce sayd thus, when the old Man, spreading his hands to heaven, cryed out, O my God, what is this I heare? Fifty yeares have I served thee day and Night in all kind of Mortification of body and spirit, and yet cannot attaine to that purity of heart which my Brother heere can preserve sound and acceptable unto thee in the midst of polluted Places and Company.

He that feeles not the taint of evill practizes scapes not free by that purity which he hath not, but by the predominancy of some more grevious infection. He that is truely good is alwaies the worse for every willing fellowship with that which is not good.

Guard. Though our cosens better abilities forbid our

descanting on the story before him, yet the weaknes of many present, whom it may hereafter no lesse concerne, enforceth mee to the remembrance of those three lamentable effects which have happened by schollers going to Tavernes, in little above the compasse of the last yeare ; that at least the feare of bodily danger may terrify them whom the preservation of a good conscience cannot overrule from this unchristian practize. Theres no Man can think that these three that are come to our notice are all the mischeifes that have lately befallen in this kind, and much lesse that they should be casuall accidents. No, verily. They bee serious admonitions intended by the Divine Providence for our instruction, that wee should learne to avoyd the sin, least wee be involved in the same punishment as they were. I have heard that the Oxford scholler, that on Midsommer Eve killed the Barber at the Popes Head in London, was a civill man, and ment nothing lesse when he went into the Taverne then the murther which he committed. Sure I am that the Cambridge scholers, in whose company the Lieuetenant was slaine at the Mitre, were some of them Persons of good integrity of life, as well as of great eminency in learning ; and he who, in his owne defence, killed that third man, was undoubtedly as secure in his owne apprehension when he went into the Alehouse from comming out guilty of such misfortune, as any Man living could bee. Theres no security then in a mans owne good minde when he enters into these places where others disorder makes him runne continuall hazard. Hee that cannot promise himselfe the mastery of the most distempered Mens harts and hands that can bee, can have no assurance of safety from the good temper of his owne. If there could a Taverne or Ale house be kept for sober mens pleasure onely, there might happily be some ground for a conceit of taking no harme in it; but being, as they are, open Randevouzes of all the debauched humours in the earth, theres no man can sett his foot into them to be merry, without manifest perill both of his Innocency, honour, and life. For howsoever good the company bee that he carries with him, yet he can give no warranty from the intension of such society, as the whole world can, it may bee, hardly furnish worse. The truth of this is so evident, as I am confident there is no Man that hath had any litle practize of Tavernes, but in his owne experiment hath found manifold proofe of it, having often seen contentions here raysed amongst the best naturd, quaerels pickt against the quietest dispositions, and injuries offered to the most harmlesse persons that could bee found. That they have not growne to outrage, nor ended in any such inconveniences as these formerly recompted, must needs be granted by them that rightly observe the matter, to have proceeded onely from the overruling mercy and goodnes of GOD, which he that goes on still tempting and abusing, after such fearefull examples as these are, hath little reason to hope of better successe then those other unhappy scholers had.

MODERAT. You neede not have gone so farre as London for a third Instance. The selfe same Mitre that you speake of was the same yeare, if I mistake not, the stage of another tragique Act that drew blood, though it brought not Death, through the exuberancy of GODS mercy. Well, whatsoever may be sayd in defence of the Lawfulnes, surely there appeares notable danger in the entrance into these kind of places; and therefore, reserving myselfe to my owne place for the making up this New Yeares guift for our good freind and cosen, Ile give it now by way of precept to my son, whom my praiers and vows have sett apart for this holy calling, that he keepe himselfe pure and undefiled from this evill usuage of the world; and whenever he is invited either to Taverne or Alehouse, let him answere, His Mother gave him charge to the contrary.

The Gresham Press,
UNWIN BROTHERS,
WOKING AND LONDON

Recent Publications.

THE TEMPLE. Sacred Poems and Ejaculations by GEORGE HERBERT. The Text reprinted from the First Edition of 1633. With Seventy-six Illustrations after ALBERT DÜRER, HOLBEIN, MARCANTONIO, and other Masters. Cheaper Edition, crown 8vo, cloth, 3s. 6d.

"By far the best edition of the poems of 'holy' George Herbert, beautifully tasteful in every way."—*Publishers' Circular.*

THE HOPE OF IMMORTALITY. An Essay incorporating the Hulsean Lectures of 1897-98. By Rev. J. E. C. WELLDON, Head-Master of Harrow School. Second edition. 6s.

"States its arguments so freshly and eloquently that it cannot but be read with interest by many to whom the study of the subject as a chapter of theology would be both impossible and distasteful."—*Scotsman.*

"The book is full of noble words, as well as of originality, erudition, and logical argument."—*Queen.*

"An extremely interesting book."—*St. James's Gazette.*

THE SPECTATOR IN LONDON: Essays by ADDISON and STEELE. With Fifty-six Illustrations by RALPH CLEAVER, and Headpieces by W. H. ATKIN BERRY, CLOUGH BROMLEY, &c. Cheaper Edition, crown 8vo, cloth, 3s. 6d.

"Excellently printed, illustrated in a delightful way, and altogether makes as charming a gift-book as could be desired."—*Spectator.*

COUNTRY STORIES. By MARY RUSSELL MITFORD. With many Illustrations by GEORGE MORROW. Cheaper Edition, crown 8vo, cloth, 3s. 6d.

"There is no wearying of these sketches of old world life and manners in country and country town."—*Manchester Guardian.*

"Mr. Morrow's pictures are clear, quaint, and amusing."—*Scotsman.*

CONFIDENCES OF AN AMATEUR GARDENER. By A. M. DEW SMITH. With many Illustrations. 6s.

"To read these sparkling, sunny, racy pages is like walking in some flowery pleasance of Arcadia."—*Daily News.*

"The book, though often fanciful, is more practical and comprehensive than Mr. Dudley Warner's 'My Summer in a Garden'; and though often poetical, less imposing and florid than the Laureate's 'Garden that I Love.' ... We should like to quote more from this fascinating volume."—*Spectator.*

TOM TUG AND OTHERS: Sketches in a Domestic Menagerie. By Mrs. DEW SMITH, Author of "Confidences of an Amateur Gardener." With Illustrations by ELINOR M. MONSELL. 6s.

"As an exponent of canine and feline individuality she stands alone. Tom Tug, the bull-dog, and Tom Jones, the rescued stray cat, are drawn with a skill only the true lover of animals can fully appreciate."—*The Sketch.*

"If you are offered a choice between 'Tom Tug and Others' and a novel 'as a novel,' pray choose 'Tom Tug.' It is a beautiful book."
Black and White.

LONDON: SEELEY & CO., LTD., 38 GREAT RUSSELL ST.

"Mrs. Marshall's imaginative pictures of the England of other days are in reality prose poems."—LITERATURE.

Stories by Mrs. Marshall.

In Large Crown 8vo, Cloth, price 5s.

THE PARSON'S DAUGHTER, and How She was Painted by Mr. ROMNEY: a Story. By Mrs. MARSHALL, Author of "Under the Dome of St. Paul's," "In Westminster Choir," &c., &c. With Eight Illustrations after ROMNEY and GAINSBOROUGH.

UNDER THE DOME OF ST. PAUL'S. A Story of Sir Christopher Wren's Days. With Illustrations by T. HAMILTON CRAWFORD.

IN THE CHOIR OF WESTMINSTER ABBEY. A Story of Henry Purcell's Days. With Illustrations by T. HAMILTON CRAWFORD, R.S.W. Fourth Thousand.

A HAUNT OF ANCIENT PEACE. A Story of Nicholas Ferrar's House at Little Gidding. With Illustrations. Fourth Thousand.

THE MASTER OF THE MUSICIANS. A Story of Handel's Days. With Illustrations. Fifth Thousand.

KENSINGTON PALACE: IN THE DAYS OF QUEEN MARY II. With Iullstrations. Sixth Thousand.

PENSHURST CASTLE: IN THE TIME OF SIR PHILIP SIDNEY. With Illustrations. Fifth Thousand.

IN THE SERVICE OF RACHEL, LADY RUSSELL. With Illustrations. Fourth Thousand.

WINIFREDE'S JOURNAL. A Story of Exeter and Norwich in the Days of Bishop Hall. With Illustrations. Fourth Thousand.

WINCHESTER MEADS IN THE DAYS OF BISHOP KEN. With Illustrations. Eighth Thousand.

UNDER SALISBURY SPIRE: IN THE DAYS OF GEORGE HERBERT. With Illustrations. Twelfth Thousand.

ON THE BANKS OF THE OUSE. A Tale of the Times of Newton and Cowper. With Illustrations. Fifth Thousand.

IN FOUR REIGNS. The Recollections of ALTHEA ALLINGHAM. With Illustrations. Sixth Thousand.

UNDER THE MENDIPS. With Illustrations. Seventh Thousand.

IN THE EAST COUNTRY WITH SIR THOMAS BROWNE, KNIGHT. With Illustrations. Sixth Thousand.

IN COLSTON'S DAYS. A Story of Old Bristol. With Illustrations. Sixth Thousand.

LONDON: SEELEY & CO., LTD., 38 GREAT RUSSELL ST.

Books on Music.

RECOLLECTIONS OF JOHANNES BRAHMS. By Dr. J. V. WIDMANN and Professor DIETRICH. Translated from the German by DORA E. HECHT. With Two Portraits. Large crown 8vo, 6s. [*Immediately.*

STUDIES IN MODERN MUSIC. Hector Berlioz, Robert Schumann, Richard Wagner. By W. H. HADOW, M.A., Fellow of Worcester College, Oxon. With Portraits on Copper. Fourth Edition. Cloth, 7s. 6d.

"We have seldom read a book on musical subjects which has given us so much pleasure as this one, and we can sincerely recommend it to all who are interested in the art."—*Saturday Review.*

"It is a real relief, amid the rambling and slipshod effusions which constitute the bulk of musical *belles lettres*, to encounter such a volume as these 'Studies in Modern Music,' by Mr. W. H. Hadow. Mr. Hadow is himself a musician of no mean attainments; but there is no parade of technical knowledge in his book. He writes like a scholar and a gentleman, his style is felicitous, and his critical attitude at once sane and generous."
Graphic.

"He writes with striking thoughtfulness and breadth of view, so that his essays may be read with much interest by musicians. It is a remarkable book, because, unlike the majority of musical treatises by amateurs, it is full of truth and common sense."—*Athenæum.*

STUDIES IN MODERN MUSIC. Second Series. Frederick Chopin, Antonin Dvorák, Johannes Brahms, preceded by an Essay on Musical Form. By W. H. HADOW With Portraits on Copper. Second Edition. Cloth, 7s. 6d.

"The three biographies are charming; and in each case the author has something both new and true to say."—*National Observer.*

"The development of form is described with many brilliant touches and with complete grasp of the subject, and the book, which will probably be considered to be even better than the former work, is most heartily to be recommended to all who wish to attain the highest kind of enjoyment of the best music."—*Times.*

"Highly finished portraits are presented of the three modern masters named, and the articles are distinguished by the same musicianly knowledge and felicity of expression as those in the earlier book."—*Athenæum.*

A CROATIAN COMPOSER. Notes towards the Study of Joseph Haydn. By W. H. HADOW, Author of "Studies in Modern Music." With Portrait. 2s. 6d. nett.

"A volume full of interest, ethnical as well as musical."
St. James's Gazette.

"Will be read with interest and profit by all concerned with the study of music, and especially with the study of the national or racial elements in musical composition."—*The Globe.*

"A deeply interesting book. . . . Should find its way into the hands of every earnest musical student in the country."—*Musical Times.*

LONDON : SEELEY & CO., LTD., 38 GREAT RUSSELL ST. .

Natural History and Country Life.

LIFE AT THE ZOO. Notes and Traditions of the Regent's Park Gardens. By C. J. CORNISH. Illustrated from Photographs by GAMBIER BOLTON. Fifth Edition. 6s.

"The book gives an account of the habits and nature of the inmates of the lordly prison-house in the Regent's Park, and some of their past or future companions. It is of absorbing interest throughout."—*Daily News*.

ANIMALS AT WORK AND PLAY. Their Activities and Emotions. By C. J. CORNISH. With Twelve Illustrations. Second Edition. 6s.

"Mr. Cornish is always entertaining and generally informing, and has indeed written a delightful book."—*World*.

"It would be difficult to find a more fascinating book."—*Daily News*.

NIGHTS WITH AN OLD GUNNER, and other Studies of Wild Life. By C. J. CORNISH. With Sixteen Illustrations by LANCELOT SPEED, CHARLES WHYMPER, and from photographs. 6s.

"A most delightful volume of essays in country life and sport and charming studies of wild life."—*Spectator*.

WILD ENGLAND OF TO-DAY, and the Wild Life in it. By C. J. CORNISH. Illustrated by Drawings and Photographs. Second Edition. 6s.

"Mr. Cornish has undoubtedly found his true vocation in describing his experiences of country scenery and animal life."—*Athenæum*.

"The chapters are instinct with a full appreciation of country life. . . . It is exceedingly well illustrated by drawings and photographs."—*Field*.

ANIMALS OF TO-DAY : Their Life and Conversation. By C. J. CORNISH. With Illustrations from Photographs by C. REID, of Wishaw. 6s.

"Quite one of the brightest books of popular natural history which have appeared in recent years is Mr. Cornish's fascinating studies of 'Animals of To-day.'"—*Leeds Mercury*.

"Charmingly illustrated."—*Scotsman*.

MOUNTAIN, STREAM, AND COVERT. Sketches of Country Life and Sport in England and Scotland. By ALEXANDER INNES SHAND. With many Illustrations by ARCHIBALD THORBURN, LANCELOT SPEED, and others. 6s.

"A thoroughly healthy, breezy book, bringing with it a whiff of sweet, strong country air. Some excellent illustrations make up an unusually delightful volume."—*Guardian*.

LONDON: SEELEY & CO., LTD., 38, GREAT RUSSELL ST.

www.ingramcontent.com/pod-product-compliance
Lightning Source LLC
Chambersburg PA
CBHW031427230426
43668CB00007B/469